The Department of State
on the Eve
of the First World War

# The Department of State
## on the Eve
## of the First World War

RACHEL WEST, O.S.F.

The University of Georgia Press
Athens

Copyright © 1978 by the University of Georgia Press
Athens 30602

All rights reserved

Set in 11 on 13 point Mergenthaler Times Roman type
Printed in the United States of America

Library of Congress Cataloging in Publication Data

West, Rachel.
The Department of State on the eve of the First World
War.

Includes bibliographical references and index.
1. United States. Dept. of State—History.   2. United
States—Foreign relations—1913–1921.   3. European
War, 1914–1918—Diplomatic history.   I. Title.
JX1706.A4  1978          353.1'09          77–22062
ISBN 0–8203–0435–2

for Julia A. West

# Contents

# Acknowledgments

It is difficult to write without the help of friends, and I want to thank the following individuals for reading the manuscript in its various forms: Edward H. Buehrig, Robert H. Ferrell, Irving Katz, and John Edward Wiltz—all of Indiana University. Arthur S. Link, the dean of Wilson scholars, most kindly read the manuscript with great care and pointed out places for improvement; I am greatly in his debt. My typists were Sister Clarence Marie Kavanaugh and Evelyn Cramer, and they did wonderful service, especially in retyping the versions of the notes and the essay on sources. During the necessarily drawn-out process of studying and writing I often looked to Helene Ciborski, C.S.J., Sister Marilynn Hofer, and Susan Jackson for "morale building," as well as to my colleagues at Marian College, Sister Susan Bradshaw, James J. Divita, William Doherty, and Sister Mary Carol Schroeder. Always there was help from the Sisters of St. Francis, Oldenburg, Indiana, especially Mother Marie Dillhoff and Mother Miriam Clare Heskamp. At the Columbia University oral history office I profited from the guidance of Elizabeth Mason. At Yale University assistance came from the head of manuscripts at the Beinecke Library, Judith Schiff, and from the late Herman Kahn. At Harvard, John Milton Cooper, now of the University of Wisconsin at Madison, showed me the arrangement of manuscripts in the Houghton Library. At Duke, Calvin D. Davis of the department of history took me around the collections. At Princeton my guides were John W. Davidson and Eugene P. Trani. At the National Archives in Washington, Milton O. Gustafson and John Macoll were most graciously helpful. Jerry Israel of Illinois Wesleyan kindly allowed me to read a manuscript chapter from his later published book. My brother, Quentin L. West, offered his advice and criticism. And I wish to thank the staff of the University of Georgia Press for all their courtesies and helpfulness.

# I

# Introduction

It stands to reason that at the moment of the most crucial turn in European and world history of modern times, the outbreak of the Great War in July and early August 1914, the diplomatic representatives of the United States should have sent home information about the coming holocaust. And yet the truth is that a month after the assassination of the Austrian Archduke Francis Ferdinand and his consort the Grand Duchess Sophie in the streets of Sarajevo at the hand of a Bosnian revolutionary named Gavrilo Princip, the American government was pursuing a somnolent course. State Department officials gave the impression of attentiveness to world-wide affairs. In fact they were no more aware of what was going on in Europe than of what was going on at the North Pole. No American diplomat in July and August 1914, so the historian Walter Millis pointed out more than forty years ago in *The Road to War*, possessed much understanding that the peace of Europe of the nineteenth century, continued almost without interruption since the defeat of Napoleon at Waterloo in 1815, was about to come to a flaming end. The American vice-consul general in Budapest sensed on July 13 that trouble was brewing and drafted a cable to Washington. Then he considered the cost of sending the cable and the probable remonstrance that would come from some underling of Secretary of State William Jennings Bryan. The secretary himself might not be too happy if his routine were disturbed by such a sudden interruption to his visits with fellow Democrats or his preparation of a talk to be given on the Chautauqua circuit. So Vice-consul Frank E. Mallett sent the news by letter, which arrived just before war was declared.

It is, to be sure, another question to ask what the American government in 1914 might have done with such information. Very probably it would have done little or nothing, since the policy of the American nation was still, in 1914, the policy of James Monroe as set out in the message to Congress of December 1823. President Woodrow Wilson in all probability would have maintained that affairs in Europe, unlike events in nearby Mexico, were none of the nation's business. Secretary Bryan was convinced that his peace treaties—his treaties of conciliation, concluded with two dozen or so nations stipulating that they should have a "cooling-off" period prior to any declaration of war—would hold. Many of the lesser government officials were on vacation. If matters in Europe did take a serious turn, everyone thought the British government could handle them. Ambassador Walter Hines Page in London had been praising the British foreign office, as well as other European foreign offices, and complaining about the supposedly inferior American State Department. Why not let the British take care of Europe's problems?

Had there been a warning of war, perhaps Second Assistant Secretary of State William Phillips, somewhat familiar with Europe, would have become excited. Counselor Robert Lansing, only a few months on the job, then might have acted. Lansing would have looked at a war in Europe as a question for international law; apply a few basic principles, he might have told the British, and that would solve the problem. Americans in general tended to look for easy, legal solutions in those days when reform and efficiency in government had become watchwords.

And yet it does not suffice to remark the lack of information and the probable uselessness of that information had it been available. The question should be, why was none available? As Seneca remarked, it is better to have useless information than none at all. The very possession of information sometimes changes one's outlook. In retrospect the historian wonders what might have happened if Americans had been better informed by their diplomatic representatives in Europe for two or three dozen years before 1914, say from the time in 1888 when a new emperor had come to the throne of Germany and the position of Prince Otto von Bismarck, eroding for some time, was thereafter steadily undermined until his resignation in 1890. It was that point at which the politics of Europe began to go awry, and it was no occasion for Americans or the citizens of any other great nation to be uninformed. If the American leadership of Woodrow Wilson's time had possessed even half of former-President Theodore Roosevelt's instinct for the solution of international troubles, it might have sufficed to warn off the new leaders of the second German empire and persuade them to restrain themselves. When in 1914 Germany's weak ally Austria-Hungary appeared to be challenged by what the Austrians considered a government of pigs in Serbia, the United States could have offered to mediate—indeed could have demanded the opportunity—and then perhaps the war might not have started. Who can tell? Maybe such an intervention would have accomplished nothing. But considering what did happen, the American government could not have made matters worse by attempting a mediation.

In the pages that follow I have tried to take a photograph, so to speak, of the Department of State in 1913–14 and to draw some conclusions. At the outset of my studies I knew that the photograph would not be altogether impressive, but I must now confess that it turned out much worse than I had assumed. The sheer amateurism of the department, the blindness of the highest officials—these stand out. No amount of retrospective good will, the need to allow for the advantage of hindsight, can absolve the responsible leaders of the United States government in 1914 for their incapacity in the business of foreign affairs. I have not, incidentally, been able to find out everything I had wished to discover. Some items were elusive. I could not discover what the rules of correspondence from embassies and legations to the department in Washington were; there appear to have been rules, but no one bothered to preserve them. But the feelings of the official reporters in foreign lands were clear enough—they did not wish to correspond with Washington on subjects of much greater importance than visas and commercial listings; they disliked sending information which, they perhaps rightly feared, would only go into department pigeonholes. The rest of the Department of State's activities seem fairly clear, and I have sought to set them out for latter-day readers a half-century and more after the guns began to boom in Europe and the world turned from ways of peace, perhaps forever.

# 2

# A Century and a Quarter

When William Jennings Bryan took over management of the Department of State in March 1913, he inherited an organization antique in size and arrangement. An individual of the present day, looking at Bryan's department and comparing it with the vast bureaucracy of our own time, would not recognize the same institution. Bryan's tenure came in an era when most department officers wore cutaway coats to work as a normal badge of office. Not many coats were necessary, for the full strength of the Washington staff was 213 officers, clerks, messengers, and manual laborers. The entire force of the American diplomatic and consular services abroad numbered fewer than 450 persons.[1] Pre–World War I secretaries might find the department's present-day functioning incomprehensible. The department has grown to an organization of monstrous complexity. It now employs some 24,500 persons at home and overseas. More than a fourth of these, including a deputy secretary, three undersecretaries, one deputy undersecretary, a dozen or so assistant secretaries, their deputies, dozens of directors and chiefs and assistants, diplomats on rotation to the department, stenographers, telegraphers, and computer programmers, occupy a huge building at Twenty-Second and C streets, in northwest Washington, D.C. The building takes up over four square blocks, eleven and eight tenths acres, of the capital's prime real estate.[2]

The department for which Bryan assumed responsibility in 1913 had developed slowly from the first days of government under the Constitution, 125 years before. "State" is the oldest cabinet department and can actually trace its lineage to the pre-Constitution era back as far as 1775 when the Continental Congress established a Committee of Secret Correspondence. This committee, and its successor under the Articles of Confederation (known as the Department of Foreign Affairs), had little authority, for both were subservient to Congress. When an enactment of a different Congress in 1789 reconstituted the Department of Foreign Affairs as an advisory branch to the new presi-

4

dent, the result was not at first auspicious. The incumbent secretary, John Jay, left the department and accepted the more prestigious post of chief justice of the Supreme Court. Shortly afterward Congress renamed the department, and matters began to improve. The new title, Department of State, indicated that its duties encompassed more than foreign affairs. Under the first secretary of state, Thomas Jefferson, and well into the nineteenth century, the State Department was a home office as well; its responsibilities included not only management of diplomacy and custody of the Great Seal but the issuing and recording of patents, copyrights, and executive pardons, caring for manuscripts of historical value, publishing census returns, and handling presidential correspondence with state and territorial governors. When over the years other offices assumed the domestic chores, the department's title, a misnomer, lingered on—the more correct one being that used under the Articles of Confederation, Department of Foreign Affairs.[3]

The numbers of personnel grew with the department's responsibilities but never kept up with the dealings of an expanding nation with foreign countries. Jefferson needed only five clerks, a secretary, and a French translator. (The duties of the last, the Republican poet and editor Philip Freneau, went far beyond his translations, which the others doubtless could have done as well and perhaps better, since Freneau could not read the language; Freneau was one of Jefferson's political assistants.) By 1800 there were ten persons in the department; in 1820, fifteen. But by 1898, when a difficult era in foreign relations began, there were still only eighty-two. In 1908 there were one hundred sixty-seven.[4]

Despite the addition of minor clerks the task of copying reports and dispatches frequently devolved upon the secretary and his chief clerk. The nineteenth-century secretaries were burdened with duties that recent secretaries such as John Foster Dulles, Christian Herter, Dean Rusk, William P. Rogers, Henry A. Kissinger, or Cyrus Vance would have assigned to a low-level assistant with an elementary knowledge of office machines. Secretary John Quincy Adams personally executed three copies of the Adams-Onís Treaty of 1819 with Spain and afterward peevishly complained that "it was considered by Mr. Madison that the public duties of the department were more than sufficient for one man. . . . For myself . . . I have found the duties more than I can

5

perform. Some of them therefore are not performed.''[5] In the days before typewriters, carbon paper, and copying machines the hand-copying of department documents lumbered along. Everything was done in an exacting, inefficient way. When Wilbur J. Carr entered the department as a clerk in 1892 he received a scolding from Sevellon A. Brown, who had been there since 1864, for addressing envelopes in fine Spencerian hand; Brown assigned Carr to practice the somewhat different style which, he said, characterized the department's calligraphy.[6]

Preservation of correspondence created headaches equal to the production of it. Adams complained that important letters frequently disappeared and that he had on his desk at one time eleven unanswered dispatches from the minister to Great Britain, Richard Rush. He instituted an elemental method of indexing departmental correspondence. But as late as 1870 when Hamilton Fish was secretary, there was still no comprehensive indexing system, and officials had to rely on the memories of the department's oldest employees. John H. Haswell, an early chief of the bureau of indexes and archives (established in 1873), introduced a system of filing and preserving papers, which remained in effect until 1909. According to this system the department grouped diplomatic and consular transactions under five headings: instructions to ministers abroad, dispatches from ministers, notes to ministers of foreign nations resident in Washington, notes from the ministers in Washington, and miscellaneous. All outgoing messages were written on fine paper and press copied, then recopied for binding in large folio volumes. The problem of finding material on a single topic was so difficult under this system that when Secretary Elihu Root came to the department in 1905 he brought David A. Salmon from the War Department to introduce the subject-number index system set up there while Root was secretary of war. Root's method soon went into effect and with the adoption of a more flexible decimal classification in 1910, and some later modifications, it bore the test of time until recently.[7]

The nineteenth-century department was a low-key operation. Records could turn up in strange places. After John Hay's death, Root's third assistant secretary of state, Francis Mairs Huntington-Wilson, recalled ''having to delve among papers in the cellar of Mr. John Hay's house to find notes of important oral assurances from a Russian representative of which no official record had been made.''[8]

6

If anything happened as a result of the paperwork, it took a detective to find out who had made it happen. Correspondence from American envoys drifted from desk to desk, picking up the stamped symbols characteristic of each official perusing documents. Diplomatic and consular officers abroad carefully learned the symbols of all department employees and sometimes could determine who had delivered reproof or approval—if the particular message, before it went out by pouch or cable, had received that much attention.[9]

As the department increased in size and complexity, secretaries of state attempted to reorganize in a substantive as well as mechanical way. Secretary Adams and his successor, Henry Clay, made important suggestions, but the first major reform in this regard came in 1833 under President Andrew Jackson's relatively obscure secretary, Louis McLane, who directed the establishment of seven bureaus, including one for the diplomatic service and one for the consular service, each responsible for a segment of departmental activity. Strangely, although the consular service already had become the largest representation abroad, numbering one hundred fifty-two officials, McLane's reform assigned two clerks to the work of that bureau and three for handling correspondence from the nineteen diplomatic representatives— an early indication of the department's low esteem for the consular service despite its value to the nation in dollars and cents.[10]

It was not until after the Civil War that Secretary Hamilton Fish, acting under pressure of an economy-minded Congress which had depleted the department's clerical ranks, took the first step toward geographic divisions and divided the diplomatic and consular bureaus according to groups of countries. Fish's general organizational setup of 1870 lasted until the early twentieth century. But for some reason the regional divisions of the diplomatic and consular bureaus gradually disappeared, so that the perennial head of the diplomatic bureau after 1897, Sydney Y. Smith, once told a visitor that the four aged clerks sitting in the four corners of his office divided the world among themselves ("but not its goods," for department clerks were notoriously underpaid).[11]

All the while the quarters of the department were barely adequate. From the closing years of the eighteenth century until after the Second World War, department personnel complained of overcrowded quar-

7

ters with good cause but little relief. Housing had posed no problem in the early years of the nation's history; Jay's Department of Foreign Affairs made do with two large rooms in a small house on South Sixth Street in Philadelphia. After several moves the department in 1820 settled into a two-story brick building of some forty rooms at the corner of Fifteenth Street and Pennsylvania Avenue, next to the Executive Mansion. This porticoed building served well until after the Civil War, although there was increasing difficulty with storage space for records. In 1866 the building was torn down to make way for an expansion of the treasury, and the department moved, not inappropriately, into the Washington Orphan Asylum, where it remained until 1875 and completion of the south wing of a brand-new neoclassical building next to the White House at Seventeenth Street and Pennsylvania Avenue which was designated the State, War, and Navy Building.

The move to Old State (as it eventually became known) closed one era and opened another. Every account of American diplomacy of Fish's time and after mentions the hideousness of this vast granite structure, its Victorian outlines so out of keeping with the surrounding classical buildings. Still, Old State was impressive in its day, even if its large entrance with its sweep of steps and noble pillars, its staircases, and high-ceilinged rooms belied the fact that the building was too small to house three cabinet departments. Secretaries of state soon were pleading for a larger edifice. Overcrowding forced one bureau and then another to seek quarters in nearby and faraway buildings, moves which had produced some fifty annexes by 1947 when the department at last moved out.

Old State gave way to New State at Twenty-Second and C. With glass and concrete additions constructed between 1957 and 1961, this later building, its core a hand-me-down from the War Department, now contains most of the department's offices and related agencies.[12]

The years passed, and the department slowly took on its present-day proportions. Nothing happened in a hurry. The operations of the department throughout the nineteenth century possessed a leisurely quality; the titles of the department's leading personages for many years remained unpretentious. For a long time the most important department officer next to the secretary of state was the chief clerk. In addition to having custody of the secretary's correspondence, this official was the principal administrator of the department's internal affairs and, after McLane's reorganization, of the bureaus. He remained the officer charged with acting in the secretary's absence even after establishment of the office of assistant secretary of state in 1853. Fortunately the chief clerk usually was an experienced employee. There were exceptions. Secretary of State Daniel Webster's first administrative act in 1841 was appointment of his son Fletcher to the office. Fletcher Webster had no experience in diplomacy. His appointment made it possible for the secretary to keep diplomatic transactions in the family while out of town on other business. When William H. Seward became secretary of state in 1861 he imitated Webster by appointing his son Frederick to the post of assistant secretary. Seward frankly admitted that he intended his son to take care of office-seekers, a large responsibility for a nineteenth-century secretary; later secretaries commonly followed this example by making the first assistant secretary the first assistant dispenser of patronage. Meanwhile the increasing administrative problems had necessitated appointment of a second assistant in 1866.

It was fortunate for the diplomacy of the United States in the nineteenth century that despite the inadequate organization, in terms of titles and housing and functions and personnel, there always seemed to be an officer of the department who could get things done. It was Daniel Webster's good judgment to take on as his chief clerk William Hunter, Jr., who had a reputation for linguistic skill and an encyclopedic memory. Hunter had entered the department in 1829. For fifty-seven years, until his death in 1886, secretaries drew on his storehouse of knowledge about treaties and diplomacy.[13] Frederick Seward called the amazing Hunter "the personification of the Department work."[14]

Before Hunter left the department a successor appeared, Alvey Augustus Adee, whose service lasted well into the twentieth century. If any official of the new century embodied the finest characteristics of the former, it was Adee. "A.D.," or "AAA," as he sometimes signed himself, had joined the diplomatic service in 1869 as secretary to the colorful if amoral minister to Spain, Daniel E. Sickles, whom Adee's great uncle, the lawyer John Graham, had defended for the killing of Philip Barton Key. He entered the department in Washington in 1877 at the bidding of Secretary William M. Evarts who had noted the young man's skill in securing the extradition of Boss William M.

Tweed the year before when Adee was chargé d'affaires in Madrid. Adee remained in the department until two days before his death in 1924. He served as chief of the diplomatic bureau and third assistant secretary of state, the latter an office established in 1874; he then became second assistant—which post he held for the remainder of his career.[15]

At the turn of the century Adee was the most indispensable of the department's employees. John Hay, who disliked department work and would have preferred "to lie in the orchard and eat the sunny side of peaches," feared that his able second assistant would wear himself out and lamented that "one Adee is all we have in the pantry."[16] Adee was a bachelor (he claimed his bachelor status was economical) and virtually lived in the department except for those weeks each year he spent bicycling around Europe searching for diatoms to examine under a microscope. He was fluent in French, German, Italian, and Spanish, and also was a Shakespearean scholar who wrote verse. But his value to the department lay more in his knowledge of precedent and rhetoric and in his single-minded dedication to improving the style of departmental correspondence. During the thirty-year period he was second assistant he composed nearly every important treaty. Few incoming or outgoing dispatches escaped his scrutiny. He detested loose language, and his infrequent losses of temper generally arose from inept wording by subordinates. No student of American diplomacy of the period can escape seeing in the department's archives his critical commentary on correspondence, usually written in red ink on green paper.[17]

Adee undoubtedly was an eccentric. He was a small man, only a little over five feet in height. Deaf from childhood, he carried an ear trumpet, which he used with discretion. He bought items of clothing in lots of thirty-six; he numbered them serially to determine the quality of the material as well as to check thieves. He kept about a dozen pairs of shoes in his office and a like number at home—all of the same pattern. He carried several spoons when eating out because, he explained, regular silverware did not fit his mouth. He lived with his brother in Washington and rarely appeared at social functions, although he was a witty speaker, full of jokes and stories.[18]

If Adee had other qualities they were bureaucratic. Huntington-Wilson admired Adee as he did few individuals in the department but remarked that the second assistant was too ready to defer to any officer who consulted him. If one wanted to test an idea, he said, it was best to ask Adee questions "slightly indicating that one's opinion was the opposite of what it really was."[19] This quality helped keep Adee in the department through the terms of fourteen successive secretaries of state.

Adee was an able man, and well might Hay worry about "Semper Paratus" Adee's health, for despite the fact that the department at the turn of the century included several able men, they were too few to meet the requirements of the time. Involvement in the Far East and Latin America after the Spanish-American War brought a marked increase in the communications of the diplomatic and index bureaus. The flow was infinitesimal compared with the 10,000 daily messages during the 1960s. But from 1887 to 1907 the annual rate rose from 36,925 pieces to 94,000, an increase of 156 percent unaccompanied by a like increase in the number of clerks. The burgeoning correspondence reflected both diplomatic involvements and a startling rise of American commerce. The nation's foreign trade had boomed from barely over a billion dollars in 1875 to close to two billion in 1898, and it soared to well over three billion ten years later. Between 1898 and 1908 immigration also doubled, an additional burden for the department.[20]

In the years before Bryan's appearance at the State, War, and Navy Building in 1913, there were slow changes in department organization, most of them for the better. Hay was no reformer, and during his tenure from 1898 to 1905 the department, despite dramatically enlarged responsibilities, remained much the same. His successor Root was a poor administrator; one subordinate thought that the New Yorker's dream of heaven was hundreds of stenographers surrounding him while he did all the work.[21] Root saw no immediate need for an overhauling of the department similar to that he performed in the War Department. What he did recognize was the demand for a change of methods used by the bureaus, which by 1909 were costing the government nearly $49,500 for outside services, and he also saw the need for reforming the diplomatic and consular services.[22] President William

H. Taft's secretary of state, Philander C. Knox, attended to the business of reorganization, and by the end of the Taft era there had been changes of some magnitude.

Such changes in department procedures as occurred in the fifteen years before Bryan's time were largely the work of two subordinate officials, one of whom had entered the department as a thousand-dollar clerk in 1892 and remained the typical civil servant long after he attained the salaries and dignified titles of director of the consular service, assistant secretary of state, and, finally, minister to Czechoslovakia. Wilbur J. Carr was born on an Ohio farm in 1870. He received his education in bookkeeping, general business, shorthand, and typewriting at two unlikely institutions, Kentucky Commercial College and Chafee's Phonographic Institute in Oswego, New York. He took the civil service examination in 1892. From that time the solemn-faced Carr was a model bureaucrat who, according to the somewhat critical Huntington-Wilson, "toed in slightly, as if from so many years of walking the straight line of Civil Service duty." [23] Within a few years he had served in nearly every one of the department's offices and in 1902 became chief of the consular bureau.

Carr was a new broom in the department. During his years as chief of the consular bureau he went at his work with reforming zeal. It took little acumen for him to see that the turn-of-the-century consular service needed reform. Although the largest of the department's branches with some three hundred men abroad by 1900, it had received little attention and had become the refuge of the spoilsmen. A large part of the problem stemmed from an inconsistent salary system; most officers depended on fees varying from almost nothing to $40,000 at Amoy and $60,000 at Liverpool. There was little or no inspection of their activities, so that consuls at remote but lucrative posts could be incompetent for years.[24] President Cleveland frequently spoke of reforming the service and issued an executive order in 1895 requiring appointees to consular vacancies paying between $1,000 and $2,500 to take an examination, but by Root's time it had "evidently come to be regarded as cruel and inhuman treatment not to pass a man. In view of the character of the examination a rejection would practically be an imputation of idiocy." [25] Carr began to push reform, discreetly as was his way. A protégé of Adee, he had learned to study all aspects of a subject before acting. From Root he learned the value of getting acquainted with congressmen. He set about talking to businessmen—they often had interest in consular reform. He talked to consuls on leave in the United States.[26]

Carr had the support of Root, the backing of President Theodore Roosevelt, and a cooperative Congress. With such assistance most of the reforms he had in mind were a reality by the end of Root's first year in office. Roosevelt on November 10, 1905, issued an executive order requiring both diplomatic and consular candidates to take examinations for entrance into the services. At the same time Root appointed a departmental committee of which Carr and Huntington-Wilson were the principal members to study and revise the examination system.[27] An executive order had no permanence, so Root and Carr sought legislation, and Root drafted and Carr steered through committee the Lodge Act of April 5, 1906, enumerating nine classes of consulates (a defect in the measure, for places, not men, were classified) and fixing their salaries. Consular officers had to pay all fees into the treasury, and moonlighting in business or law was forbidden to individuals earning a salary of over $1,000. The president was to appoint five inspectors, and consulates were subject to their perusals every two years. A stronger executive order, dated June 27, 1906, established appointments and promotions according to civil service regulations.[28]

As chief of the consular bureau Carr put these enactments of 1905–6 into operation. He moved slowly but with such thoroughness that his consular reforms became models for attempts to improve the diplomatic service, which because of its aristocratic character and political import was more difficult to change. Carr's immediate superior, Third Assistant Huntington-Wilson, disagreed about the procedure for examinations, favoring oral examinations. Carr believed them subject to error and political influence. The outcome was a compromise; examinations became both written and oral, each part of equal value in determining the total score. The consuls found Carr a formidable but kindly examiner. He was a likable chief who had a knack for making his consular visitors tell all they knew.[29]

In some ways Carr was an anomaly in the Department of State. He was dedicated to reform of an overseas service with several hundred offices and workers, but his experience was entirely vicarious. He never served in a consulate, although he probably knew more about consular work from reading inspectors' reports and listening to visitors than did most consuls general. Although he listened attentively to Adee's descriptions of annual European jaunts, he did not go to Europe until 1916, twenty-four years after he entered the department, and he never visited the other continents.[30]

Carr, one should add, was not ambitious in the ordinary sense, although he welcomed the praise and salary advances he received as he rose in the small hierarchy of the department. He described himself as "conscious always of an inferiority of preparation and of mind, lacking in information but by determination and endless hours of labor doing what better educated and more highly placed men had failed to do." He tended to favor as consuls men who had worked hard rather than men of native intelligence or education.[31] In frequent moments of a loss of confidence in his work he spoke of returning to the Ohio farm, but he was no farmer and had built his life around improvement of the consular service. Like Adee he became a sort of living tradition. A veteran consul, Robert Skinner, wrote in 1922, "How can one write of his *connection with* the Consular Service—he *is* the Consular Service."[32]

In addition to handling the consular service, Carr worked to improve the department's financial system. At Root's request he assumed the work of budget director without title. He tightened up the bureau of accounts, appeared before Congress to appeal for funds, estimated departmental appropriations, reorganized the cipher and telegraph offices (unlike most departmental employees, he was interested in cryptography), and compiled lists of laws relating to the department and the diplomatic and consular services. As the years passed his workload was extraordinary, and he was happy.[33]

The second reforming official in the State Department prior to the First World War was an unlikely person, Secretary of State Root's third assistant secretary, Francis Mairs Huntington-Wilson. Born in Chicago of wealthy and politically influential parents, Huntington-Wilson had gone abroad four times before he was nine years of age. He graduated from no Kentucky Commercial College, but from Yale in 1897. His acquisition of a diplomatic appointment after graduation was typical of the procedures of his era. Armed with letters from Senators Shelby M. Cullom and William F. Mason of Illinois, from Senator Mark Hanna who was a friend of a Yale classmate, and a "great many" other movers and shakers of American *fin de siècle* politics, he visited former Secretary of State John Sherman, a friend of his grandparents, but finding that "the poor old gentleman's memory had quite failed," he did not at first get an appointment. His father, he later wrote in his memoirs, then "breezed into Washington, took Senator Cullom and Senator Mason to the White House . . . saw President McKinley, and returned with the promise that I should be commissioned Second Secretary of Legation at Tokio."[34]

In the capital of Japan the young Yale graduate easily rose to be first secretary of legation and found time to write an article on the diplomatic service for the *Outlook*, an important reason, he thought, for his later rise in the department in Washington. Not long after the article's publication in 1906, Root called Huntington-Wilson home to make him third assistant secretary; the diplomatic officer had requested a transfer to the locality which, he later said, he considered "the fountainhead of American foreign policy." In his memoirs published a half-century later he confessed that he had begun his diplomatic career "knowing nothing of international law, diplomatic procedure, of commerce, and little of history." By 1906 he believed he had learned enough about these matters to undertake a reorganization of the department, which he found in deplorable shape.[35]

When Huntington-Wilson turned to the business of reorganizing the department he had the confidence of a Yale man; perhaps he might have done better had he attended the Kentucky Commercial College. He thought department personnel "the honest plodding type of civil service employee . . . preoccupied with living on their meagre salaries; were good conscientious workers but lacking any very broad knowledge of the world or particular taste for foreign affairs." His duties as third assistant, he discovered, were simple. He was responsible for finances but had only to sign vouchers prepared by the bureau of accounts. He was head of the consular service, or thought he was, and had only to sign instructions prepared by Carr and by Carr's assistant, Herbert Hengstler. He was in charge of protocol and commented, "After my hard work in Japan, here surely was a sinecure."[36]

Lacking suitable employment for his talents he set about composing regulations for consular and diplomatic service examinations and planning reorganization.

To Huntington-Wilson's credit he was an able draftsman and had sound ideas about the services. As were many diplomats of his day, he was concerned with the nation's economic interests. Latin America and the Far East appeared the regions for greatest development. He thought many of the policies regarding Latin American and Far Eastern affairs "unrealistic," principally because no machinery provided the secretary and the president with information. He began to urge regional departmental bureaus manned by experts. In the summer of 1906 he drafted an administrative chart and thirty-seven pages of recommendations, salary scales, and general suggestions for promotion and transfers and presented the compendium to the secretary of state.[37]

Secretary Root thoughtfully pigeonholed Huntington-Wilson's plans. For one thing, they entailed additional personnel and larger appropriations at a time when Root was attempting to use his influence with Congress for consular reform. For another, the secretary had come to dislike their author. Although he appointed Huntington-Wilson he had come to regret his choice, discovering his third assistant to be "of a mean disposition, ungenerous, rather formal and quite lacking in a sense of humor, dangerous, suspicious, egotistical, and ready to take offense."[38] President Roosevelt's opinion was even lower; TR detested the address "excellency," and when the third assistant drafted a presidential message filled to the margins with that title, Roosevelt was furious and called the message "fatuous and absurd" and, worse, "ungrammatical." Huntington-Wilson was so offended he tendered his resignation, but Root smoothed his third assistant's—and the president's—feelings. Considering the secretary's changed opinion of the third assistant it is remarkable that Huntington-Wilson remained in the department after this and other similar contretemps. One explanation has it that Huntington-Wilson had received his transfer to the department largely through the efforts of his beautiful wife, the former Lucy James, whom he had met and married in Japan. Her looks and intelligence reportedly had impressed Secretary of War William H. Taft when he visited Tokyo; back home, Taft introduced her to Root, who was so dazzled by the lady that it was impossible to refuse requests on her husband's behalf.[39]

On one issue only did Huntington-Wilson win out over his adversary, Root, and that was in his proposal for the department to be broken into geographic divisions. At the outset Root opposed the idea, but on this point the third assistant apparently was able to gain support of a close friend of the secretary—First Assistant Secretary Robert Bacon who possessed, so another diplomat later commented, what the third assistant lacked, the power and influence to break through "the crust" of the organization of the department.[40] Huntington-Wilson's superior in Japan, Ambassador Lloyd C. Griscom, had warned of the importance of getting along with Bacon.

Bacon talked to Root, and the secretary decided to establish a bureau of Far Eastern affairs with the third assistant secretary as director. Huntington-Wilson balked. That would mean giving up his position as an assistant secretary. Perhaps that was what Root had in mind. At Huntington-Wilson's request the secretary recalled two young diplomats from their Far Eastern posts, William Phillips and Percival Heintzleman, to become departmental "messengers" who sat behind a screen in the third assistant's office and carried on the work of the new Far Eastern bureau. They shortly became chief and assistant chief, respectively, of the bureau. The new bureau was functioning so smoothly by 1909 that Root began to change his mind about establishing other geographic divisions.[41]

Huntington-Wilson's saga at the department well illustrated the small-bore qualities of affairs of state as conducted at the State, War, and Navy Building prior to the World War. As Roosevelt's term came to a close, the third assistant secretary sensed plans to remove him from the department to make room for Phillips's promotion to his position. Phillips had pleased Roosevelt on many scores; not only was he charming and a Harvard man but he was a member of the tennis cabinet. Huntington-Wilson had told the president, in the presence of the Swedish crown prince and Swedish minister, that he preferred golf. This blunder drew from Griscom, who overheard the remark, a whispered "You damned fool!"[42] After his tactless remark the third assistant came to believe that he had no further chance of remaining in the department. With inauguration of a geographically sectional bureau and with the acceptance of his policy of bringing diplomatic and consular service personnel into department offices (such as happened in his own case), he had accomplished nearly all his goals. He received an appointment as minister to Argentina early in January 1909. But then his luck changed, for reasons impossible to know. The Sunday before Huntington-Wilson was to leave for Buenos Aires, Root's successor Knox (who became secretary after Robert Bacon had served in an interim capacity) called him in and asked, "Would you be willing to give up being Minister to the Argentine Republic and to stay in the Department as my second in command?" The minister-designate was astonished for he had talked to Knox at length on only one occasion. He liked what he knew of the man, however, and accepted on the spot.[43] He moved into the first assistant's office on March 6, 1909.

During the Knox era, which lasted until 1913, Huntington-Wilson operated in a congenial atmosphere. Through his office door the first assistant "could see the new Secretary, impeccably dressed, sitting at his enormous desk behind a huge Partegas Invincible cigar which, small as he was, he looked quite important enough to dominate."[44] Assuredly Secretary Knox could dominate Huntington-Wilson, of whom one observer wrote that he always glanced over both shoulders before beginning to speak.[45] The first assistant willingly became Knox's closest associate, even filling in for the secretary at dinner engagements when Knox, whose wife was deaf, chose not to go. President Taft disliked Huntington-Wilson nearly as much as had Roosevelt and could not comprehend the friendship. "I would just like to sit on Wilson once and mash him flat," the president was reported to have commented.[46]

Fortunately for the first assistant's professional and personal well-being, Huntington-Wilson dealt more with Knox than with the president, who allowed Knox a considerable freedom in foreign affairs. With Knox's backing and one hundred thousand dollars from Congress (the Tariff Act of 1909 imposed increased responsibilities and the secretary had pleaded successfully for funds to meet the emergency), Huntington-Wilson carried out the plans he had submitted to Root in 1906. The project proved to be the first internal reorganization of the department since 1870.[47] He built his reform on two features. He proposed creation of the post of undersecretary of state, subordinate only to the secretary and the president and acting as head of the department in the secretary's absence, and he set up regional divisions staffed by experts.

The proposed new post of undersecretary was not established at that time. As long as Knox was in office, Huntington-Wilson as first assistant was in fact an undersecretary, although he did not attend cabinet meetings in Knox's absence. He received a slightly higher salary than the second and third assistants ($5,000, to their $4,500). Creation of an undersecretary fell victim to Knox's establishment of the office of counselor, a post paying its holder $7,500 annually, for the secretary's friend, Henry M. Hoyt of Pennsylvania. The counselor was to be a skilled international lawyer who would act as legal adviser to the secretary in matters requiring such expertise. When Hoyt resigned in November 1910, Chandler P. Anderson assumed the position. Observing that his salary was second only to that of the secretary of state, Anderson asked for freedom from direction by the assistant secretaries and requested his office to be made a presidential appointment—a privilege Huntington-Wilson had sought for himself. The first assistant was not happy, and friction ensued until 1913 when both men resigned and President Wilson appointed John Bassett Moore as counselor with the right to be acting secretary, resolving the issue contrary to Huntington-Wilson's plan.[48]

Knox's first assistant had more success with establishment of geographic divisions. Besides the already tested bureau (now termed division) of Far Eastern affairs, headed in 1909 by Ransford S. Miller, there soon were divisions of Latin American affairs under Thomas C. Dawson and later H. Percival Dodge, Western European affairs supervised by Knox's third assistant secretary, Chandler Hale, and Near Eastern affairs directed by Evan E. Young. Each division handled diplomatic and counsular correspondence "on matters other than those of an administrative character" relating to countries within its area.

The distinction between Western Europe and the Near East was arbitrary—by today's definitions almost laughable. The Near East included Germany, Austria-Hungary, Russia, the Balkan nations, Turkey, Greece, Italy, Abyssinia, Persia, and Egypt. The small size of WE and NE indicated the department's greater interest, in the days before the World War, in Latin America and the Far East. The division of Western European affairs, dealing with nations of such large importance to the United States as Britain and France, consisted of only three staff members besides its supervisor, who as third assistant secretary of state had additional duties of managing departmental protocol, administering the diplomatic service and several bureaus, and directing questions relating to international conferences. The chief of NE and his one assistant were experts on Greek and Turkish affairs.[49]

The only other new division established in 1909 was the division of information. Its earliest director was Philip H. Patchin, who was succeeded after his resignation by Sevellon L. Brown (not to be confused with Sevellon A. Brown, the earlier-named department employee). The information division performed services of some importance, preparing and distributing correspondence concerning foreign relations to the diplomatic and consular services and to the bureaus. It undertook the editing of *Foreign Relations of the United States*, the annual series of diplomatic documents published since 1861. Its chief, one assistant, and four clerks began work at 8:30 A.M. daily, reading and digesting American and foreign newspapers, sending summaries to the secretaries and heads of bureaus by 10:00 A.M. To increase information available to the public concerning foreign affairs Huntington-Wilson directed that papers explaining state matters be made available to the newsmen he received daily at 10:30 A.M. and 3:30 P.M.[50]

Huntington-Wilson had a penchant for new titles and categories, and his reorganization designated officials above the clerks and below the first assistant secretary either as "administrative" or "advisory" officers. The second and third assistants, whose duties remained nearly the same as before, together with the director of the consular service, a new post established for Carr, comprised the administrative officers. Huntington-Wilson had intended Carr's position to be that of a fourth assistant secretary, as it was in all but name, for Carr received the same salary as the second and third assistants and the same independence. The counselor and solicitor, who dealt with questions of municipal and international law, mostly claims by and against the United States, were advisory officers. Huntington-Wilson sought and secured appointments of a third adviser, called a resident diplomatic officer, an experienced diplomat whose advisory duties were to the secretary and the first assistant. This officer—Dawson, and later Dodge, both experts in Latin American affairs—received an annual salary of $7,500. For reasons of economy and politics the office lapsed in 1913.[51]

Beneath the advisers in rank and salary were the chief clerk and the division and bureau chiefs, designated "other administrative officers." When Carr moved to the higher rank, the former librarian of the department, William McNeir, became chief clerk. He directed internal business of the department, including supervision of the clerks and translators, purchase and distribution of supplies, management of the mail and telephone services, and finally, upkeep of the department's stables and numerous fireplaces. McNeir, together with the law clerk, the chief of the bureau of appointments (who for some unknown reason now had charge of the Great Seal), and the chief of the bureau of indexes and archives, which included the telegraph room, came under Huntington-Wilson's direction.

The remaining department bureaus—the diplomatic bureau, the bureau of rolls and library, the bureau of accounts, all supervised by the third assistant, the consular bureau and the bureau of trade relations, both under Carr's jurisdiction, the bureau of citizenship, under the solicitor—did not undergo major changes. The examination requirement for diplomatic and consular candidates enacted by Roosevelt's orders of 1905 and 1906 and Taft's of November 26, 1909, increased the work of the bureau of appointments, which kept the efficiency records. The bureau of accounts, despite Carr's earlier labors, remained an archaic organization. The bureau of trade relations, established in 1903, now included two commercial advisers who received $4,500 each, and a clerical force of thirteen. In September 1912 a departmental order abolished this bureau and replaced it with the office of foreign trade advisers, a key agency in the developing department.[52]

Huntington-Wilson left the department in March 1913 and later lamented that his program had been lost "in complicated details," that the system he had envisioned was ineffective because of the "clash of innumerable personalities."[53] Its breakdown was inevitable once Knox and Huntington-Wilson left. The system was designed for them only—especially for the difficult and supercilious first assistant secretary. Some observers noted that the reorganization of 1909 had not in fact changed the structure of the department but had increased its personnel and its problems. By the end of 1909 there were 210 employees, an increase of about one-sixth of the total force before reorganization. Most officers had retained their former positions or had moved to similar ones.[54]

Reorganization had not corrected the discrepancies in salaries, and higher salaries for the counselor and the resident diplomatic officer assured that the prestige of these offices would surmount that of lower-paying posts, including Huntington-Wilson's first assistantship. The initial indication of instability within the organization, besides the feud between the first assistant and the counselor, was abandonment early in 1913 of the distinction between administrative and advisory officers.[55] From that time the counselor and the solicitor ranked directly below the secretary, with the three assistants and the director of the consular service following, an arrangement commensurate with the respective salaries.

Officers were still grossly underpaid, and the best men often chose to leave the department for higher pay and less drudgery. A business expert appointed by Taft to examine the machinery of government, Major Charles Hine, reported in 1910 that "the working of the State Department indicates the most modern type of organization and an intelligent development of the most progressive methods. . . . So far from . . . needing much expert assistance, it is in a position to set an example as to fundamentals of organization and methods for many large business corporations."[56] A year later, however, the department's organizational handbook, which cited Hine's praise, described the situation in the division of Latin American affairs, remarking that it was fairly typical of department offices. The amount of work performed by the division was "so great that, owing to the smallness of the force, it is necessary for practically the whole force to remain after the regular office hours each day to keep the work up to date." The chief of the division was working overtime fifteen hours, and the seven other members of the division, eighty-five hours among them.[57]

The department early in 1913 thus displayed features of both the nineteenth and twentieth centuries. Improvement had begun. Carr had succeeded in his effort to reform the consular service. With the inauguration of examinations for entry into the lower ranks of the diplomatic service, through the executive orders of 1905, 1906, and 1909, that branch too was entering the modern world, albeit slowly. Huntington-Wilson had introduced experts into the department in a manner unknown to the late nineteenth century. But departmental personnel, especially those whose service had begun years before, still thought narrowly of their positions, their special work within the department, rather than in broader terms of international relations. The department in March 1913 hardly resembled an efficient operation. Its membership included a strange assortment of unimaginative bureaucrats, former diplomats, and a few experts in international law and diplomacy.

# 3

# Mr. Secretary Bryan

The appointment of the erstwhile boy orator of the Platte, the perennial Democratic candidate for the presidency, William Jennings Bryan, to the secretaryship of state in 1913 was an almost natural development of American politics, although it might have seemed strange to an outside observer. The Commoner, as Bryan was known, represented the type of progressivism in domestic politics and international relations for which most Democrats had voted. In domestic affairs the Nebraskan was a champion of popular democracy and free silver. In foreign affairs he was an anti-imperialist. He viewed international politics as no different from daily dealings among Christian gentlemen and had declared he would never participate in diplomatic negotiations leading to war. To many good Democrats such a viewpoint, such a declaration, seemed very sensible.

The political friendship between the new president, Woodrow Wilson, and his secretary of state was of recent vintage in 1913. For years Wilson had resented Bryan's influence in party circles. When Wilson had been a professor at Princeton and then president of the university aspiring to the presidency of the United States, he had despised the type of devotion that led, every four years, to the spectacle of Bryan's addresses at the Democratic national convention and the invariable reaction on the part of his followers. Denouncing him as a lunatic with no mental rudder, Wilson opposed Bryan within the party in 1896 and 1904. In 1908 he recommended that the party expel Bryan and the Nebraskan's followers, a suggestion that inspired the *New York World* to comment on the Princeton president's conviction that the minority party was too large and that a loss of several million voters would improve its chances in the election. After Bryan's third defeat in 1908, and the Princetonian's election as governor of New Jersey two years later, Wilson's newfound progressivism led him to take a different view of Bryanism. The Commoner noted with approval the governor's change but accepted friendship slowly. Mrs. Wilson realized that her husband's refusal to speak from the same platform as Bryan would harm his presidential chances, and the two Democrats met in March 1911. Both men were surprised at each other's sincerity and accord on progressive principles, particularly on the tariff.[1] As president-elect, Wilson owed a large part of his victory to the thrice-defeated presidential candidate, even though Bryan joined the Wilson campaign belatedly.

Bryan's position in the presidential campaign of 1912 had been doubtful at the outset. In the convention at Baltimore a Bryanite from 1896, Senator Champ Clark of Missouri, received the votes of the Nebraska delegation which Bryan headed. The trend to Wilson had begun on the tenth ballot. Only on the fourteenth ballot did Bryan shift Nebraska's votes to Wilson, announcing he would switch them back if the detestable New York delegation, which had declared for Clark, decided for Wilson. Bryan thus had lent Wilson dramatic but not decisive assistance. An inveterate worker for the party, he afterward gave Wilson support in the campaign, in the late summer and early autumn addressing crowds as often as ten times daily.[2]

After the election few observers doubted that Bryan would receive a major appointment. The one mentioned most frequently was the secretaryship of state. But at first it looked as if Bryan might become governor-general of the Philippine Islands. His interest in foreign affairs hitherto had extended primarily to granting independence to the Philippines. After opposing war with Spain in 1898 he had become convinced that Spanish rule in Cuba constituted a barbaric violation of the independence its inhabitants deserved and formed a volunteer regiment that saw service in the wilds of Florida. Leaving the army the day the peace treaty was signed in Paris, he opposed the territorial additions of that treaty as imperialistic and immoral. He then withdrew opposition and the treaty passed, as he became persuaded that only the United States, possibly with himself as president, would grant the Philippines the independence they wanted. He soon learned that he had miscalculated. His incessant efforts for Philippine independence nonetheless led him to suggest early in 1913 to President-elect Wilson, through Wilson's friend Colonel Edward M. House, that he be allowed to serve as governor-general of the islands for a year before becoming a cabinet officer. Wilson's enthusiasm for Philippine independence was lukewarm at best, and the effort failed. Bryan then moved to unseat Governor-general William Cameron Forbes, who opposed independence, and replace him with a person more amenable to that design. With Bryan's endorsement the president appointed Francis Burton Harrison as Forbes's successor.[3]

Bryan had yet another concern about foreign affairs, and it was initially unclear whether that concern would permit his acceptance of the secretaryship of state. The negotiation of treaties of conciliation would, he believed, prevent nations from going to war on slight provocation. The Commoner believed that nations could settle nearly every dispute by peaceful means, that violence was irrational, and that in his lifetime with his own efforts he could achieve a world without war. Would Wilson allow him to negotiate such treaties? Fortunately the two men seemed of one mind on this subject.

Attempting to discover if Bryan would take the secretaryship, Colonel House sensed a mundane problem bothering the Commoner. Bryan had written Wilson on Christmas day asking if he might make some arrangement to continue lecturing for pay on the Chautauqua circuit and also keep the editorship of the newspaper the *Commoner*, which he had owned and edited since 1901. Wilson replied that Bryan could continue those duties.[4] Later House visited Bryan in Florida and noted that the latter's new residence would probably cost in the neighborhood of $25,000, a lot of money for one who had houses in Nebraska and in Mission, Texas. House observed that Bryan in 1913 was worth some $200,000, made largely through lecturing.[5] The salary of the secretaryship of state, upped in 1911 from $6,000 to $12,000 (a raise Bryan once had opposed), would be less than that accorded an ambassador, and House recognized Bryan's need to continue lecturing and editing. He also foresaw that this activity could become a target of criticism for the administration.

Another problem with the appointment was that Wilson still distrusted Bryan's judgment. During the first weeks after the election Wilson seemed to be looking for some way to show gratitude to Bryan and at the same time keep him out of sight. He distrusted Bryan's judgment of men, and as secretary of state Bryan would be in a position to influence appointments. House talked to Mrs. Bryan—whose poise and intelligence he praised to the president-elect—regarding appointment of her husband to the ambassadorship at the Court of St. James's, an idea that had appeal because the Bryans' daughter had married a Britisher and was living in London. Wilson and House considered Russia an honorable place of exile but knew Bryan would not accept that post.

Still, most Democratic leaders believed Bryan's inclusion in the government would benefit the administration. Even among political opponents there were those, including the editor of Theodore Roosevelt's journal, the *Outlook*, who acknowledged that the new president could achieve none of his programs without support of the progressive Nebraskan.[6] Indeed, it might be better to include him; ties of loyalty to the executive would bind him to the administration. As Finley Peter Dunne's "Mr. Dooley" noted, paraphrasing President Wilson, "I'd rather have him close to me bosom thin on me back."[7]

And so Bryan was appointed. "It is a great pleasure," he wrote Wilson from Miami, "to be associated with one who moves so steadily forward and is so little disturbed by criticism issuing from irresponsible sources. . . . I would prefer to hold no office at all but I am persuaded that I can render more service near you."[8] By inauguration day Bryan and Wilson seemingly had buried differences, and the new secretary of state, as triumphant in anticipation of his first major national office as the new president could have been in his, rode in the inaugural parade in a car immediately following the president's. Some observers, including a proud and only slightly embarrassed Bryan, noted that the cheers for the secretary of state sounded louder and more numerous than those for the newly inaugurated president.[9]

What, then, would Secretary of State Bryan do in the Department of State? Employees in the State, War, and Navy Building awaited the arrival of the new secretary with trepidation, for they feared his often cited desire to reward deserving Democrats. Bryan's initial remarks to the assembled personnel on March 5, 1913, increased their nervousness, for the Commoner, according to the printed speech distributed to them beforehand, said ominously, "I am not prepared to discuss tenure of office. . . . I have not had time to learn from the president the general policy that will be impressed upon the various depart-

27

ments." According to Carr, Mrs. Bryan was more explicit, noting while on a tour of department offices "how it must have been a pleasant place to work and weren't they all sorry to leave." [10]

In subsequent weeks and months it became clear that the role of spoilsman was occupying an inordinate amount of the secretary's time and energies. At the outset of his tenure perhaps as much as nine-tenths of the secretary's mail came from office-seekers. Moreover, his several hundred weekly visitors ardently sought favors. The secretary gave unstinting attention to each applicant for office, especially if the applicant had voted for Bryan in one of the presidential elections or was related to someone who had.[11]

Bryan's spoils system touched directly on department offices in Washington. Huntington-Wilson and Adee were asked to remain, but the former resigned almost at the outset of the administration. He later wrote that the department had been "debauched and weakened by the political appointments of Bryan." He had little opportunity to observe the debauchery as during most of Bryan's tenure he was out of the country, as well as out of favor.[12] His successor, a former governor of Wyoming, member of the Democratic National Committee and long-time Bryan man, John E. Osborne, became the secretary's highest ranking appointment within the department. Other appointees, such as the counselor, John Bassett Moore, received their offices from the president with Bryan consenting. Among lesser officers Bryan secured the appointment of Joseph W. Folk of Missouri as department solicitor; he briefly had supported Folk as a presidential prospect in 1912. When Folk resigned, there was another Bryanite, Cone Johnson of Texas, to take his place.

To replace the chief clerk of the department, William McNeir, with Bryan's confidential secretary, Benjamin G. Davis, Bryan had to get McNeir's consent, as the office was classified under civil service. Carr was annoyed. "Thirty-three years in the service," he wrote of McNeir, "and I doubt whether Bryan even knows what his duties are! . . . A wife who is almost an invalid. A sister in the hospital, and income about to stop. But Bryan does not care. He is thinking only of his own fortunes and the political debts he can pay or create." Moore wrote on McNeir's behalf, at the behest of the latter's brother, and Bryan offered the position of librarian which McNeir had held before he became chief clerk, at a reduced salary. Moore thought McNeir should fight the matter. The chief clerk, a shy person, knew that to do so would make his position unbearable and decided to accept the lower-paying job.[13]

As foreign trade advisers Bryan turned to another former secretary from his campaigns of 1900 and 1908, Robert F. Rose, and a presidential elector from Kentucky and former law officer of the treasury department, William B. Fleming. The trade advisers were of some importance within the department, especially at a time when the administration was arguing a new tariff bill. Unfortunately neither had experience in the work. Counselor Moore wrote that Rose's appointment was "one of those deplorable manifestations which Mr. Bryan constantly makes of the utter lack of administrative sense and the entire absence of an appreciation of ability, experience, and training as qualifications for office."[14]

The counselor, whom Bryan reportedly insulted in April 1913, by asking the well-known authority on international law if he knew anything about the subject, learned that the secretary could recognize the qualities of personnel once he had seen their usefulness. Bryan told Moore that the chief of the diplomatic bureau, Sydney Smith, was so valuable that he ought to be paid $10,000 a year, an amount Moore considered excessive although he agreed with the assessment of Smith's ability. Moore discovered that most of Bryan's appointees within the department, including the much criticized foreign trade advisers who at first seemed absurdly incompetent, were good men who lacked knowledge but were willing to learn and in time gave at least passable service.[15]

The secretary was annoyed to learn that Carr's consular service operated under rules of civil service classification, as he wanted Democrats in these places. Carr reported the secretary as "cold-blooded about it—speaks not of efficiency, fitness or long service, but merely of places for Democrats." Bryan's treatment of consuls was heavy-handed. The secretary told the wife of the consul at Barcelona, Mrs. Henry H. Morgan, that the department would handle her husband's case on the basis of his record but added what came to be a refrain, "What about all the Democrats that have been waiting twenty years?"[16] Bryan insisted on filling the post of consular inspector with a Democrat. Regarding a certain applicant for such a position who had been in the service for twenty years, he wrote President Wilson that the "only reason for not recommending him is the feeling that the man who inspects these consulates should be in hearty sympathy with the Administration, because we have to rely so largely upon his judgment in judging the good behavior of our consuls." Wilson yielded to this request that all new inspectors be loyal Democrats but balked when the secretary asked him to revoke Roosevelt's executive order regarding classification of consuls and diplomatic secretaries according to merit. Bryan told House he thought many consuls "unfit" and deserving of dismissal, but Wilson insisted he would uphold the order of his predecessor. The president did admit to exceptions. An executive order removed the consulate at Jerusalem from the rule so that Bryan could appoint an aged clergyman. The new appointee died shortly after arrival at the post.[17]

More important for the future of American diplomacy was the secretary's attitude regarding chiefs of diplomatic missions abroad, positions not bound by civil service or executive order. Bryan in 1906 had told the ambassador to Italy, Henry White, that the Democrats, once in office, would send only Democrats abroad. Horrified, White later wrote that "it never occurred to him for a moment that the slightest training was necessary, or the interests of our Government should be in any way hampered . . . by the substitution of a 'good Democrat' possessing no knowledge whatever of the intricacies of European diplomacy for the man who spent many years of his life in close contact with all these questions."[18] The minister to Panama, H. Percival Dodge, showed consternation in July 1913 when Bryan told him that no favor would go to career diplomats, for the secretary preferred men "fresh from the people." Dodge had been in the diplomatic service since 1897 and told Moore he intended to get congressional support for remaining in Panama. He was replaced by a loyal Democrat from Kentucky named, perhaps not incidentally, William Jennings Price.[19]

The secretary and President Wilson both wished to democratize the diplomatic service, for they regarded the ambassadors and ministers Roosevelt and Taft had appointed as representing an aristocracy of Republican wealth and talent, which was true enough. Bryan deplored the lack of "prefixes" in front of Democrats' names, which prevented many good men from acquiring the prestige necessary for serving their country. Perhaps knowing the importance of what Roosevelt had called the hyphenate vote, that is, citizens of foreign birth or antecedents, the secretary thought that it would be appropriate to recognize naturalized citizens by accrediting them to their nations of birth. He was also concerned that there be a diplomat from nearly every state, and in May 1913 he wrote the president about a vacancy in Venezuela: "If Gonzales is selected from South Carolina, McMillan from Tennessee, Lamar from Florida, and Leavell from Mississippi, a number of the Southern states will be taken care of. You already have some Virginians in mind, and Texas has been recognized in Thomson, although . . . it would be well to take another diplomatic position from Texas if we can do so." After comments on appointees from Oklahoma, Arkansas, and New Mexico he added, "I will speak to you later about Alabama and Louisiana."[20] The secretary wrote Wilson in February 1914 regarding the appointment to Stockholm of a Connecticut man of Swedish descent, which geographical combination aptly summarized his views on qualifications for appointments abroad. He had, he said, four reasons for objecting to the appointment. First, Connecticut had few Swedes, and "it would be well to appoint one from a section where there are a great many of that nationality and thus get a larger benefit from it." Second, the minister from Sweden resident in Washington (perhaps noting some of Bryan's earlier hyphenate appointments) preferred someone not Swedish-American. Third, the Connecticut man was barely a Democrat, certainly not one of long standing, and his appointment could not benefit Democrats in his state. "Fourthly," Bryan wrote petulantly, "in our last conversation I understood you to agree that the Swedish post should be given to Arkansas in lieu of the Uruguay mission."[21]

One of Bryan's devices for rewarding Democrats was a temporary appointment. When Jacob Gould Schurman retired from the Greek legation in 1913, Bryan sought out an ex-Populist from Massachusetts, George Fred Williams, because the president's choice, "an original Wilson man," Professor Garrett Droppers of Williams College, could not immediately leave his academic duties. "We have so many deserving Democrats and so few places to give. . . . If you do not approve of the suggestion in regard to George Fred Williams, would you like to have me look about for a good Democrat who would like a winter's stay in Greece?" Williams got the winter's vacation in Athens, despite President Wilson's intense dislike for the man who had led the campaign in Massachusetts against his candidacy in 1912.[22]

The worst of Bryan's appointments were in Latin America, where there were positions which the Republican dollar diplomats had filled with career men. In addition to Dodge's removal from Panama, there was the replacement in Ecuador of Montgomery Schuyler, a diplomatic officer since 1902, by Charles S. Hartman, a free silver Republican who had left the party for Bryan in 1896. For Cuba a Democratic editor of Cuban descent, William E. Gonzales of South Carolina, mentioned above, replaced Arthur M. Beaupré, who had been in the diplomatic service since 1897. The appointment was distasteful to Cubans because Gonzales's father, a revolutionist, had removed to the United States in 1850. Edward J. Hale, seventy-four years old, replaced the veteran Lewis Einstein in Costa Rica. George Weitzel, a former assistant chief of the division of Latin American affairs, was succeeded in Nicaragua, a difficult post, by Benjamin L. Jefferson, who had to be shown the location of his assigned country on a map. A land agent from Louisiana, John Ewing, replaced Charles D. White in Honduras. White had been in the diplomatic service since 1904. Ewing later had Bryan appoint his brother as his aide, who was reported to have received the president of Honduras while suffering from an attack of delirium tremens.[23]

Most of Secretary Bryan's patronage cases involved smaller missions. The president recognized that Bryan owed debts to his followers and gave him a free hand in appointing men to posts of lesser importance. Wilson selected most of the ambassadors, particularly those for Europe and the Far East, although Bryan's political shrewdness sometimes proved helpful. The secretary's objection to the appointment of Thomas W. Gregory of Texas as ambassador to Mexico, on the ground that loyalty to Texas would make Gregory an interventionist in Mexican affairs, demonstrated a wisdom neither Wilson nor House had acquired. Bryan "beamed with satisfaction" when he learned that Gregory had withdrawn, perhaps at the colonel's urging, whereupon House happily told him he "would expect several ambassadors and ministers and a bunch of consuls in exchange."[24]

Bryan might have spent less time rewarding Democrats and more learning about foreign policy. William Phillips became third assistant secretary of state in 1914 and later said that although he liked Bryan he realized, "like everyone else, that he was a poor secretary of state and that his ignorance with regard to the conduct of foreign relations was abysmal." [25] Aside from a few long-held principles, such as anti-imperialism and belief in conciliation treaties, world issues had troubled Bryan scarcely at all. A domestic politician, he had small regard for the cultural achievements of other nations. On a trip to Europe in 1903–4, and on a world tour from September 1905 to August of the following year, he spent his time studying the politics of nations he visited and lecturing on democracy to those personages he met, including Czar Nicholas II. [26] He read little and knew almost no history. Nor did he know much of geography. The American minister to the Netherlands, Henry van Dyke, reported, perhaps erroneously, that the new secretary of state did not know that the Dutch possessed an empire in the East Indies (in a book describing his travels, *The Old World and Its Ways*, published in 1907, Bryan had included a chapter on those islands, entitled "Netherlands India"). [27]

There was a problem other than Bryan's ignorance: he was disorganized. Entering the department he had called upon several of its members, including Alvey Adee, Francis Huntington-Wilson, and Wilbur Carr, to brief him on foreign affairs. They found the secretary "seemed hardly to follow a definite line of thought," a lamentable contrast with Secretaries Philander Knox and Elihu Root. [28] Counselor Moore agreed that the trouble with Bryan was "his apparent inability when present to give consecutive thought or really intelligent consideration to anything brought before him. He never seemed to have a reasoned judgment on anything or any real appreciation of what he was doing." [29]

Bryan was disorganized in more than just thought. In the department he was willing to extend a welcome to anyone who had voted for him, provided the man could get into his office. In his department routine everything was confused. The secretary altogether disregarded protocol regarding admission of foreign diplomats, much to the annoyance of ambassadors and ministers who, after waiting in outer offices for more than an hour, often were shown in to the secretary's office behind lesser officials. [30] Carr in April 1914 described Bryan's office at the height of the Mexican crisis. "The room had a large congregation of newspaper men in it when I saw the Secretary today. He was replying to their questions and Bob Rose and the other Rose were taking stenographic notes of the questions and answers. Long was standing near the Secretary. The British Ambassador was sitting nearby waiting for an interview. Kelly was sitting at his desk looking on and Davis and I were waiting with papers for Bryan to sign."[31]

Under these circumstances much department work went unfinished. Papers sent to the secretary's desk remained there for weeks or disappeared. As often happened in the case of the counselor Moore, through whose hands nearly all department matters were supposed to pass, Bryan picked up papers and sequestered them before Moore could get time to read them.[32]

Ministers and ambassadors abroad became aware of the disorganization at home. To their queries on routine matters they received no replies and sometimes waited weeks for answers on matters of policy. Later researchers in department archives would discover that reports and memoranda on important issues affecting policy in 1913–14 usually carried the stamp or signature of the secretary, but the date indicated a long gap before reading. Henry P. Fletcher, who at the time was minister to Chile, later recalled that he always telegraphed Bryan when the matter was important, for the secretary respected telegrams. Another Latin American envoy commented that he found it more effective to give the item he wanted relayed to the secretary to the Associated Press, and Bryan would read it in the *Washington Post*.[33] The American ambassador in London, Walter Page, and the first secretary of the embassy in Berlin, Joseph Grew, complained of the lack of communication. Page blamed the secretary and suggested to Colonel House that the president appoint Phillips to oversee communications, checking the dispatches Bryan handled. When Phillips eventually arrived in the department, he undertook to survey Bryan's correspondence, checking every outgoing letter from the secretary's desk. Bryan did not object.[34]

One result of Bryan's disorganized routine was that President Wilson himself was forced to circumvent the secretary of state by using executive agents. The employment of William Bayard Hale, John Lind, and Colonel House in the diplomatic crises of Mexico and Europe in 1913–14 adversely affected relations between the department and other foreign offices, in addition to demoralizing department personnel trained for the work now often performed by amateurs.

Bryan multiplied his difficulties as secretary of state by poor communication with the press. The secretary, it developed, was secretive. He disliked reporters, who, he remarked, had a "faculty of reading between the lines, above the lines, and below the lines."[35] The secretiveness of course should not have been a surprise. For years Bryan had been wounded by reporters, and he was sensitive on this score. He also was by nature guarded. "No man," someone wrote, "had Bryan's confidence; no man could speak for him or tell what he would do in a given case. As long as he was secretary of state he maintained his uncommunicative, determined attitude."[36] He angered newspapermen whose questions on foreign affairs he regarded as improper. Bryan's friends were equally offensive to reporters. Senator Ben Tillman of South Carolina, who had referred to Democratic office-seekers as the biblical "wild asses of the desert . . . athirst and hungry," commented when he saw reporters standing around the department offices, "Bryan, I didn't know that you had two herds of wild asses around here."[37] With the president's consent Bryan issued a statement in July 1913 that no questions would be answered concerning foreign policies until the president thought such answers would promote the public interest. This roused reporters such as Vincent Starrett of the *Chicago News* who came to regard the secretary as an "eminent fathead," of "portentous ignorance, egotism, and vulgarity."[38]

The result of Bryan's bad relations with the newspaper reporters was that everything he did came under intense press criticism. A teetotaler, he refused to dispense alcoholic beverages to the Washington diplomatic corps, and almost immediately there was a contretemps. The "grape juice incident" took place at Bryan's first diplomatic banquet, on April 21, 1913, and created a furor in the newspapers. There were innumerable references to "grape juice diplomacy." The publicity annoyed the secretary. The majority of letters he and his wife had received were approving, he said. Admirers deluged the Bryans with cases of grape juice and other nonalcoholic drinks, which the secretary gave to department personnel.[39] But whatever Bryan said or did in regard to the substitution of grape juice for hard liquor during his tenure at the state department, newspaper reporters did their best to make him look foolish.

Then there was another cause célèbre. In summer of 1913 newspapers reported that the secretary intended to continue lecturing for pay. In reply Bryan tried to explain that he had found the work on the Chautauqua circuit necessary not only to maintain his public image but to supplement his income which, after tithing, he found inadequate. He needed the money, he said, to meet insurance payments. He was not, one should add, the only government official to lecture for pay. Vice-president Thomas R. Marshall and Speaker of the House Champ Clark were out on the circuit that summer, but being less in the public eye they did not receive the criticism. There seemed indeed to be a double standard. Angered by Bryan's desertion of him at the Baltimore convention in 1912, Clark cheekily told reporters it was dishonest for an officeholder to make money by lecturing. Hostile reporters seized upon the secretary's proposed lecture tour to ridicule him as a carnival performer who displayed his wares on the same stage with jugglers, minstrels, and performing seals. They criticized him for the hours and days spent away from his office. "We have no quarrel because the Secretary of State wishes to meet crowds of his fellow citizens and draw inspiration from them," the *Nation* commented. "But we do protest emphatically at what is now going on—a Secretary of State cutting short conferences with foreign Ambassadors to rush off to a little town in West Virginia or Maryland to earn his $250; then returning to Washington by sleeper for a few hours at his office, and finally dashing off again for a wild night ride by auto or a train journey to some obscure hamlet."[40]

Bryan came to the department with the dream of securing treaties of conciliation—"cooling-off" treaties, they came to be called—with as many nations as would consent to sign such agreements, and even on this score he found himself criticized by the press. His peace plans were well known; he had been working on them since his visit with Count Alexei Tolstoy in the winter of 1904. An editorial in the *Commoner* on February 17, 1905, was the first suggestion of his plan that international disputes be submitted to a commission or court of arbitration, with the reservation that the government of each country could reject the findings if it found them incompatible with its honor and integrity. Bryan believed that a cooling-off period during which the "peace forces of a nation might have a chance to be felt and heard" would forestall war.

He had sent the first draft of his proposal to the White House early in April 1913. On April 24 at noon he told the assembled Washington diplomatic corps of his plan. In addition to calling for a permanent commission of one citizen from each signatory, one from another state chosen by the signatories, and a fifth member selected by agreement of the parties, the plan accepted the principle of independent action. A provision that there be a moratorium on changes in naval or military programs during the cooling-off period ranging from six months to one year met opposition from the Senate and from foreign countries, and Bryan abandoned it. In all, thirty nations signed conciliation treaties, and of these bilateral instruments twenty eventually went into effect. Bryan considered them his most outstanding triumph while in office, indeed the triumph of his lifetime.[41] But the treaties drew fire from critics at home and abroad who accused Bryan of wasting his time, and Ambassador Page wrote House of the rumor that Bryan was coming to England to urge his peace plan and declared that if this should happen he would resign, as the British had no respect for "grape juice diplomacy."[42] An exaggeration, but many people did tend to disregard the treaties. History itself dismissed them. No nation ever invoked them, and although these instruments are still theoretically in force, membership in the conciliation commissions has long since lapsed with the deaths of the appointed commissioners.

Bryan's diplomacy, one must conclude, was that of a well-meaning amateur, and this was his weakness as secretary of state. For nearly two decades, since 1896, he had been a domestic political leader of large stature. In 1913–14 he still could exert an enormous influence over his many devoted party followers. But in diplomacy he was by any analysis an amateur. His abilities were quite insufficient to guide properly his cabinet department at a time of uncommon crisis during the year and a half prior to the outbreak of the greatest war the world had ever seen.

# 4

# Supervisors: Wilson and House

In the making of American foreign policy it may not be a crucial matter if the secretary of state is ignorant both of the broader aspects of international affairs and the more immediate problems of administering his department. The ambiguity of the American Constitution allows the president, as commander-in-chief and as chief executive, to determine in large part the government's relations with other powers. No one realized this fact more than the newly elected president in 1913, Woodrow Wilson. If as governor of New Jersey, Wilson had by most accounts little knowledge of the intricacies of foreign affairs, the former professor and college president was a student of the Constitution. Better than most presidents-elect he understood the prerogatives of the post he was to hold for eight years. As president he assumed control of matters in which he was by nature or choice interested; in particulars of policy outside this range he allowed each cabinet department to manage on its own. To an individual unacquainted with the president at the outset of the new Democratic administration it might have appeared that Wilson's relations with the State Department would be as vague as his involvement with the Department of Agriculture—whose secretary, David F. Houston, often was to complain of the chief executive's lack of interest. The president's conviction that his office gave its holder power and responsibility, his ambition to be a statesman, and the increased American involvements in world affairs all combined to make his direction of State Department matters more immediate and, more often than not, to cause him to ignore or bypass that department.[1]

The new president was as little prepared for the responsibilities of statesmanship as was William Jennings Bryan, who in fact had traveled more widely and had at least a speaking acquaintance with contemporary world leaders. Wilson's political experience was far inferior to Bryan's. In some other respects their backgrounds were similar. Both men were deeply religious Presbyterians of Scots-Irish ancestry;

both had trained in public speaking and as college undergraduates had excelled at debating. There may have been, it is true, considerable differences in standards of debate at the colleges each attended, but Bryan's style of oratory pleased most Americans of that era every bit as much as did Wilson's.

Wilson's life from college to the presidency is well known and needs no recital. After the years of graduate work at Johns Hopkins, the teaching at Bryn Mawr and Wesleyan University in 1885 to 1890, the twenty years as Princeton professor and president, the two years in the governorship of New Jersey—in this passage of a quarter century and more there was hardly an item of foreign affairs that had touched Wilson's immediate concern. It would be wrong to state that he was totally ignorant of such matters. Although he spoke no foreign language, he read, besides Latin and Greek, both French and German. From 1898 onward he had realized the increasing importance of the United States as a world power. In 1899, when he was seeking a candidate for a new chair of political science at Princeton, he wrote to Walter Page and Albert Shaw asking for nominations of an individual acquainted with "the new world affairs into the midst of which we find our country thrown."[2] Wilson taught courses in comparative government and was especially conversant with the British constitutional system. But any knowledge he had of foreign affairs was more theoretical than practical. Certainly he did not anticipate the extraordinary international problems that would involve his country while he was in the White House.

If the new president had never held a high regard for Bryan and had appointed him to head the State Department only for political reasons, once Bryan was in the State, War, and Navy Building and Wilson in the White House they seemed to get along. Each man admired the other's sincerity and idealism, and on certain points such as their attitudes toward the tariff, monopolies, and the financial power of Wall Street, the two were in harmony. They both had a deep interest in world peace. They were advocates of a new "moral"—as contrasted with "dollar"—diplomacy. In fact these appeared indistinguishable to some State Department members. Wilson completely shared Bryan's belief that relations between governments were and should be no different from relations between Christian gentlemen. Diplomacy should be removed from the market place (without destroying its commercial advantages) and also should cease to be the preserve of an aristocracy or bureaucracy. For these sentiments there was not complete enthusiasm among some of Wilson's and Bryan's underlings; to would-be dollar diplomats, aristocrats, and bureaucrats such ideas seemed hopelessly naive. To these two leaders, moral diplomacy was as absolute a requirement as Christianity, and in the grand struggle for principles that beset all the generations of mankind it was as certain to emerge victorious.

Both Wilson and Bryan believed that good governments should be recognized and bad ones not, although neither clearly defined their standards. The British government was entitled to equality of rates for passage of its ships through the Panama Canal because a previous treaty said so; a Christian gentleman kept his promises. In European affairs, which had about them something sordid because of their connection with aristocracy and royalty, the rule should remain abstention; whatever the problems of Jews in Russia and Eastern Europe, they must be alleviated without American intervention. As for the sort of representatives the United States should send abroad to advance its ideals, Wilson and Bryan agreed that the finest American diplomats would come not from the professional diplomatic service but from the thousands of young men who supported the Democratic cause in 1912.

The president's support of Bryan's cooling-off treaties was heartfelt and sincere, even if presidential faith in the willingness of nations to abide by such agreements in a crisis was somewhat less than that of the secretary of state. Colonel Edward M. House told Sir Edward Grey in 1913 that the president was "not altogether *en rapport* with Bryan's peace plans" but would allow the secretary to go as far as possible on the matter.[3] In sum, if the personalities of Wilson and Bryan were in some respects poles apart, the convictions of the two men regarding foreign policy were essentially the same.

The president and Bryan were publicly tactful about each other. Wilson received numerous letters complaining about Bryan, especially when he undertook the Chautauqua lectures. Understanding Bryan's political importance and the value of the secretary's loyalty, the president did not comment. Perhaps he should have, for he had given Bryan permission to resume the lectures. Bryan in turn was more openly loyal to his chief, insisting that the *Commoner* carry no criticism of a Wilson appointee, print no picture of himself except with the president or another cabinet member, and refrain from running letters or stories unfavorable to administration policy.[4]

Wilson had small regard for professional diplomats and department bureaucrats, and this prejudice applied even to those individuals he appointed. Upon sending appointees to their posts he gave most of them no instructions and thereafter paid little attention to their reports unless they were amusing, as were those of Walter Page, or agreed with his beliefs. One might have thought this behavior toward his representatives abroad somewhat odd or at the least unconventional or perhaps incautious. There was, however, a considerable consistency in Wilson's attitude toward the administration of foreign affairs. When the young Professor Wilson was trying to extricate himself from his teaching duties at Bryn Mawr in 1887 (he heartily disliked teaching political science to young women), he had applied unsuccessfully for the position of first assistant secretary of state. It had not occurred to him that the post needed someone who had experience and knowledge of diplomatic procedure. He believed only that a stint in the office would improve his teaching. By 1913 he did not seem to have changed his ideas. He considered the members of the various State Department offices unimportant in the forming of American policy and considered both the department and the diplomatic service sinkholes for unambitious or indifferently talented persons.[5]

Wilson's view of professional diplomacy appeared clearly in the case of a Princeton graduate, John Van Antwerp MacMurray, who aspired to a position in the diplomatic service. In 1905 young MacMurray had asked Wilson for a recommendation. It was Wilson's policy to write few such recommendations unless he considered the person especially worthy, as he did MacMurray, whom he believed to be a brilliant writer. The then college president had written in reply that such a career as MacMurray desired was useless and had no future. He advised the young man to continue his study of letters. "My feeling of uneasiness in all such cases," he wrote, "rests chiefly on my knowledge of the great temptations connected with foreign secretaryships. There is little of serious importance to do; the activities are those of society rather than those of business; the unimportant things are always at the front; there is no provocation to study; impulses are cooled and principles are exposed to rust." MacMurray ignored this advice and entered the service with Wilson's later blessing. After the president of Princeton became president of the United States, Mac-Murray, who had served in Tokyo and St. Petersburg and was then on duty in the department, was offered the post of minister to Siam. Mac-Murray turned it down because he did not want a political appointment lacking permanence and preferred to remain a diplomatic secretary awaiting the day when appointments to ministerial positions might be solely on merit. By this time, late in 1913, Wilson was beginning to grasp the importance of the diplomatic service. He allowed MacMur-ray to go to Peking as first secretary of legation and continue a career in which he later achieved a considerable prominence.[6]

Upon winning the election in 1912, Wilson told friends that he intended to appoint only the "best men . . . exceptional men, out of the common run."[7] This was surely an admirable if not altogether novel pronouncement by a successful candidate. His view of who constituted the best men, it was soon apparent, was traditional, coinciding with Bryan's views of deserving Democrats. As was his prerogative, the president reserved for himself the appointment of major officials within the department and abroad, leaving to Bryan the posts of less importance. There was, however, a certain care here. Ordinarily Wilson did not make any appointment in the various departments without consulting the pertinent cabinet officers, and in order to avoid much time-consuming labor he left the business of requests for office to the cabinet heads, to his secretary Joseph P. Tumulty, and to Colonel House. Such was the case with State Department appointments. Within Bryan's department Wilson personally selected, with House's advice, John Bassett Moore, William Phillips, and Robert Lansing. The entire cabinet had agreed that Alvey Adee should remain as second assistant secretary. Wilson objected to Bryan's selections of John E. Osborne and Joseph W. Folk, for he thought them incompetent, but in keeping with his general policy of noninterference with the cabinet heads' dispensation of patronage, he allowed them to enter the department.[8]

Wilson attempted, although with little enthusiasm, to maintain both the letter and spirit of previous executive orders regarding the consular and diplomatic services, notably the two orders of Theodore Roosevelt. He was more successful in the case of the consuls, in part because they had legal protection in the Lodge Act of 1906, in part because Colonel House took an interest in maintaining the integrity of the consular service. On House's advice the president in 1913 reminded Bryan to set a date for examinations for the diplomatic service, as many young men were seeking appointments. Encouraged by House, the president sought passage of an act which would do for the diplomatic service what the Lodge Act had achieved for consular officers. Bryan's opposition interfered with this plan, as did Wilson's understanding that passage of such an act would alienate important Southern and Western senators seeking diplomatic appointments from their states.[9]

Wilson's methods and motives in making diplomatic appointments showed him no less a spoilsman than Bryan. He claimed a "general principle that those who apply are the least likely to be appointed," yet nearly every successful diplomatic appointee had sought preferment because of some contribution to the Democratic party.[10] Wilson avowed that he would not nominate rich men but learned he had to do so, for the expense of maintaining an embassy or even a small legation was too great for most of Wilson's "best men." His first diplomatic choices were not poor men, although all were Democrats—or thought to be persons "in sympathy with us"—as the president told Moore.[11] Charles W. Eliot, John R. Mott, Henry B. Fine, and Cleveland H. Dodge were individuals of considerable means. All of them rejected diplomatic posts on grounds of the expense. Wilson was forced to turn to such persons as James W. Gerard and Henry Morgenthau of New York, men of more wealth than Wilsonian principles. The editor of the *North American Review* and *Harper's Weekly*, George Harvey, had assisted Wilson's political ambitions since 1902. He had been off-again, on-again in support throughout the presidential campaign and in 1913 was piqued not to receive the London embassy he claimed Wilson had promised him. So perhaps he was a biased observer. But he wrote in 1914 that of all the president's major diplomatic appointments only Walter Page had not been a heavy contributor to the campaign. Page, he wrote, had given only $100.[12]

Wilson sought to appoint to Austria or France the Democratic national chairman, William F. McCombs, who considered himself personally responsible for the victory of 1912—not because McCombs was suited for either diplomatic post, as Wilson publicly claimed and reiterated to McCombs, but as he admitted to his wife, to House, and to McCombs's rival, William Gibbs McAdoo, because he wanted to remove McCombs as far from his presence as possible. By early 1913 McCombs was plainly unstable, probably an alcoholic (he reportedly downed a bottle of whiskey daily, and House thought he was taking drugs). For months he alternately accepted and rejected the Paris embassy, citing reasons of expense, health, the lack of prestige of an ambassadorship, and countless other objections. "I am going to let him have just as much rope as he requires to hang himself," Wilson laughingly told his wife. Colonel House added that while it might be hard on the French people, "something was due to the Governor" and himself.[13] The result was that the Republican Myron T. Herrick remained in Paris knowing that his appointment was to end sooner or later, if only McCombs would accept or another man could be found.

In a letter to a Princeton friend Mrs. Wilson intimated that the offer of the Berlin post to Dean Henry B. Fine was not solely because of the Princeton professor's talents. Fine had sided with Wilson in the academic battles of 1906–10, and her husband and she were eager to watch the chagrin of Wilson's one-time academic opponents when Fine received a position. Fine, unfortunately, claimed he did not have sufficient financial resources. Nor, it appeared, was he willing to risk the possibility of failure in working for Wilson again, for he rejected the offer even after the president arranged for Cleveland Dodge to maintain Fine in Berlin.[14]

The greatest contributor to the president's campaign of 1912 was Charles R. Crane of Chicago, and Wilson wanted to reward the plumbing magnate. He decided on Russia. The president must have understood that Crane's name was well-known to the State Department, for during Taft's regime Crane had received appointment as minister to China, only to lose the post by tactless statements to the press concerning his instructions as he was en route to take ship. Philander C. Knox and Francis Huntington-Wilson, after investigation of the matter, had rightly cashiered Crane, who later had used the incident to advance his position in the Democratic party. In 1913 he turned down Wilson's offer of St. Petersburg, vacant for more than a year because of Russian failure to heed American requests to cease persecution of the Jews, although he made it clear that he would reconsider the offer at a later date.[15]

When Crane slowly bowed out, this gave Wilson and Bryan an opportunity to secure a temporary appointment, and the person recommended by Senator James Hamilton Lewis of Illinois was a Joliet newspaperman, Henry M. Pindell. The offer flattered Pindell, but word leaked to the press, in the form of letters Senator Lewis claimed were forgeries. It appeared that the senator had offered the appointment to Pindell by explaining that it would be a good vacation with no need to do any work. The editor of the *New York Tribune* could not "recall anything more diverting than the view of Mr. Pindell, of Peoria, being taken up to a high place by the Hon. 'Jim Ham' Lewis and shown a vision of himself hobnobbing with the crowned heads while Mrs. Pindell and the little Pindells got 'social positions.'" Wilson denied he had offered the appointment but said that he considered Pindell completely fit for the post. The president had not yet acquired the prejudice against Senator Lewis which would lead him to remark to House in 1916 that he "did not want to do anything Senator Lewis of Illinois would even indirectly feel was done for him." In 1913 he was disposed to bail out the senator.

What to do about the Pindell problem? Both Lewis and Pindell were in embarrassing positions, especially because, unknown to them, the Russian ambassador in Washington as well as the American chargé d'affaires in St. Petersburg, Charles S. Wilson, informed the State Department that Pindell would be persona non grata because of publicity given the case. There ensued a maneuver in which Wilson made the offer to Pindell to spare him public embarrassment, on the condition he would reject it after senatorial confirmation to spare the president embarrassment. Informed of this byzantine procedure the Russians were told to keep it confidential. The Senate duly confirmed Pindell, and Pindell duly resigned. Department officials were appalled, especially by the president's deception of the Senate, which had no knowledge of the arrangement. The Russian post remained vacant until after the outbreak of war in August 1914, when it went not to Crane but to another large contributor to the Democratic campaign, George T. Marye of California.[16]

The president found the Far Eastern posts difficult, for both he and

Bryan agreed that they should go to men of Christian principle. Wilson considered the leader of the international Y.M.C.A., John R. Mott. Disappointed by Mott's refusal ("one in a thousand," Wilson called him), the president considered Norman Hapgood, the former editor of *Collier's Weekly* who had been ousted from that position because of support for Wilson, but asked House to find out if he were an orthodox Christian. House questioned Hapgood on his religious beliefs and decided he had few. The president continued to search. The Wisconsin professor-reformer Edward A. Ross, whom Crane had recommended, was found politically if not religiously unsound. Finally Professor Paul Reinsch, also of the University of Wisconsin, was selected; this seemed an ideal appointment, for he was a professed Christian and an acknowledged expert on Far Eastern affairs.

Despite the fact that Japan rated an ambassadorship while Peking rated only a minister, the appointment to Japan seemed to present less of a problem, and here the solution proved political. George Guthrie of Pittsburgh, the third member of his family to be mayor of that city, had been a contributor to the Democratic campaign, and he sought the Tokyo appointment. Although Wilson had no great liking for Guthrie, the former progressive mayor received the nomination to Japan shortly after Wilson's inauguration. Neither Wilson nor House seems to have raised the question of Guthrie's religious orthodoxy.[17]

As appointments gradually were made, it became necessary to relieve the incumbents, sometimes a delicate and difficult chore. Wilson's manner of removing Republican appointees was not always tactful. It was the custom for ambassadors and ministers to submit resignations upon the election or re-election of a president, and the majority of incumbents had done so in 1913, but many of them waited for weeks or months after March 4 to receive word of what they were to do, and some of them certainly hoped to stay on. A few career men openly asked for extensions, notably Taft's minister to Constantinople, William W. Rockhill, a diplomat of long experience who asked that his appointment be extended sufficiently so that he could have the honor of serving under three Democratic administrations. Upon returning to Washington on vacation Rockhill learned that Henry Morgenthau, who had served as chairman of the Democratic finance committee, was to receive the post. Morgenthau's appointment went beyond reward for service to the party, for before Rockhill's time the Turkish post had been filled by a Jew. The president possessed only contempt for Morgenthau, who wanted to be secretary of the treasury and at first turned down the ambassadorship because he resented the religious tradition. Felix Frankfurter, who worked with Morgenthau during the World War, could write in long retrospect that "he hadn't a brain in his head," and that "it was something new to him; that you had to have an idea before you expressed it," but despite this consider-able handicap Wilson in 1913 wanted Morgenthau to represent Jewish interests in the Ottoman empire.[18]

As for other presidential contacts with the Department of State—with, say, department officers in the State, War, and Navy Building—they were largely indirect. With exception of Bryan, whom Wilson saw frequently and often talked to by telephone, the president's only direct connection with the department was through the counselor—Moore, and later Lansing. In the secretary's absence Moore and his successor attended cabinet meetings. As a result the president got to know the counselors, but he knew almost nothing about most of the other officers of the department. Because Moore and Lansing were Democrats picked by the president the arrangement seemed satis-factory.

Actually the president's relations with Counselor Moore were far from satisfactory, at least as Moore viewed them. Wilson so often disregarded his advice. Moore complained bitterly that Wilson did not deal with legal matters in an educated manner because the president had become, as early as his Princeton presidency, too much the politi-cian to pursue serious scholarship. A jovial person, Moore found the president as cool in dealings with people as he appeared on July days in his white summer suit complete to white stockings and shoes. Moore resented the fact that Wilson, even when informed, did nothing to relieve the burden imposed on the department's counselor by new appointees' inexperience and the secretary's lack of administrative ability.

As an individual with some years of experience in departmental novelties, Moore was particularly annoyed by the president's use in foreign affairs of special agents lacking department approval or even department knowledge. The first of these appointments, John Lind of

47

Minnesota, became the president's special representative in Mexico City. (An earlier emissary, William Bayard Hale, had gone to Mexico at Wilson's request and, although he had no official capacity, his subsequent report, much to Moore's disgust, was regarded with interest at the White House.) Newspapers announced the Lind appointment before department officials knew of it. Moore agreed with critics who noted that Wilson's idea of a good representative in a crisis area was a man who had no knowledge of the subject and disliked the personages involved. Such a person would be capable, so the theory went, of giving the president more objective advice than would experts or perhaps the department's counselor. This view had some merit, for the previous administration's appointees in Mexico, particularly Ambassador Henry Lane Wilson, had behaved in decidedly unneutral fashion. But it was, as Moore thought at the time and Frankfurter later commented, "a hell of a way to run a railroad." [19]

Mexican affairs occupied the major part of Wilson's dealings with foreign countries until the late summer of 1914, and increasingly he ignored the advice on Mexico proffered by department officials. Communication between the White House and the department generally remained on such a personal level—as in the case of the frequent telephone calls between the secretary and the president, all unrecorded—that department personnel were understandably demoralized. They could busy themselves drawing up instructions, reading dispatches and notes, interviewing ambassadors and ministers, and the resultant information could be filed according to the department's new and efficient filing system, but when a decision had to be made, the men who did it seemed to be the president and Bryan or, even more likely, one of Wilson's informal advisers such as Colonel House or a special emissary. Department personnel, the experts, were left standing at the switches as the train, perhaps, went down the wrong track.

Lower department personnel in Washington were not the only individuals ignored in the conduct of foreign affairs. Bryan had some reason to feel that he was occasionally outside of the president's diplomatic arrangements. Much of the contemporary commentary about Wilson ignoring Bryan was an exaggeration. The president, however, notably circumvented the secretary in the touchy case of the California alien land legislation, advising the California legislature directly after instructing Bryan not to do so—Bryan who was politically far more knowledgeable of the situation and the legislators, and who at presidential request had traveled out to the West Coast.

When it came to consulting Congress on foreign affairs Wilson likewise often failed to do so, as when he raised Peru's legation to an embassy without congressional authorization, in violation of a 1909 Act of Congress. His dealings with the foreign relations committee of the Senate, admittedly a weak group, were sometimes quite offhand, verging on the irresponsible. His early dealings with Congress on foreign affairs showed either a desire to be offhand or unwillingness to pay attention to the detail of foreign relations. When questioned early in 1914 by an opponent, Senator James A. O'Gorman of New York, as to how many governments had recognized Huerta, Wilson said he did not know and had to ask the secretary of state. His speeches to Congress on the Panama Canal tolls question and on Mexico showed he had not read the mountain of diplomatic correspondence or consulted those persons who had.[20]

Several months after resigning as counselor of the department, Moore confessed to his wife that he had "less confidence in Wilson than in any other man" he had known. He condemned Wilson's "supercilious ignorance" and (presaging the future) his "readiness to misrepresent and to create false appearances in order to give false impressions."[21]

Behind President Wilson in foreign affairs, of course, stood a man for whom the well-informed Moore, probably the best expert in international law this country has produced, had an uncertain respect, namely the slight, quiet figure of Colonel House of Texas, the president's adviser, friend, confidant. This was the "enigmatic" House, who many people believed was the power behind Wilson. The wealthy, soft-spoken colonel had been a figure in Texas politics before he met Wilson in 1911. He preferred to be called "Mr. House" rather than by the honorary title that Governor James Hogg of Texas bestowed on him. He held no formal post in the administration and refused to hold an office until the Paris Peace Conference in 1919.

The colonel's reticence about publicity was the result of several factors in his background, upbringing, and personal preference. He had been in ill health from childhood, having fallen on his head from

49

a tree at the age of twelve and contracted a fever and then malaria; he always suffered intensely when the weather became warm, as was the case so often in Washington. A small man with slight appeal to the public, House had known early in adult life that he had no future as an officeholder, although he was attracted to politics. For some years before Wilson's election his ambitions had been intensely political; he hoped to advise men in power, perhaps becoming a president-maker. House sought out Wilson in 1911, and the two men recognized the ground for friendship—House perhaps more than Wilson.

There was nothing strange about the friendship between House and Wilson although the personalities of the two men seemed as opposite as those of the president and the secretary of state. House sensed Wilson's peculiar trait, a need for approval by a devoted follower, and he recognized Wilson's capacity for greatness. Sooner than did Wilson he recognized that the area in which to achieve prominence in American history was no longer domestic affairs, but foreign relations.

House's talent for using friendship to achieve his goals was remarkable. In 1913–14 his friendship with Wilson was at its height. There should be no question, incidentally, of House's admiration for Wilson. The mawkish letters of affection, the terms of endearment which today seem so unmasculine, the passages in House's diary which remark the pleasure of Wilson's companionship before and after the inauguration, all those expressions were sincere. But if House liked Wilson, he hoped to use him. Wilson gave House opportunity to fulfill a justifiable ambition. The two personalities worked easily together and, one might add, in the best interest of the nation and progressivism. House could temper Wilson's idealism; he could shield Wilson from persons who irritated the president. He was a good listener who commented shrewdly, usually with approval, on Wilson's ideas. Wilson helped himself by allowing his friend, whose insight on matters of diplomacy was sometimes better than his own, a certain latitude in the administration of and, occasionally, the direction of foreign policy. An admirer of the colonel, Phillips, stated many years later that House had an "uncanny grasp of foreign situations and injected himself where he thought he could be of help." Phillips thought that House never usurped the authority of the State Department, "but sometimes he did go pretty far in representing that he was speaking for the president." Ambassador James W. Gerard, who wrote House frequently, claimed that the colonel was invested "with all the powers of the President from the first."[22]

House in many ways was a practical man. He was more of a progressive than Wilson, and his dislike for Tammany hence was greater; his ideas of democracy and the benefits of government in the interest of the people were closer to those of Bryan. This was evident in the colonel's novel, *Philip Dru: Administrator*, published anonymously in 1912, a literary horror in which the hero assumed a dictatorship of the United States, reformed the government according to populist-progressive-parliamentarian ideals, and resigned when his work was complete. Philip Dru represented what House would have liked to be and wanted to accomplish. But the colonel possessed a healthy streak of practicality and was willing to deal with persons less progressive than himself or the president, including Tammany hacks, to achieve his goals.

House's relation to the Department of State was as unique as his friendship with the president, and in some sense he made up for Wilson's lack of contact with the Washington department and with representatives abroad. The colonel had known Bryan longer than he had known Wilson, and it was in part through House's efforts that the two leading Democrats came together. House's friendship with Mrs. Bryan, whom he admired for her intelligence and perception, enabled him to approach the secretary indirectly through Mary when he could not get some point across to William. The families had been neighbors in Texas, where Bryan owned a house. The colonel indeed could report on Bryan's real estate transactions from close range. Bryan trusted House and may have realized that it was through the colonel that Wilson agreed to give him a position in the cabinet. House's political acumen made him aware of the desirability of Bryan's appointment and assistance for passage of progressive legislation.

Although House liked Bryan, he was aware of the secretary's shortcomings. During trips to Europe in 1913 and 1914 the colonel learned how Bryan's personality failed to impress foreign statesmen, of how foreigners regarded Bryan's peace plans. When war broke out House was quick to warn Wilson not to send the secretary abroad because European statesmen regarded him as a comical visionary.

House remained friendly with Bryan and was careful never to show his hand in such a way as to embarrass the secretary. The colonel's conversations with foreign diplomats in Washington, with whom he was on closer terms than Wilson or any man serving the State Department, were accomplished at the house of Phillips, often in secret, so Bryan would not be offended. According to Phillips's later account, Bryan usually knew of these meetings but did not voice objection—if he had any. House openly defended Bryan and warned his country club friends he would resign if any of them showed resentment of his bringing the secretary there. He showed special concern about Bryan's feelings when after arranging with Sir Edward Grey's secretary, Sir William Tyrrell, to communicate privately by cable, he urged secrecy saying, "If Mr. Bryan should find we are doing this I am afraid he would be hurt." Bryan came to resent the president's use of House rather than himself as an intermediary for peace, but it was a slowly increasing resentment; he did not blame the colonel until the time of his resignation in 1915.[23]

House possessed closer ties to the Washington department than either Bryan or Wilson, even though the colonel seldom visited department offices. His supervision was largely through appointments. Besides Bryan's apointment he was instrumental in arranging those of Moore, Lansing, and Dudley Field Malone, and when Malone resigned, of the Republican Phillips who had left the department at the end of Roosevelt's regime but remained on the rolls of the diplomatic service. Had House not backed Phillips, he would not have gained his appointment, for Bryan thought Phillips supercilious and, worse, of the wrong party.[24]

House was the president's adviser on ambassadorial and ministerial appointments, more so than Bryan, and thus had private ties to the diplomatic service. At times the colonel seemed almost to dictate to Wilson, as when he wrote that the president should "do nothing about the Belgian mission until he heard from me concerning it."[25] It was House who recommended Walter Hines Page for London. House and Page were friends, and their correspondence witnesses the importance of House's advice to Wilson on department and diplomatic matters. The colonel had a hand in the appointment of Gerard, whom he thought the president underrated (Wilson detested him), and unsuccessfully urged the continuation of Myron T. Herrick in Paris. He managed the nomination of Morgenthau, for whose personality he had little admiration but whose political value he appreciated. He saw to it that the Republican appointee in Chile, Henry P. Fletcher, remained. This latter arrangement was a coup for House, for the able Fletcher was a dollar diplomat, a close friend of the principal advocate of American bankers' participation in a Chinese consortium, Willard Straight, and his opinion of Wilson's Latin American policy was at the least ambivalent. House even induced the president to have Fletcher's post raised to an embassy.[26] In one of his less shrewd maneuvers the colonel took part in the sending of the anti-Catholic Lind to Mexico. Nearly every diplomatic aspirant came to House, either to seek preferment or to ask advice.

During the first two years of the administration House's closest connection with the department was his friendship with the third assistant secretaries—Phillips and the latter's predecessor, Malone. Knowing that Bryan was a spoilsman he saw to it that these two young men secured control over the appointment of diplomatic and consular officers.[27] Upon his initial visit to Europe in the spring of 1913 he learned the importance of the diplomatic and consular officers in the embassies, legations, and consulates, and wrote about their responsibilities to the president, who belatedly directed the colonel to take the lead in seeing that such appointments were made on merit rather than for political reasons. House received letters from the embassies and legations, particularly from his friends in London and Berlin, suggesting promotions and replacements within the diplomatic service, and he would pass them to the third assistant secretary who in turn recommended them to the president. In similar fashion he controlled consular appointments. Somewhat later, in 1914, the colonel discovered the importance of ability among the chiefs of mission, the ambassadors and ministers, a fact he obviously had not grasped when urging the appointments of McCombs and Morgenthau. By August 1914 he had discovered that many ambassadors and ministers were incapable of handling even minor crises, and with Phillips's support he was urging the president to reconsider some of the major appointments, especially those backed by Bryan.[28] It was partly because of his efforts, and in part a result of wartime necessities, that several career diplomats re-

53

moved from office in 1913–14 for political reasons returned to diplomatic work after war began.

House was a constantly busy man in his unobtrusive way, and it was through the two holders of the office of third assistant secretary that the colonel cleared up some of the difficulties of communication about which envoys and diplomatic secretaries complained so bitterly. He wrote to the most frequent complainer, Walter Page, and likewise to Fletcher early in 1914, that he intended to see that "Billy" Phillips, soon to be appointed in Malone's place, be given the task of keeping the embassies and legations informed.[29]

The remarkable factor in House's operations was that there was so little indication that other department officers realized what House was doing. Moore's long and detailed memoranda of interviews and department happenings rarely mentioned House, although they missed few other diplomatic and nondiplomatic events and personages. Nor did Wilbur J. Carr's diaries during 1913–14 mention him; the careful director of the consular service knew what the third assistants were doing but seemed altogether unaware of House's importance.

Did House show as much ability in looking into the future as he did in subtly manipulating the department's bureaucratic machinery? His vision of the future of American foreign policy always had been broader than that of Wilson—at least as one might have measured the visions of the two men in the years 1913 and 1914. He would begin talking to the president in 1914 about a proposed Great Adventure by which the United States would take the lead in establishing permanent peace and harmony within the international community through pacts of disarmament. During House's trip to Europe the preceding year Page suggested that the president visit England and perhaps the Continent to establish a position of world leadership. House's imagination, according to Page, "turned red" at the prospect. The president rejected the suggestion because at that time he believed a trip abroad by an American president would be unwise—especially any visit that might imply an alliance. Some months later, and after long conversations with Page's first secretary of embassy, Irwin R. Laughlin, who had returned to the United States on vacation, House asked for and secured permission from the president to tour Europe in Wilson's stead, to discuss disarmament with European leaders, to view the tense European scene, to feel out American diplomats on the feasibility of the Great Adventure.[30] Afterward, he thought, he could visit the Latin American nations to build a similar arrangement for hemispheric solidarity. In giving House permission in 1914 to go to Europe once more, Wilson again bypassed the department. He did not tell Bryan the nature of House's mission and the colonel went armed only with letters of introduction from the president. That was sufficient for the heads of state he was to visit—"everything," as Foreign Secretary Grey commented.[31]

House left for Europe in May and returned in late July when the situation in Europe was clearly out of hand. The Great Adventure came to naught, for House was a political technician and no student of the extraordinary combinations and collisions of the nations of Europe. In frequent letters to the president during that fateful summer, the most beautiful summer in many years when for days and days the lovely weather continued without letup, he told of visits with European leaders, particularly of his visit with the kaiser. He was naive about the friendliness and warmth with which he was received, the agreeableness of the leaders, their assurances of sympathy with his plans. Europeans undoubtedly did not know what to make of this representative with the title of colonel, although his importance was well known to such Britishers as Grey and the latter's secretary Tyrrell, with whom House had conferred earlier over Mexican questions. Most of the European officials were especially uncertain of House's ability to carry through his proposals. They found him pleasant, cosmopolitan, well read, his visit generally more impressive than would have been a mission by the secretary of state.[32] House misinterpreted their careful reaction to his tactful questioning as evidence of agreement with the Great Adventure. But the Europeans could scarcely agree to the suggestions of an unofficial representative, even though a representative and close friend of the American chief executive. House should have known that. So too should have Wilson. As with Bryan's conciliation treaties, it was another sad piece of amateurism in foreign affairs.

# 5

# The Department

For old diplomatic hands such as William W. Rockhill, the nomination of John Bassett Moore as counselor of the Department of State in April 1913 compensated for the appointment of William Jennings Bryan to the secretaryship. Of all Democrats available to advise on foreign policy, Moore appeared best qualified. "A little fat jovial man," he was fifty-two years old when he replaced Chandler P. Anderson. He had entered department service in 1885, the first clerical appointee certified by civil service examination. Upon recommendation of a fellow native of Delaware and close friend of Moore's family, Secretary of State Thomas A. Bayard, he had become third assistant secretary of state only a year later. In the course of his subsequent work in the department and as a professor at Columbia University, he brought together a series of reports on international legal problems, which culminated in 1906 in publication of the eight-volume *Digest of International Law*, a work students of the subject immediately recognized as definitive. Moore had left the department in 1891 to take the Hamilton Fish professorship of international law and diplomacy at Columbia, a chair he held until 1924, but the duties of teaching and direction of doctoral students did not prevent him from serving as first assistant secretary during the Spanish-American War and as counsel and delegate on several arbitration commissions. In 1912 he became a member of the Permanent Court of Arbitration at The Hague. Added to his credentials was the fact that he was an impeccable Democrat, and in 1913 political friends thought him the ideal replacement for either Philander C. Knox or Francis M. Huntington-Wilson.[1]

President Wilson considered Moore the perfect choice to balance Bryan, who, when approached on the subject early in March 1913, agreed, though perhaps not for the same reason as the president. The secretary had never heard of Moore, much less of the office Wilson wanted Moore to fill. According to Moore's account Bryan quizzed him regarding his political affiliations, his qualifications as a lawyer, and his former service at the department. Moore had never held a diplomatic post, and he considered service abroad a disqualification for department service. He believed nothing was more dangerous to a nation than the presence in its foreign office of an expert with a bias for or against a country in which he had served as a diplomat. The secretary learned enough from this encounter to conclude that Moore "would quite likely object to being made subordinate to the assistants" and advised the president to accept the lawyer-professor's conditions for assuming the counselorship.[2]

Moore set down three conditions in a letter to the president of March 13. He wanted independence from the direction of the three assistant secretaries, permission to remain on the International Commission of Jurists and the Hague Court, and assurance that he could continue teaching at Columbia until May 1. He told the president that he might be able to persuade the trustees of the university to grant him a year's leave of absence but he hesitated to ask for more. In fact he had already asked a former student, then serving as librarian for the Supreme Court, Edwin M. Borchard, to serve as substitute lecturer and law librarian at Columbia and in this invitation remarked that the term of employment would probably be two years.[3]

The president told Moore there would be "no sort of trouble about meeting the conditions," but the Columbia professor still hesitated. He feared hindrance by other department officers (Huntington-Wilson was still in the department) and also the possibility of being used as a political pawn. He knew that Huntington-Wilson had served as acting secretary and was not likely to wish Moore in that position any more than he had wanted Anderson there. Huntington-Wilson resigned on March 19, and that made almost inevitable the designation of a replacement by a political appointee of Bryan's choosing. When Moore visited Washington early in April the secretary introduced him to John E. Osborne, who already was occupying the first assistant secretary's office without appointment.[4] Moore foresaw further trouble and wrote Bryan and Wilson suggesting that the president use Section 179 of the *Revised Statutes of the United States* to give the counselor authority to serve when necessary as acting secretary. The president replied that he thought the suggestion a good one, but he advised Moore not to publicize it as to do so might embarrass the not yet appointed Osborne.

Moore drafted a form authorizing the counselor to serve as acting secretary, and Wilson and Bryan approved—the latter hesitantly, at first suggesting that the order be given separately on each occasion the secretary left town. In the meantime Wilson sent Moore's name, but not Osborne's, to the Senate for approval.

The Moore appointment proved fraught with theoretical difficulties. The implication of Wilson's initial request that Moore not announce the fact that as counselor he was to serve on occasion as acting secretary and the absence of Osborne's name in the nominations was lost on Moore until Chief Clerk William McNeir told him the situation was becoming a subject of department gossip. After consultation with Columbia's legal experts and the chairman of its board of trustees, George L. Rives, who once had served as first assistant secretary of state, Moore wrote an angry note to the president. "In these circumstances, I feel that I must, in justice to you, to the Secretary of State, to Governor Osborne, and to myself, as well as in the interest of a harmonious public service, withdraw myself, as I now do, from a situation which, having already given rise to forebodings of personal disappointment, manifestly can be relieved only by such action on my part." [5] It was Wilson's turn to be alarmed. Fearful that the administration was on the verge of losing an illustrious appointee, he and Bryan told Moore that Osborne had agreed to the counselor's occasional assumption of the position of acting secretary. As a matter of fact Osborne had not been asked, but Bryan was certain, so he told the president, that "we shall be a happy family here in the department and I own he and Mr. Osborne will be the best of friends when they become acquainted with each other." Wilson wrote Moore that he had sent his name to the Senate in good faith and that Moore could accept on his own terms. Still not mollified, Moore replied peevishly that he would "take the place of Counselor just as it is, without any change whatever in its present status, with the mutual understanding (which, in order to prevent further misconception, I can in appropriate terms and on proper occasions make public) that I am within a few weeks to vacate it." The president now tried to soothe Moore by restating that it was all a misunderstanding and that he was sure Moore had "the disinterested devotion to the public service which would . . . drop this little contretemps into oblivion." [6]

Moore stayed almost a year as counselor with full authority as acting secretary, but he was not an individual to drop any matter into oblivion. The unpleasantness surrounding his appointment presaged trouble between the counselor and his superiors, especially the president. Moore soon recognized that Bryan, with all his ignorance of department matters and the duties of the various offices, bore him no ill will and was grateful for the counselor's presence. Moore's principal advisory duties were to the president; Moore was the latter's chief adviser on foreign policy during Bryan's absences from Washington. Moore disapproved of administration foreign policies from the first. He came gradually to the knowledge that the president approved Bryan's appointments of deserving Democrats and would not interfere with the secretary's policies because Bryan "had been so nice." He eventually came to believe the president was trying to use him in a plot to get rid of Bryan and, unwilling to cooperate in such a maneuver, conceived an intense dislike for Wilson and all his works. He was certain that while the president might prefer him to Bryan as secretary of state, Wilson's moralistic view of diplomacy was not merely at odds with Moore's legalism but prevented use of the secretary of state's advice unless it agreed with his own views. The only Wilsonian policy Moore could approve in principle was the attempt to secure the cooling-off treaties.[7]

Moore's stay as counselor was unhappy for him and for the department. He considered the changes in administration after 1898 to have been confusing and inefficient, and he complained especially of the new decimal filing system, which he found so cumbersome that he claimed he never could have compiled his *Digest of International Law* had it been in effect. He treated the new arrangements with disdain, complaining that there were too many bureaus and divisions and assistant secretaries under the reorganization of 1909 (he seemed to forget there had been the same number of assistants in 1898). He was no less disturbed by the lack of help he received and by the fact that he had to handle so much work himself. The truth was that Moore did not want to delegate responsibilities and insisted on doing most of the work himself rather than turning it over to inexperienced politicos. Overworked and irritated, he found that other things in Washington had changed since earlier days. He discovered no peace in the Cosmos Club, to which he belonged, for its membership now seemed concerned more with "quantity rather than quality in food."[8] He unburdened himself by describing department activities in long memoranda and letters to friends. He did know more about the department's affairs than anyone else there, including the secretary of state. As acting secretary he frequently was responsible for drafting important communications, and diplomatic representatives found they could deal more quickly with him than with Bryan.

Moore's stay in the department became steadily less pleasant. The announcement of the administration's policy of nonrecognition of the Victoriano Huerta regime in Mexico was a decision Moore heartily disliked. Asked for his opinion, he had advised recognition; he considered the alternative contrary to established precedent regarding recognition of de facto governments. He pointed out to Bryan the incongruity of recognizing the Chinese republic, behaving no less brutally toward opponents, and the nonrecognition of the new Mexican government. Bryan, who had come to like Moore, laughingly agreed, but not in Wilson's presence. From the outset Moore was responsible for handling nearly all the correspondence related to the Mexican question. The president increasingly ignored his advice. When Wilson sent John Lind to Mexico, Moore read about it in the newspapers and, as Felix Frankfurter later recalled, exclaimed, "My God! This is the first I knew of that!" He never saw Lind's dispatches until they had been analyzed by the president, and sometimes not even then.[9]

Rumor arose in the late summer of 1913 that he would shortly resign, but Moore did not give up easily. To his wife he wrote that if his coming to the department had been foolish, resignation at that point would be more so. "No one could deplore more than I do," he wrote, "the mistakes that have been made, and no one could be less responsible for them than I am, but I will trust to time for the revelation of the truth and will do nothing to embarrass the Government in its difficulties."[10] Throughout the Mexican crises of late 1913 he maintained more humor than humility. The Austrian ambassador, Constantin Dumba, requesting information regarding Mexico, asked, "And the Monroe Doctrine, is it to be pensioned?" Moore answered, "Pension the Monroe Doctrine! What treasury could bear the provision for so great a Potentate, even in retirement? Would Europe 'chip in'?"[11]

Rumor of Moore's resignation persisted, and when he left Washington early in September 1913 for a short vacation, newspapers reported that he had gone away in a huff. Moore wrote Huntington-Wilson, who had left the department in a similar manner some months before, that he was sorry to have been thought "capable of such an unbecoming lack of serenity." [12] The rumor died upon his return to Washington, to rise again with more reason in November after a conversation between Moore and the president in which the counselor disagreed sharply regarding the legality of armed intervention in Mexico. At that time Moore drafted a letter of resignation in which he discoursed at length on department inefficiency, but he never sent it. Unlike Huntington-Wilson, he preferred, when he had to, to go quietly. [13]

Late in January 1914 he decided it was time. He told the minister to Colombia, Thaddeus A. Thomson, "in absolute confidence" that he intended to resign that spring. Thomson told House, who reported it to the president's physician, who relayed it to Wilson, giving as Moore's reasons the incompetence of the department personnel and the fact that two of Thomson's letters written from Bogotá had never reached the counselor. Moore's official explanation to the president was different. He had told the president earlier that he could secure only one year's leave of absence from teaching duties at Columbia. A former college president could hardly disagree, even though he might know that the university's trustees would have given Moore an extension. On February 2, 1914, Moore wrote Bryan of his intention to return to Columbia and added that he was sending the president his resignation to take effect on March 4. Newspapers, especially those hostile to the administration, used the occasion to berate Wilson and Bryan for ingratitude to their most distinguished public servant. [14]

Moore remained silent publicly but in letters to friends explained his point of view. "I cannot say," he wrote former Assistant Solicitor Frederick Van Dyne, whom he had aided in securing a transfer from the department to the position of consul general in Lyons, "that I left the department without regret. . . . I felt for several days a sense of profound melancholy over the condition in which I left the department. Nevertheless, I had learned that as long as I would remain, nothing whatever would be done to improve the conditions there." His decision to leave had come upon hearing that Bryan planned a Latin American trip in September 1914; the counselor was unwilling to perform the duties of secretary while Bryan enjoyed himself abroad.[15]

Moore had considered his position within the department in 1913–14 that of a drudge rather than adviser on foreign affairs and blamed Wilson as much as Bryan for failure to see that the department obtained the services of qualified personnel. But he himself was not without blame. As Mrs. Bryan quickly recognized, he was "full of his own importances," overly sensitive and critical, too much the professional international lawyer to assume a subordinate role in a bureaucratic machine. Unlike Wilbur J. Carr, who admired him to the point of considering him indispensable, he was no bureaucrat and was too sure of his legal rectitude to accept decisions contrary to his judgment.[16] He wasted his talent in a position requiring more pliability. Instead of assisting in the functioning of the department, his presence perhaps added to its demoralization.

Department morale improved, at least by a fraction, with appointment of Moore's successor, Robert Lansing, almost as distinguished an expert in international law. Four years younger than Moore, Lansing had married the eldest daughter of former Secretary of State John W. Foster and had served as legal counselor on more arbitration commissions than any other American. Since Wilson's election his New York political friends had sought an appointment for him within the department; unlike Moore, who three times had rejected the post, Lansing wanted to be the first assistant secretary of state. Recommended by such prominent Democrats as Frederic R. Coudert of New York City and by Moore, Lansing failed to secure the appointment in 1913 largely because of Bryan's desire to have his friend Osborne.[17]

Lansing at that time approved Wilson's policies. He earlier had opposed Secretary Knox's dollar diplomacy. He thought the president's Mexican policy correct and "likely to succeed," and in January 1914 wrote A. Mitchell Innes of the British legation in Uruguay: "President Wilson is making a tremendous impression upon the people. . . . He has the same energy and determination as Roosevelt without the latter's impulsiveness and brutality. Furthermore, he is showing himself to be a constructive rather than a destructive statesman. He is building up what Roosevelt so successfully tore down."[18]

Upon entering the department Lansing did not fear subordination to the assistants and made no demands. Carr described him as "weak, irresolute, lacking in information" and thought he showed "little familiarity with situations now arising," but as Lansing took hold of the affairs of his office, Carr recognized the virtues of methodical application to detail and soon remarked that the department showed an "absence of feverishness and more deliberation" when Lansing acted as secretary in Bryan's absence. He noted that the counselor, like former Secretary Knox, kept a clean desk without appearing hurried.[19] The polished, handsome Lansing was a quiet person who did not reveal himself even to those individuals with whom he worked. William Phillips described him as a "reserved man who gave out little of himself . . . a constant student of the Bible . . . not in any sense brilliant, and sometimes painfully slow in reaching a decision." Whatever his deficiencies the department ran more smoothly.[20]

The post of counselor thus passed easily from Moore to Lansing. As for the number three position in the department, the first assistantship, it proved more difficult to arrange. Perhaps the problem was that the job gave the appearance of more authority than it possessed.

The initial holder of the post was Huntington-Wilson, who quickly did himself in. During the first week the Democrats were in office Huntington-Wilson, surprised and cynical about President Wilson's invitation to remain (the president feared too rapid a transfer of offices, especially the entry of Osborne), spoke at the White House in favor of recognition of Huerta's regime, nonrecognition of the Chinese Republic, and continuation of the Chinese consortium as the "indispensable instrument of American policy in China." These were suicidal arguments, but Huntington-Wilson had never been noted for tact. He wrote Bryan on March 16 of difficulties with Counselor Anderson, still in the department. The first assistant thought the counselor's office "an excrescence upon the symmetrical organization of the Department" and asked Bryan to grant him full powers of acting secretary, as Knox had given him, in order that he would not have to confer with Anderson in the secretary's absence. He noted that elimination of both the first assistant and counselor and substitution of an eight-thousand-dollar undersecretariat was in order and he would be glad to give Bryan the gist of his other plans for reorganization any time the secretary desired. In passing the letter to Wilson, Bryan wrote only that he had suspected the situation existing between the two department officials, and since Huntington-Wilson's appointment was temporary he would honor his request to act as secretary. Bryan's reply to the first assistant was courteous and sympathetic, as were all relations between Bryan and Huntington-Wilson, but three days later, upon reading of the president's repudiation of the Chinese consortium, Huntington-Wilson lashed out at Wilson, excoriating the administration for "radical departure from the practice . . . whereby the knowledge and experience of the various officials of the foreign office is made use of in the study of great questions of foreign policy." He announced his immediate resignation, which Wilson unperturbedly accepted by return messenger. To Bryan, on a Western trip, the president telegraphed what had occurred and made clear that the secretary's return to Washington was unnecessary.[21]

Osborne became the next incumbent. Before Huntington-Wilson's time the office of first assistant had been a political plum bestowed by the secretary; Bryan wanted to have it so once more. He desired a man well able to deal with office-seekers, as he told Moore, "to help him 'let them down easy.'" Osborne seemed admirably suited for this task.[22] Born in New York State in 1864, Osborne after completing high school had worked for a Vermont druggist and then had studied medicine and received a degree from the University of Vermont. Removing to Rawlins, Wyoming, Dr. Osborne accepted appointment as secretary surgeon for the Union Pacific Railway. He established a drugstore, which developed into a profitable wholesale drug company. Nothing if not enterprising, he took up sheep raising and at one time was the wealthiest sheep rancher in the state. Mayor of Rawlins in 1888, governor of the state five years later, he was a representative in Congress from 1897 to 1899. Vice-chairman of the Democratic congressional committee in 1898, he was on the Democratic national committee at the time of his appointment to the State Department. He was both a Bryan and a Wilson man, having known enough to pick the correct Democratic candidate at least a year before the national convention. He was a close friend of Bryan, who had given him advice about buying land in Texas. Like Huntington-Wilson, he possessed a beautiful and charming wife who made a favorable impact on Washington society.[23]

Osborne created several impressions during his three-year tenure as first assistant. He certainly lacked knowledge of foreign affairs and the department's administrative procedure. He handled all his own accounts, apparently not knowing how to use clerical assistance. Moore thought him a trial, as the counselor did most political appointees. Fortunately for Moore, Osborne during his first year frequently was absent from the department on political business. Carr varied in opinion, finding Osborne at one time "a rather good judge of men" and fair and considerate as an examiner for consular appointments; at another time "weak," indecisive, without force as an administrator; at still another lacking in frankness, "cold blooded." The latter appraisal may have been true enough. Osborne had the distinction of possessing shoes made from the skin of George (Big Nose) Parrott, an outlaw lynched by a Wyoming posse in the 1880s shortly after the future governor's arrival in Rawlins. He had had a large square of skin removed from Parrott's body and had it tanned and made into shoes which he displayed with pride.[24]

The president's decision to ask Alvey A. Adee to remain as second assistant secretary of state met unanimous approval of the cabinet, all of whom recognized that Adee despite his seventy-one years was indispensable because of his knowledge of diplomatic procedure. It is difficult to imagine what Bryan and Adee must have thought of each other's manner of handling affairs; neither left a record of any encounter. Although during the early weeks Adee signed most of the department mail, he was unwell, and both Carr and Moore noted that he was "no longer capable of carrying the burden of work" he had performed almost singlehandedly under Secretary John Hay. Adee had spoken of retiring since 1909 and wrote Moore early in 1913 that if he were to take a rest it might be well to get it before he was "too stiff and infirm" to enjoy it. Moore replied that the problem of a successor would be difficult, and Adee remained. In October 1913 Moore wrote Adee a brief note on the occasion of the second assistant's taking a vacation. The note indicated something of the condition of the department, for as Adee told Moore, to whom he returned the note in person "with an air of trepidation," its content expressed what "had sometimes been borne in on him, yet it might be thought to convey certain implications." "Don't hurry back," Moore had written. "Try to feel that a foreign office should be characterized first of all by complete emancipation from the trammels of tradition and entire freedom from the prejudices which knowledge and experience seem unfortunately to engender." It was the kind of note Adee thought Secretary Hay would have marked, "Burn this before reading."[25]

If under Secretaries Hay, Elihu Root, and Knox the first and second assistants had been personages of some importance, in Bryan's department it was the third assistant who, next to the counselor, held responsibilities. This was chiefly the doing of Colonel House, who recommended both of Bryan's third assistant secretaries, Dudley Malone and William Phillips.

Malone was an interesting appointment. The son-in-law of Senator James A. O'Gorman, he admittedly would have preferred the higher paying position of collector of the port of New York. He had spent all his life in New York City, receiving a law degree at Fordham and practicing law. The president became acquainted with him through Malone's relationship to O'Gorman, but the son-in-law had no use for the senator (later he divorced O'Gorman's daughter) and frequently urged Wilson to silence his father-in-law, especially when O'Gorman opposed progressive measures, which was most of the time. Malone stood in high favor with the Wilsons; Mrs. Wilson had wanted him appointed the president's private secretary in place of Joseph P. Tumulty. Ray Stannard Baker later described Malone as a "highpowered, emotional Irishman, brilliant and erratic" who made warm, lasting friendships, and this Malone seemed to do with both Wilson and House, as well as with Bryan, whom Malone idolized. As much as they liked the young lawyer, Wilson and House were uncertain of his abilities and so had refused to place him in the New York position he wanted.[26]

As third assistant secretary Malone concerned himself almost exclusively with the consular and diplomatic services.[27] He did not know much about the consular service, Carr thought, bewildered by the manner in which the personable young Irishman broached the subject. Carr and Bryan had drawn up a list of appointments, many of which Carr did not approve, and sent it to the White House. Wilson took no action, but several days later Malone told Carr to draw up a new list, that this was to be an honest deal, "cards on the table." Such language mystified the somewhat stuffy director of the consular service, who perhaps had never played a game of poker. Carr mistakenly thought Malone too much the politician to be concerned with improvement of the consular service. As for Moore, he rejected Malone out of hand, referring to him as "Third Assistant Secretary of State and son-in-law of Senator O'Gorman or vice versa." Moore complained that he was in the department even less than Osborne and that the gregarious Malone, who later described himself as a "Sinn Fein Irishman" and prided himself on his physical resemblance to Winston Churchill, put on airs.[28] On one occasion the assistant chief of the division of West European affairs, Charles Lee Cooke, came to Moore in distress. Cooke was in charge of protocol, and Malone had directed him to print name cards that omitted the "Third" in front of the title "Assistant Secretary of State." Cooke thought that of all directions he had received in his long stay in the department this was the most troublesome. Moore told him the matter concerned the other two assistants rather than himself, but that the law stated that the secretaries received their appointments according to rank. Cooke decided to have the cards printed both ways and let Malone take responsibility for violating the law.[29]

Malone's heart remained in New York City. He maintained his law practice there even while third assistant, continued his activities in New York politics, and late in 1913 nearly broke with President Wilson over the mayoral candidacy of the anti-Tammany John P. Mitchel. Malone wanted to campaign for Mitchel, who was running on a fusion ticket, but Wilson advised against it. Malone threatened to resign, and House supported him; shortly after this rift Malone, thanks to the colonel, received the appointment he had wanted, collector of the port of New York.[30]

After Malone departed, the third assistant secretaryship of state remained vacant for several months, to Moore's anguish. From the first Phillips was front-runner. Then serving as secretary of the Harvard Corporation, he was House's favorite. Phillips had to overcome handicaps. Known for his wealth, he also was a Republican and had ties with the Roosevelt and Taft administrations. The grand-nephew of Wendell Phillips, "Billy" Phillips in 1913 was in his mid-thirties. He had entered the diplomatic service in 1903 when he had become private secretary to Ambassador Joseph H. Choate in London. In the days before diplomatic examinations that initial appointment qualified him for the position of second secretary of legation in Peking, whence he was recalled to the department when Huntington-Wilson inaugurated the division of Far Eastern affairs. After a year as head of the division Phillips had become third assistant secretary in 1909. When Senator Eugene Hale of Maine threatened Knox with cutting off an appropriation if his son were not given Phillips's position, Knox sent Phillips back to London as an embassy secretary. Returning to the United States in 1912, he remained on the department rolls, an unusual concession to a diplomatic service officer not on duty.[31]

House set to work in Phillips's favor, even having him telephone Moore asking for the counselor's recommendation, a request which probably earned Phillips a rebuke. The counselor told House he could not speak for Phillips because Bryan might object and said he would recommend Phillips only if Wilson raised the question. Ambassador Walter H. Page wrote Wilson and House praising Phillips's behavior when on duty in London and suggested that Phillips might be the man to straighten out communication snarls between the department and the embassies (Malone had done some of this sort of work, but not enough to satisfy Page).[32]

Wilson summoned Phillips to the White House early in January 1914 and asked him to negotiate privately with Luis Cabrera, an agent of the Mexican leader Venustiano Carranza, keeping only Bryan and himself informed of the operation. The intent was to test Phillips's loyalty and his skill. It was a dangerous scheme and Phillips accepted warily. For the next several weeks he avoided the department, entering the White House each evening through the east entrance to confer with Wilson in the second-floor library, meeting Bryan in a carriage when the secretary and Mrs. Bryan drove to dinner engagements. Each time he reported news of negotiation with the Mexican agent Wilson would look over the report, discuss it, and type out an instruction for the next day's work. Bryan listened to Phillips's reports and accepted the arrangement as "quite normal."[33] The negotiation completed, the president asked Phillips to take the post of third assistant secretary, which by then had been vacant for five months. Wilson sent Phillips's name to the Senate only two hours after the resignation of Moore as counselor, giving the latter justification, had he needed any, for his belief that the administration would not fill important department vacancies so long as he was there to do the work.[34]

Phillips appeared in the department as a breath of administrative fresh air. He sought to satisfy Page's complaints about lack of information, going directly to the secretary about it and receiving a promise to communicate more systematically with the ambassador. He examined every piece of Bryan's outgoing correspondence regarding foreign affairs. His responsibilities as third assistant included not only the management of Bryan but the division of West European affairs, and he inherited Malone's duties of handling diplomatic and consular appointments. A believer in the merit system for service officers, Phillips worked conscientiously to raise and maintain the quality of personnel, commenting to House that "there was plenty of dead timber to be weeded out."[35] There were other duties. As third assistant, he was in charge of protocol, an odious task he was glad to leave to Cooke's expert care. He served as liaison between the department and Colonel House, often meeting in House's residence or at his own for discussions with foreign diplomats.[36]

Phillips got on well with Bryan despite Bryan's initial doubt about a young Republican brahmin around the office. The two men became riding companions in the early morning in Rock Creek Park, for Bryan was trying to lose weight. Phillips was on good terms with the new counselor, Lansing, and when the latter went on vacation in the summer of 1914 they communicated frequently on department matters. He soon was doing such a good job that when Osborne began to talk about resigning in 1914, House suggested to Wilson the idea of a promotion for Phillips. Wilson agreed, but Phillips pleaded he was unfit for the administrative position Osborne held (long afterward another secretary of state, Dean Acheson, recalled that Phillips was a poor administrator), and, anyway, Osborne changed his mind, at least for a time.[37]

Early in 1914 President Wilson, upon recommendation of Bryan and Lansing, prepared to accept another Republican, Chandler Anderson, as solicitor of the department. That important legal position was then in the hands of the former governor of Missouri, Joseph W. Folk. Having had some difficulty getting along with Bryan, Folk was resigning to take a much higher paid position as chief counsel for the Interstate Commerce Commission. Bryan had supported Folk as a possible presidential candidate in 1912 before turning to Champ Clark and then to Wilson. The secretary had wanted Folk as attorney general in 1913, but Wilson's opinion of the governor was possibly similar to Brand Whitlock's, who wrote that he hoped the president-elect was not appointing Folk "under the mistaken supposition that Folk knows very much about fundamental democracy." Bryan thought Folk had all the qualities needed for government service—"official prominence," national reputation, progressivism, friendship with Wilson, "identification with the religious life of the nation." In July 1913 Wilson finally consented to Folk's appointment as solicitor of the State Department, but the appointee did not occupy that office until September 22.[38]

Folk seems to have been almost a cipher in the Department of State. The only extant evidence of his work relates to his sitting in on an oral examination for the consular service. Before his appointment and during his tenure, legal work was carried on by three assistant solicitors. Wilson and Bryan asked Counselor Moore to select two of the three in return for accepting Bryan's selection of the solicitor and one assistant. Moore rightly thought this an attempted "deal" and told the president so, but in the end the assistant solicitors were Moore's men and the solicitor was Bryan's man. The counselor resisted briefly the appointment of Lester Woolsey, the only man on duty in his office, as one of the assistant solicitors. A former law department clerk, Fred K. Nielsen, and Moore's friend Borchard, who had turned down the Columbia University position, were the other two assistants.[39]

When Folk resigned the grand department question became who would be his successor. Anderson did not receive Folk's chair, for President Wilson had learned of the greater party loyalty of Cone Johnson of Tyler, Texas, an important delegate at the Baltimore convention of 1912, whom Bryan recommended. Another Texan, Thomas W. Gregory, who eventually became Wilson's attorney general, later described Johnson as a "brilliant man, with no deep seated convictions, who had been on both sides of almost every great question . . . in the last twenty years." Johnson did have one deep-seated conviction that endeared him to the secretary of state. According to House he was "an intense prohibitionist." Johnson learned the duties of his office quickly and by the summer of 1914 was acting as legal adviser to the secretary almost as often as was Lansing. His selection proved one of the best the secretary made, for the solicitor's readiness to see both sides of a question balanced the president's and Bryan's failures.[40] After the appointments of Lansing and Johnson one could not complain about the department's competence in legal matters, for the two lawyers and their assistants were experts.

The oldest department post, that of chief clerk, had meanwhile gone to Benjamin G. Davis of Nebraska whose record as a civil servant dated from 1887 when he had entered the War Department as a clerk. Between that time and appointment to the position of Bryan's confidential clerk on March 5, 1913, Davis had served through all the civil service grades. As has been mentioned, Bryan wanted him as chief clerk and forced Chief Clerk McNeir to take a large salary cut by accepting a lower post. McNeir had been willing to take the position of librarian, a post he once held, but became chief of the bureau of accounts and disbursing clerk. Department resentment of Chief Clerk Davis in 1913 (there were later complaints that he had "too many relatives in the department to enable him to escape criticism or to inspire confidence") stemmed as much from the demoting of McNeir as from his lack of ability. As custodian of the secretary's files Davis maintained good order, and he was careful with money.[41]

Unfortunately Davis had no control over Bryan's personal files and could not be held responsible for the losses of correspondence crossing the secretary's desk, losses much complained of by department officials. The man responsible for those personal files, at least for twenty months, was a young Cornell graduate, Manton M. Wyvell. When Bryan had visited Ithaca during the campaign of 1900, Wyvell had been a football player and president of the Bryan Club. The club had attended Bryan's meeting and started counter demonstrations against hecklers. Bryan was so impressed that he invited the club president to join him on the tour, and the young man accepted. A dozen or so years later and Wyvell was in the State Department. Wyvell's ignorance of department protocol, his sheer lack of tact, was abysmal—he reportedly referred to Ambassador Sutemi Chinda of Japan in his hearing as "the little Jap."[42]

During the Bryan regime Carr remained as director of the consular service. Despite misgivings about Bryan, about Democrats, and about the fate of consular reform, Carr stayed. The secretary openly distrusted him, thought him a Republican, and wanted to get rid of him. Bryan's attempts to take the consular service off the merit system caused Carr much distress. Carr was bewildered when Malone took over the duty of recommending consular places, though perhaps relieved once he understood the arrangement. Malone's successor Phillips assumed the task after consultation with Lansing, who agreed that because the president did not know Carr, the third assistant should continue the supervision of appointments while allowing the director of the consular service authority "both as to the consular service and legislation." The process made Carr nervous. Asked to prepare a paper on the diplomatic and consular services for the Foreign Trade Convention in May 1914, he wrote in his diary: "A poor paper, but the best I was able to prepare in the tired and overworked condition in which I am, and in view of the fact that there are many things which ought to be said, but which cannot be said because they are either contrary to policy of Dept. or have not been decided upon by Mr. Bryan."[43]

Carr continued to handle the financial matters of the department as he had since Root's time, even though this was not part of his prescribed duties. Because Bryan gave little thought to department appropriations and did not seem aware of how much was coming in or going out, the responsibility was difficult. Neither Bryan nor Osborne, who as chief administrator of the department should have assisted him, gave Carr any help when he went before congressional committees to explain requests for funds. He was distressed that Democrats in Congress, on an economy binge for party advantage, wanted department appropriations kept so low. The strain told on Carr's nerves, and his opinion of his own capabilities, never great, declined. He wrote in May 1914, "I do nothing—neither play, sing, recite, dance, nor play cards . . . only a listener. A selfish life I have led to have so few qualifications of interest to others."[44]

The chiefs of the three regional divisions under separate control (the third assistant secretary headed the division of West European affairs) were among the victims of the Democratic sweep. The chief of the division of Latin American affairs, William Doyle, resigned in April 1913 to accept employment with a Philadelphia concern at twice his departmental salary, although he would have preferred to remain in the department. Bryan wanted him replaced by a Democrat sympathetic to the administration and picked Boaz Long of New Mexico who had no experience in Latin American or department affairs and who, it developed, was a "dollar diplomat." Long's position during the first year of the Wilson administration was, along with that of the counselor, the most influential in regard to Latin American affairs.[45] A career man who headed the division of Far Eastern affairs after 1909, Ransford Miller, resigned late in 1913 to be replaced by the able Edward T. Williams, a former missionary who had served in diplomatic and consular posts in China. Williams was secretary of legation in Peking at the time of his assignment to the department, and as chargé d'affaires early in 1913 had gained favor with the administration by recommending recognition of the Chinese Republic. He was strongly pro-Chinese, as was his successor in Peking, possibly to the detriment of American-Japanese relations.[46] John V. A. MacMurray replaced Williams in China, leaving the division of Near Eastern affairs without a chief; to the latter division Bryan appointed the dean of the Illinois College of Law, Albert H. Putney, who had the backing of Senator "Jim Ham" Lewis. The new Near Eastern chief was the author of *Putney's Law Library* (twelve volumes) and reportedly had prepared the entire work in six months. While in the department he was contemplating a history of the world to be written jointly with Senator Lewis.[47]

Despite Carr's fear that the bureau chiefs would lose their positions under the Democrats, there were few changes. Remaining in their positions were the able and experienced chief of the diplomatic bureau, Sydney Smith; the chief of the bureau of appointments, Miles Shand; the chief of the bureau of citizenship, Richard W. Flournoy, Jr.; the chief of the bureau of indexes and archives, John R. Buck; and the chief of the bureau of rolls and library, John A. Tonner. To head the bureau of information Bryan secured a Democratic newspaperman, John H. James, whose wife was the niece of Bryan's running mate in 1896. The presence of several experienced men as heads of bureaus undoubtedly saved the department from utter chaos in the early weeks of Bryan's tenure, but the fear of dismissal and the necessity of breaking in new men remained throughout 1913 and 1914. The chiefs of bureaus vainly sought their own promotions within the department,

73

even minor ones; Flournoy, who had been in his post since 1909, was dissatisfied and complained that his position had gained little recognition and led to nothing.[48]

Two Bryan men, Robert Rose and William Fleming, came into the office of foreign trade. To clear the way for Rose, who had served the secretary in two presidential campaigns, Bryan arranged the transfer of Evan E. Young to the consulate generalship at Halifax. Young was a Republican and the secretary thought it essential that there be only Democrats among the trade advisers. Upon entering the department Rose went to Carr and told him he knew nothing of the work, asking for reading. Carr "outlined enough reading to keep him busy," but noted that he thought the young man had "not the mind" for a trade adviser. Rose had said to Moore, "Well, *there's* one thing certain; I don't know a damned thing about this business." Moore pronounced Rose's statement the literal truth. After Rose had been in office several months the counselor collected some of the adviser's drafts, which Moore had corrected several times over, clipping them together with a memorandum praising Rose's sincerity but noting his total absence of talent. Rose had remarked to Moore that Bryan was "the greatest man on earth since Christ." Moore added that "there can be no doubt that if Mr. Bryan had turned Rose into a real Trade Adviser he would have been entitled to claim a miraculous power hardly short of that exhibited by his prototype at Cana of Galilee."[49]

Moore thought more highly of Fleming, an elderly judge who had told his predecessor Charles M. Pepper that he "didn't know what foreign trade was." Fleming was eager to learn and took direction from Moore to the extent that the counselor pronounced his drafts creditable and noted "but for Judge Fleming, the office of the Foreign Trade Advisers would have broken down completely."[50]

These were the men who managed foreign affairs from Washington in 1913 and 1914. Beneath them were about 125 clerks, all on civil service rolls, whose pay ranged from $1,800 down to half that amount. Most of the clerks, not quite one out of ten of them women, had been working in the department for at least five years. It was still possible for a clerk to rise within the department to become chief of a bureau or even better, but it was happening less frequently than at the turn of the century. Bureaus and divisions were ridiculously understaffed. The division of Near Eastern affairs included only the incompetent Putney and one clerical assistant. The division of West European affairs was no better off with two clerks, for its chief was third assistant secretary of state, and his assistant, Cooke, was preoccupied with details of department etiquette. Priority both in number and quality of personnel still rested with the division of Latin American affairs where assistants were commonly diplomats taking their turns in the department. Including its chief and assistant (Calvin Hitch, who spent a large part of his time in a Georgia sanitarium), the Latin American division numbered ten. The largest bureau was indexes and archives with twenty-eight clerks. Second was Herbert Hengstler's consular bureau with nineteen employees, many of them with experience abroad, supervising 291 consuls and vice-consuls. Smith's diplomatic bureau employed fourteen clerks, and handled correspondence from 121 diplomatic personnel abroad.[51]

Lack of money complicated the problems of communication within the department. During 1913 and 1914, Chief Clerk Davis issued orders that the telephone and telegraph were not to be used for private communication and cables were to be limited.[52]

Secrecy was another problem, for the department was a hotbed of gossip, and there were few rules governing who could read dispatches. During the Mexican crisis Bryan ordered that confidential documents be clearly marked, placed in sealed envelopes, and opened only by members of the department listed in the order and not by their clerks. Information continued to leak. Newspapermen and politicians wandered in and out of department offices, and all knew that red or blue tags appended to documents meant that someone thought the item "urgent" or nearly so. Occasionally information on foreign affairs appeared in the newspapers before department officials read the dispatches.[53]

General department orders were fairly rare items. If the secretary or another officer wished to issue an occasional order or direction, he did so orally or by attaching a note to a memorandum or dispatch, which as often as not the person receiving it discarded. With arrival of new department officers, the order of signatures or stamps required on a document frequently changed, and if one of the signers or stampers was missing from the department there was slight regard given to precedence.[54]

In the department in 1913–14 experienced employees, one may conclude, shared the blame for failures with the newcomers. Moore viewed every failing of inexperience in the worst light, as did Carr and the majority of the Knox and Huntington-Wilson holdovers, many of whom, like Flournoy, were disgruntled because they had not received promotions. Early appointments to high office, Malone and Folk especially, were men whose interests and talents lay outside the department. Carr declared it was "an open secret that scarcely anyone in the Dept. is in sympathy with Adm. Certain it is that there is not one safe or profound man there. Phillips is weak and inexperienced although most attractive and helpful; Lansing is not well informed and lacking in grasp of questions besides being somewhat weak. Osborne well meaning but hopeless from a Dept. point of view. Adee interested only in bicycle trips. . . . The weakest Dept. we have had."[55] The older hands, whatever their qualities, did not seem able to surmount the administrative disorder.

# 6

# Ambassadors in London and Berlin

The amateur was a fixture in the State Department in Washington in 1913—of that fact there could be no doubt. American representatives abroad, those individuals whom Theodore Roosevelt described as stuffed dolls, were no better. They were political appointees and not the products of training and experience. Often chosen for financial or political contributions to the Republican or Democratic parties—as many ambassadors are even today—they were expected to display enough diplomacy to get along in their assigned domains and reflect credit upon the administration which had appointed them. The system, if such it was, worked because there was so little serious business for a diplomatic representative to attend to. Indeed, all that was necessary was to behave. Robert Underwood Johnson, editor of *Century Magazine* and a friend of many American diplomats of the time, wrote President Wilson in April 1913 that ambassadors "need only have character, intellect, tact and sufficient breeding to keep their hands out of their pockets when on view." It was a matter of following a few rules. One had to call on people and, if those people fortunately were not at home, leave a card with the butler. One American minister to Italy, after a little experience in the diplomatic game, defined man as a card-leaving biped. Any American could do it.[1]

If showing good manners was the prime requisite of an American ambassador, then Walter Hines Page, the cultivated Southerner who inhabited the embassy in London, was a good ambassador. He had no experience in foreign relations prior to going to London, but by the standards of the time that was not necessary and in fact might have given him some erroneous ideas.

Page's background, diplomatic and otherwise, aptly illustrated the good and bad features of United States diplomacy abroad at the beginning of the present century. A native of North Carolina, he was nearly fifty-eight years old when chosen for London in April 1913. Admittedly he was no political hack. After studying Greek at Johns Hopkins he had taken up journalism because he found the impartiality of classical scholarship too demanding for his temperament. He became a reporter and editor for the Missouri paper, the *St. Joseph Gazette*, then traveling commentator for the *New York World*, then free-lance critic and editor of the *Atlantic Monthly*, and finally publishing partner in the house of Doubleday, Page, and Company. He was founder and editor of *World's Work*.

Page had known Wilson for a long time, and this acquaintance rather than political influence arranged his entry into diplomacy. In that sense his case differed from many of the appointments of his era. The two men had met in 1882, and three years later when Wilson's first book, *Congressional Government*, appeared in print, the journalist wrote a laudatory review. Young Wilson thanked young Page for his "appreciative reference." Through the years the letters between the two went back and forth. When Wilson sought a nominee for a newly founded chair of politics at Princeton in June 1899, he wrote Page asking him to suggest someone having practical knowledge of that field, especially its international aspects. Page touted Wilson as a presidential candidate as early as 1907 and campaigned for him in 1911 and 1912. Before the returns were in on election day Page congratulated Wilson on the high level of the campaign and, presuming a victory, suggested that the new president call Congress into extra session to lower the tariff and prepare the way for rural credit societies, seek the advice of experts regarding the plight of the farmer, and deliver his message to Congress in person. Wilson accepted most of these points, although it seems certain that similar ideas must have been coming from other correspondents.[2]

At first it was not clear what Wilson would do for Page. The latter's interest in problems of the farmer led to public speculation that the president would appoint him secretary of agriculture. Page was no expert on this subject, but he had been brought up in rural North Carolina, had long maintained an interest in the plight of his section, and knew that the South's problems were similar to those of other areas—that farmers throughout the country had problems with credit, that as free enterprisers they sold their goods at low prices and bought manufactured items, products of a closed market, at high prices. His agricultural wisdom would have justified appointment as secretary of agriculture. A year later in 1914 when living expenses were on the verge of forcing Page to resign as ambassador, Wilson and House would offer the secretaryship to him and he would be tempted, but in 1912–13 he was not seeking it. He knew that friends were suggesting his name and in self-defense wrote the president-elect in December 1912 that "I have not written to you about any man who knows that I have written to you about him nor about any man who has asked me to write about him. As for some of my friends who are writing to you about me, I know of no way to stop them since they do not tell me till they have written."[3] Eventually Wilson appointed another Southerner, David F. Houston. Page also came close to being appointed secretary of the interior. Perhaps the miscellaneous duties of that post and the fact that he was a progressive constituted sufficient reason for installing a literary man who kept abreast of the currents of opinion in the country and could sense the larger issues of wealth versus commonwealth. But many Democrats now believed there might be too many Southerners in Wilson's cabinet, and that a Southerner also should not hold the interior post because of that office's connection with Civil War pensions. Although Wilson authorized House to offer the Interior Department to Page, there was a reconsideration and eventually the offer went to the less controversial Franklin K. Lane.

At the outset Wilson did not consider Page for the London embassy. The president-elect twice proposed the post for the retired president of Harvard, Charles W. Eliot, who abruptly rejected it because he heard of Bryan's nomination as secretary of state and did not wish to serve under such a man "at the Court of St. James's, or any other Court." Eliot was a man of dignity and perhaps felt offended to be offered a position by the erstwhile president of Princeton, for whom he apparently had little admiration. President Cleveland's attorney general and secretary of state, Richard Olney, seemed ideal for London. But many Democrats agreed that the crusty Olney (like another suggested nominee, Henry Adams) was "too old and too irascible," and besides, Olney was not interested. (As for Adams, who had finished his *Education* in 1905, he was virtually unable to write by 1913 and in poor health.) Wilson's political and literary friend George Harvey considered himself "a man of the proper calibre," but House concluded—with some prescience—that the editor of *Harper's Weekly* and the *North American Review* "was rather too crude for the position." Harvey was an extremist, an enthusiast, as Wilson was to discover to his sorrow; Colonel Harvey would turn against his former friend and by the time of the battle for the League in 1919–20 would do everything imaginable, and some things unimaginable, to hurt Wilson's cause. Moreover, Harvey was addicted to drink, as President Harding discovered and the people of two nations could confirm when Harvey became ambassador in London in 1921.[4]

Slowly as other names for London receded for one reason or another, the focus of opinion became sharper, and coming into the center of the picture was Walter Page. Edward M. House and William G. McAdoo, both friendly, promoted Page's cause. On March 26, 1913, a telephone call from House announced the president's choice. With characteristic obliqueness House greeted the candidate with "Good morning, your excellency!" Confused and agitated, Page expressed disbelief, but he was deeply pleased. "It had come to me," he later wrote, "without the slightest thought of such a thing. I had confidence in the President's character and purposes. . . . Did any man have a right to decline to do an important public service unless there was some insuperable private reason?"[5] This was an interesting if almost banal reaction. As for the position coming to him without his having done anything to obtain it, that was the usual statement of Americans seeking public office; it was expected. It created about the same impact as "Good morning."

Page had a feeling that he could accomplish something of importance. Was this a premonition? No American envoy to London within memory had accomplished anything of importance. Did Page actually believe he was going to do something of historic importance? He could think of no private reason why he should not take the post, especially when he considered the advantages—association with prominent persons, social opportunities for his family, an occasion for his son's entry into the publishing firm and editorship of the magazine, experience for his daughter soon to graduate from Bryn Mawr. The last was not without risks. Page told House he feared young Katherine might marry a foreigner. House suggested that the ambassador arrange for his daughter to spend much time in the United States but confided to his diary that Page's small means was probably her chief protection.

So it was decided. Reassured, delighted, Page hardly needed Wilson's urging, which the president expressed in his typical way ("Pray say yes and make me content!"). On March 28 he called House and imitating the latter's manner announced acceptance with the words, "I have decided to turn my face toward the East." To the president he wrote of pleasure over the opportunity for "high adventure. . . . Thus even things never dreamed of come true—in this glad year."[6]

As with other envoys during Wilson's administration, Page received no instructions. He afterward noted that the president "knew no more about the task" than he, and "of course, the Secretary of State knew nothing; his ignorance was taken for granted. . . . The upshot of it all was that I had no idea what I was to do, where I was to live, nor what it would cost me."[7]

There remained the unanticipated task of seeing the secretary of state. No hint came from the president that the ambassador should see the secretary before he went to London. A critic of Bryan since 1896, Page had never met him nor heard the Nebraskan speak. When Page left Wilson's office on April 12, 1913, it was House who queried, "Have you seen Bryan?" The colonel took the ambassador to the department for a ten-minute visit. The secretary treated Page well and diplomatically said he approved of everything the president had told him.

It did not occur to Page at the time—or apparently to anyone else—that a visit to the British ambassador in Washington and to the chairman of the senate foreign relations committee might have had advantages. Perhaps it was just as well it did not. Ambassador James Bryce, author of the famous treatise on American government, was retiring that month. Upon return to England he was to be elevated to the peerage. His successor Sir Cecil Spring Rice had not yet taken over the embassy. Spring Rice was to have little influence with the new Wilson administration. As for the senate committee, it was a moribund group in 1913, not of the importance it later achieved.

Arriving in London late in May 1913 in the midst of the social season, Page spent part of his first weeks acquainting himself with the embassy. His quarters were less than impressive. Forced to live for three months at the Coburg Hotel, he found the residence "a crowded and uncomfortable nightmare." As for the embassy, the ambassador confided that his heart sank when he first viewed it, "the least suitable place for the dignity of the United States outside of a tenement in 'Spodunk.'" The occasion was his initial visit inside a United States embassy. He was hardly prepared for the democratic simplicity he encountered. He was appalled that his chancery was in a London shopping district, the entrance the same as to the flats occupying other floors of the building. His private office was "dingy with twenty-nine years of dirt and darkness, and utterly undignified." In the corridors he encountered "immodest looking women," lively occupants of the flats above. For all this he paid $1,500 annually from his ambassadorial salary, augmented by a $7,000 allowance for chancery expenses and $3,200 for clerk hire. He reckoned his financial needs, including house rent, as at least $50,000 a year (on a salary of $17,500) and presumed that other ambassadors in London—"excepting the Turk, who doesn't count"—spent a great deal more.[8] In this he was right. He perhaps recalled, too, that his Republican predecessor Whitelaw Reid had lived in unrepublican ostentation in the land of John Bull; the wealthy New Yorker had maintained two huge houses, one in the city and one in the country, and the servants who kept his country establishment in running order numbered forty-four. The new ambassador was making his acquaintance with a fact of life for an American envoy in a major capital—the huge cost of maintenance. He did his best under the circumstances. Within a year he moved his living quarters, albeit not the chancery, from 133 Victoria Street to 6 Grosvenor Square, where with twenty-seven bedrooms, a ballroom, and a reception hall, he and the family could expect to live more comfortably if less economically.

What was Page to do about the cost of being American ambassador to the Court of St. James's? During the first year rent and social obligations cost him more than $30,000 from his own savings, hardly in keeping with his pledge to reporters, made shortly before he left for England, that his establishment would be modest.[9] Pleas to the president for payment of the rent on 6 Grosvenor Square drew a promise that the Diplomatic and Consular Bill then pending would allow $15,000 annually for the London embassy. House was urging Third Assistant Secretary William Phillips to see the bill through Congress.

Even so, its passage would not greatly relieve Page, for with the rental of embassy offices raised to $5,000 in 1914 and clerk hire an increased expense it would do no more than reduce his annual personal losses to $25,000.[10]

The embarrassment of Page's situation, already considerable because of the condescending sympathy extended by British officials, increased when friends offered to pay his rent. One of these friends was the tobacco magnate, James Buchanan (Buck) Duke, like Page a North Carolinian residing in London. Duke was an amiable fellow who had made a huge fortune by supplying his countrymen with the estimable Bull Durham tobacco, which could be chewed or smoked. Years later when seeking a way to dispose of some of his fortune during the prefoundation era he arranged to supply an immodest amount of money to Trinity College in Durham on the condition that it be renamed, with equal immodesty, Duke University. Buck Duke would eventually go to his reward from a huge sarcophagus located in a gothic cathedral constructed on the Duke University campus; the Duke family was buried in the manner of British royalty in a side aisle. Fearing the consequences of accepting funds from an American so unrepresentative of Democratic progressive principles, Page drafted a letter to the president warning of the risk and advising against accepting the offer. The ambassador offered to quit rather than place himself under protection of such a man as Buck Duke. Page finally threatened to resign: "Oct.ʳ," he wrote piteously, "is the length of my tether."[11]

The financial picture brightened. The letter brought President Wilson's reply that the ambassador should renew the lease of the house on Grosvenor Square for the next year, and the president would arrange for the money. The arrangement, $25,000 annually, was with the president's wealthy friend, Cleveland Dodge, who himself had turned down a diplomatic post on the ground that the place would cost him $100,000 yearly. Dodge could have afforded London. Preferring to support other diplomats and retain his income from various sources, notably the huge Phelps-Dodge Corporation, he sent the cash, whenever Page needed it, to House, who handed it to the ambassador's son Arthur.[12] The increased rental of the old chancery provided an excuse to seek new offices, and the new income enabled Page to secure for the same amount quarters at 4 Grosvenor Square, where he lived and worked in a style House thought unnecessarily lavish but which Page felt befitted an American representative abroad.[13]

In the meantime Page was learning his social duties. He had the assistance of an able first secretary of embassy, Irwin Laughlin, who had been chargé d'affaires after the death of Page's predecessor Reid in December 1912 and was a diplomat of several years' and several posts' standing. Laughlin initiated Page into the ways of British society which the ambassador, despite complaints about traditionalism and the tiresomeness of it all, hugely enjoyed. The knee breeches and little sword required of ambassadors for court functions amused and delighted him.[14]

All the while some work was going on. Page was surprised at the amount of work—the stream of American callers demanding time, assistance, and often, money; the letters; "looking up the oddest assortment of information that you ever heard of"; making speeches on every conceivable subject; attending the round of dinners, receptions, and dedications. Page did manage to avoid most of the dances.[15]

Withal he visited the foreign offices almost daily. The visits were many in 1913–14. The subject of most of the foreign office discussions during the prewar months was the same that occupied the department at home—"that infernal Mexican situation." The exuberantly patriotic ambassador viewed the Mexican imbroglio and such other subjects as the Panama Canal tolls controversy and the signing of Bryan's conciliation treaty with Britain from the same vantage point. Enamored of British life and manners, he was no less a product of American democracy, and he saw his office as that of spokesman for all that was most republican and Anglo-Saxon in American aims. Impressed with what he considered the candor of British leaders he threw himself into the task of drawing the two English-speaking peoples together, perhaps into an informal alliance. Most Americans he knew would not accept a formal alliance, but the ambassador believed that the two Anglo-Saxon nations could learn from each other how best to rule the world.[16]

He was fortunate in these early stages of his ambassadorship to have the foreign office in a friendly mood toward Americans. This mood resulted in what many Americans considered striking diplomatic successes. Among them was the settlement of the differences over Mexico. During the early stages of the crisis with Huerta, the president and the ambassador found the British position contrary to their own. Presumably British recognition and support of the Huerta regime resulted from purely economic motives, notably oil interests. London's ambassador in Mexico City was Sir Lionel Carden, who had made himself odious to Americans during Taft's administration when he was British envoy in Cuba. Carden was an Huerta supporter. Wilson and House, no less than Page, regarded his presence in Mexico as tantamount to a slap in the face and were determined to get rid of him. Page looked upon the whole situation as a classic example of American moral superiority in foreign affairs. Having succeeded early in gaining the friendship of prominent Englishmen, particularly the foreign secretary, Sir Edward Grey, and also King George V, Page used his charm to assist in the removal of Carden and to gain assurance of a "hands-off" policy in Mexico. In fact the British government was more concerned with maintaining good relations with the United States than with obtaining oil, however important the oil to the royal navy. As events turned out, it did not lose the oil.

The Mexican affair convinced Page, had he needed convincing, of his country's moral superiority, and he therefore worked hard to settle the dispute over the Panama Canal. He had come to London convinced that the Panama matter could be resolved to Britain's satisfaction. He believed, as did most American legal experts, that the act of Congress passed in Taft's time exempting American coastal shipping from tolls was a breach of the earlier agreement with Britain that the ships of no nation should receive advantage in transit of the canal. This was not a matter of Democratic politics—the issue in Congress was nonpartisan even in Taft's time; in Page's opinion it was a question of "honour and rightmindedness." The ambassador's outspoken agreement with British opinion regarding Panama may have endeared him to his hosts if at times it had quite the opposite effect on American readers of press reports. His speechmaking on this subject sometimes led to criticism, but he seemed not to realize it. At one point he came close to "pensioning the Monroe Doctrine," or so it appeared, in an address which drew much criticism from the American press, amused commentary on the duties of ambassadors from Finley Peter Dunne's Mr. Dooley, and a gentle admonition from the president. By the summer of 1914 the offensive tolls act had been removed from the books.

The ambassador succeeded in persuading the British to enter into one of Bryan's cooling-off treaties. Enthusiastic from the start for renewal of the arbitration treaty between the two nations, he worked for the conciliation treaty with much less verve, for it was Bryan's idea. The ambassador was appalled when the suggestion reached him that Bryan might visit Britain in 1914 to speak in favor of the treaty. His distaste for the secretary had not abated, and he dreaded the thought of Bryan, about whom he had heard so many British officials speak with tolerant amusement, arriving in London to be entertained. House hastened to assure him that the news of Bryan's coming was only rumor.[17]

Page sometimes had his complaints, which he transmitted to friends in the United States, but generally he seemed to do all right as ambassador. He never maintained that the country he represented had no faults. After all, it was noticeably stingy about his expense account. The State Department was the target of his greatest criticism, especially when he compared it with other more apparently efficient foreign offices. Washington, he complained, was "a deep hole of silence toward ambassadors." His letters to the department went unanswered, confidential queries received replies which appeared first in the newspapers, the embassy received no word of what transpired between the department and the British embassy in Washington, and the head of the department was a fool. The ambassador could ill conceal such feelings. He was fortunate, at least before August 1914, in having both Wilson and House as sounding boards for his chagrin, and his moodiness found expression in long letters to them. Hearing a rumor that Bryan might resign if a war with Mexico broke out, he wrote House that the threat was idle for Bryan had "nothing to resign to." He believed the secretary of state was the only man in the department who did not realize its confusion. House was the usual recipient of such complaints, which Page frequently urged the colonel to burn; Wilson received generally description and discussion of British manners, politics, and policy. The witty editor, self-styled connoisseur of prose, filled pages with amusing comment.[18] The president and House were pleased with Page's informative descriptions. "Your letters," Wilson wrote characteristically, "are a lamp to my feet."[19]

The British were pleased with Ambassador Page and with his charming wife, and the famous newspaper proprietor Lord Northcliffe told House that Page was "one of the best Ambassadors the United States had yet sent to England." Business between the two countries, the publisher of the *Times* went on, was now dispatched quickly and with understanding. House took the compliment to himself. Northcliffe was referring to Page's handling of the Mexican and Panama Canal tolls controversies. He also was referring, alas, to the ambassador's outspoken pleasure in the British way of life. Page's initial success in London and his increasing partiality for his hosts was a slippery foundation for the work soon to be demanded of an ambassador dealing with a belligerent nation, as England was to become.[20]

Unlike the appointment of Walter Page, the nomination of the new ambassador to Germany, James W. Gerard, came from a begrudging president only after other men turned down the Berlin post for lack of money. Gerard had no such handicap; reportedly he had contributed some $120,000 to Wilson's campaign, most of it not recorded. But Wilson had two reasons for disliking him: the Tammany Democrat had supported Champ Clark in 1912 and also suggested Theodore Roosevelt for Democratic candidate that year.[21]

Judge James Gerard was a controversial choice for ambassador to Berlin. Whatever a contemporary or later observer might have said about Wilson's naming of Page for London, the Gerard choice raised more questions and, perhaps, more opportunity for criticism. The judge was no Tammany hack, as people then and later claimed. His background was as impeccable as that of Page in terms of having attended the right schools and, for a while, having done the right things. A member of a wealthy New York family, he attended private schools in England and the United States before entering Columbia College in 1885. He earned a master's degree in political science at Columbia. He studied law, also at Columbia, and in 1892 was admitted to the bar. But at that point, according to some lights, his career veered into uncertainty. Much more the politico than Page, he joined the Tammany organization upon advice of his father. This was an understandable decision, for to be elected to public office in the city of New York it was usually necessary to have a Tammany affiliation or endorsement. If a reformer crept into the mayor's office, as happened occasionally, sooner or later he had to creep out. What seemed so deplorable to Wilsonian progressives was that Gerard kept defending Tammany. It was all right to take things from Tammany, especially political favors, but not to defend it. Gerard's honesty bothered many Americans who had gone to good schools, listened to good talk in good homes, kept themselves upright, and stooped for Tammany support only when the light of publicity was turned off. The less said about Tammany the better.

While supporting Tammany, Gerard enlarged the fortune he inherited. He was a director and large depositor in the Knickerbocker Trust Company when it collapsed at the outset of the panic of 1907, but managed to survive that disaster. The crash coincided with his nomination to the New York State supreme court; Gerard thought the collapse of the bank, by giving him publicity, assisted him in winning a bitterly contested campaign for the judgeship. In those years he also helped develop a mining property, the Cinco Minas, in Mexico. He maintained an interest in it after he became ambassador and scoffed at persons who considered the venture an undue exploitation of Mexican natural resources.[22]

Gerard honestly kept his ambitions in public view. He wanted an ambassadorship and worked to get it. Before the presidential election of 1912 he told McAdoo and House that he had Senator James O'Gorman's and Boss Charles Murphy's support. McAdoo (imprudently, House thought) informed Gerard that the Tammany boss's backing was fatal to success, but Gerard paid no attention. He continued to seek House's assistance, sometimes directly, more often through New York political cronies. He was surely aware of Wilson's dislike. Rudolph Spreckels, a progressive reformer from California and a political independent, turned down the Berlin embassy. The president-elect in January 1913 told House, who was mentioning Gerard, that he would not give ambassadorships to rich men, especially not to Gerard. House was frank with the New Yorker about the slim chances. But Gerard knew that the Berlin post, "that hoodoo job," demanded a wealthy man. He also was sure of the secretary of state's friendship. His father-in-law, Marcus A. Daly, one of the owners of the Anaconda mine, had given about $300,000 to Bryan's campaign of 1896, and the secretary could hardly forget it. Gerard correctly attributed his eventual appointment less to House than to a combination of Tammany, O'Gorman (whose cooperation in the Senate, it was noted, Wilson needed), McAdoo, and especially Bryan.[23]

The initial offer was Spain, and Gerard refused it, for Madrid was not then of embassy rank. O'Gorman told him the post might gain the higher rank, and Gerard agreed to reconsider. He and his secretary sailed for Europe on vacation with the matter unsettled. Gerard's secretary, Lanier Winslow, cabled House anxiously on June 10, 1913, that the judge was "inclined to refuse Spain" and asked the colonel's assistance. House replied he could do nothing but advise Gerard to take Spain in hope of a better place if he achieved the expected good record. Gerard accepted the advice and readied himself for Spain. In the meantime Wilson, no doubt at House's urging, changed his mind, cabled Berlin to secure the agrément, and notified Gerard, then on board the *Imperator*.[24]

Returning to the United States to prepare himself, the judge received as little information regarding his new duties as had Page. According to his later account department members told him, "Oh, just go over and be an ambassador!" They said that a major part of the work would be making short speeches. He saw the secretary of state before he left. He saw Adee, at whose feet, he reported later, he sat, but it is doubtful that Adee's advice could have been of much service.

Berlin was a very important assignment, and was to become more important than Gerard, Adee, Bryan, House, or Wilson could have dreamed. The responsibilities of Berlin in 1913 already were heavier than those of London. The ambassadorship had not proved easy for Gerard's predecessors. Since 1900 there had been a succession of unpleasant incidents involving American envoys, most of whom for one reason or another had met with the kaiser's displeasure. Emperor William II had entered into his peculiar responsibilities in 1888 and from the outset proved impetuous, rash, difficult, irritable, unpredictable. He was altogether unlike his cousin who occupied the throne in London and already was becoming a friend of Page. His psyche required a considerable preparation. Unfortunately Gerard did almost nothing to study up on Germany before he found himself in the embassy in Berlin. He made a minor effort to learn the language but did not get far.

Perhaps he knew that the emperor spoke fluent English. As for the deeper diplomatic problems, whether over the kaiser or other aspects of German-American relations, Gerard was in the dark. He would have to rely for advice on other people, and on experience, which is not always the best teacher.

Where would Ambassador Gerard find advice? He was not going to get much from the department in Washington. House told him to expect little information and suggested that he write every ten days regarding embassy business. The colonel was to visit Germany from time to time and through his contacts there and elsewhere would help Gerard.

There would be a considerable amount of necessary socializing in Berlin. Young Joseph C. Grew, Harvard '02, was the first secretary, and Joe Grew and his pretty wife had taken Berlin society to heart. They could acquaint Gerard with the problems of an empire containing twenty-five constituent states, all of which maintained legations in Berlin. The city had more diplomats than any other capital in the world. Coupled with local expectation of courtly display among the diplomatic corps, the result was a glut of social activity. Gerard had quizzed Page in London about dress before going to Berlin. "Such things," Page wrote House, "as we never think of here till we begin to dress to go to a function, and then we ask our valets." Grew urged Gerard to adopt a court uniform. The ambassador had an elaborate one made. But after consulting Washington he received word that to wear it would offend republican simplicity.[25]

The problem of a house was complicated, in Berlin as in London. Finding his millionaire predecessor's house "ridiculously unsuited," Gerard rented the Hatzfeld Palace on the Wilhelmplatz, directly across from the chancellor's palace and the foreign office, for $16,000 a year. He had said he would not spend money ostentatiously, but he knew that display suited German taste—Berlin was an ostentatious city— and he had the money to oblige. In addition he leased a shooting preserve eighteen miles from the city.[26]

Mrs. Gerard proved an asset to her husband's career in Berlin. Gerard's wife knew how to entertain lavishly, and she did her best. It was effective. She also proved capable of controlling the many personalities among the wives of the embassy's diplomatic secretaries. This was no small task in Berlin. Before the arrival of the Gerards, Mrs. Grew had been the center of American diplomatic functions, and a rivalry developed between the two wives. For a long period, to the temporary strain of Grew's marriage, the two women were not on speaking terms. Gerard appeared not to notice. He was fond of pretty women and surrounded himself with them at receptions, dinners, and court functions. He let the intramural argument run its course. Mrs. Gerard seems to have triumphed over her young rival.

The Mexican question, Bryan's peace plan, and commercial agreements were the items on Gerard's diplomatic agenda before August 1914. In retrospect it would have been difficult for anyone to have discovered anything more irrelevant to the great political problems of Europe. The German government in 1913 may not have anticipated the holocaust, but it sensed the absurdity of the agenda of the American embassy and proved uncooperative. If one is to judge by reports both by Gerard and others, the German government was far less amenable to persuasion by the ambassador in Berlin than was the British government by Page.

Whatever its unimportance the work was wearing. The strain of the job, both the work and the play, wore on Gerard; by early 1914, Grew noted that the ambassador had become irascible. The first secretary found him increasingly difficult to deal with, slapdash and tactless. He could be quiet, logical, and dignified, but he lost his temper in interviews with critics, attempting "to cow the wretched individual by volleys of curses." Grew remarked wittily that "the Ambassador has picked out the two callings for which he is least fitted, Judge and Diplomat." [27]

Gerard was friendly with high officials although he disapproved of the system that accorded so much authority to military officers and the nobility. According to the imperial German constitution established by Bismarck in 1871, access to the emperor was the privilege not merely of civil officials, notably the chancellor, but of the military. This meant that the chancellor could not control his military colleagues unless he could gain the cooperation of the emperor. William II was aware of his pivotal position and used it to rid himself of Bismarck in 1890. A succession of chancellors, some weak, others wily, managed to keep the appearance of stability upon a government that was unstable, as so much depended on an unstable personality, the emperor. Gerard found the arrangement difficult for the work of the embassy. Although he was successful in presenting the American position on Mexico to the foreign office, his success was much less than that of Page in London. As for Bryan's peace plan he made no progress, for the military high command considered such an agreement incompatible with its interests. Not much came of the effort for commercial agreements in 1913–14, although the ambassador understood issues of finance.

The ambassador's mission meanwhile lay under a cloud at home because of lack of support by President Wilson, who showed little confidence in the ambassador's ability—"too little," House thought. The colonel pointed out to his friend "the governor" that Gerard showed "remarkable diligence" if not always success in matters of commerce. The ambassador had "no vision," House admitted, but he doubted if Wilson could have found a man for Berlin whose mind turned so consistently in the right direction. A young American in the Berlin embassy during Gerard's tenure years later said that Gerard was a much better ambassador than most people thought. But the president of the United States was an opinionated man. Wilson believed Gerard was a token to unpleasant necessity, an obeisance to Tammany Hall. To the man who lived in the White House, Gerard seemed the personification of the Tiger. Soon Wilson hated Gerard. House more than anyone outside the president's immediate family knew how to approach his chief, but backed away from taking Gerard's part. The colonel realized that when Wilson showed resentment or irritation there was nothing to do but move off and try again some other day. In Gerard's case the day never came. Until the end of his ambassadorial career he enjoyed no confidence from the president.

# 7

# Ambassadors Elsewhere

Walter Hines Page and James W. Gerard were to become the most important of President Wilson's ambassadorial appointments after the outbreak of war. American envoys at other large European posts were no less important in the days preceding August 1914, and perhaps their problems and personal foibles more clearly point up the difficulties of the Democratic party, long out of office, in setting up a diplomatic establishment. In their appointments, like those to London and Berlin, politics no less than wealth and social grace could not be ignored. Just as Wilson learned his lesson early concerning the need for wealthy men in European capitals, he like Secretary William Jennings Bryan recognized the desirability of making and maintaining political friendships, even when this meant replacement of a skilled envoy with one of inferior talents.

Page's colleague in Paris during 1913–14, Myron T. Herrick of Ohio, was a Republican appointed by Taft, but the wealthy Herrick remained in France as long as he did because of the difficulty of locating a worthy and willing Democratic replacement. As popular with the French as Page was with the British, he was perhaps more effective as an ambassador. Herrick's labors in Paris moved Edward M. House to write to Wilson in June 1914: "It is the general impression that our Ambassadors are more or less ornaments and that they accomplish but little of value, but now and then you find one that is doing effective work and Herrick is among these."[1]

The ambassador to France had a background which if not literary, like that of Page, was in other ways similar. His military attaché, friend, and eventual biographer, T. Bentley Mott, would remark that the ambassador had been a "provincial" when President Taft sent him to France in 1912. Born in a log cabin, Herrick had demonstrated many of the qualities of the self-made man. He had been a school teacher, a failure in a St. Louis business transaction, a newspaper writer, and a salesman dealing in dinner bells and parlor organs, before he earned enough money to attend Oberlin Academy for a year and a half and Ohio Wesleyan for two years. He removed to Cleveland at the age of twenty-one and entered the law firm of J. E. and G. F. Herrick as office boy and student; three years later he opened his own law office. A series of successful business ventures led to an entry into banking, and he rose from secretary and treasurer to president and chairman of the board of directors of the flourishing Society for Savings, one of the leading banks of Cleveland. He was a director of several railroads (it is remarkable how many of the pre–World War envoys advanced their careers through railroads). He became president of the American Bankers Association in 1901. Having formed a political friendship with his fellow citizen of Cleveland, Marcus A. Hanna, he was elected governor of Ohio in 1903. Wishing to reward a prominent Republican and at the same time avoid the embarrassment of having an appointment rejected by the Senate, President Taft in 1909 offered a choice of the secretaryship of agriculture or the French post. Herrick's daughter-in-law determined his answer with the words, "I vote for Paris." [2]

Unknown in Europe when he arrived in 1912, Herrick presaged House's remarks concerning his effectiveness by telling Taft that he "did not expect to just sit down and be an ornament, if that was what an ambassador was supposed to be"; he "wanted to accomplish something, and the thing . . . most in mind was a sound plan for financing the farmer." This seemed an incongruous goal for an ambassador in any European capital, most of all Paris, but Herrick took leaves to attend agricultural conferences throughout Europe and completed a study on farm credits; a book, *Rural Credits*, appeared in 1914. [3]

Herrick showed a certain provincialism and disregard for formality. He despised the traditional barrier between diplomats and French government officials and attempted to break it down by calling on the latter socially. In this effort he enjoyed little success before the war. But the French liked him. Most of all they admired his common sense, coupled with his accomplishment in entertaining. The ambassador did not have Page's financial worries. It was not until the 1920s that the United States purchased an embassy building in Paris, and at that time Herrick, back on a second tour of duty, paid for it out of his own pocket. Before the war he lived in a style described enviously by his colleague in Brussels, Brand Whitlock, as "embarrassing to a very poor minister on his way to his post," in the impressive building on the Rue François Premier outfitted by his wealthy predecessor Henry White.[4]

If Herrick had little admiration for French culture and made no effort to speak French, his hosts did not seem to mind. A woman who had lived long in Paris once answered an American who lamented the ambassador's failure in this regard: "What earthly difference does it make? The Venus of Milo has no arms, the Aphrodite of Praxiteles has no legs and the Winged Victory of Samothrace no head; don't let us be too exacting about Mr. Herrick!"[5] These seem to have been the ambassador's own standards.

Herrick's handicap in 1913–14 was neither financial nor linguistic, but the knowledge that his diplomatic career shortly would end. He had written Secretary Philander C. Knox in February 1913 that he hoped the Wilson administration would leave him in Paris until he had completed his work on land credits and until the six-month notice of the lease on the embassy had expired. Aware that he would "sooner or later have an opportunity to return to private life under this administration," he wrote House urging that the new appointment be from the West or Middle West. "There have been men here in France representing our country," he wrote, "whose horizons did not extend so far back as the Mississippi River and who seemed to think that their affiliation could be only with the old French—the Faubourg St. Germain—who, as you know, do not represent the Government in power, that is, the bourgeoisie."[6] There was some difference between the manner of life and thought of the bourgeoisie and life in Ohio but Herrick seemed unaware of it. He was hardly the representative of ordinary American ways of life that he believed himself to be.

It was in the summer of 1913 that Herrick suggested to President Wilson the prospect of an exchange of visits between the French president, Raymond Poincaré, and the American chief of state. Walter Page had suggested a similar visit by Wilson to England, and the president had turned it down, saying he would not break precedent by leaving the country while in office. Assisted by President A. Lawrence Lowell of Harvard, Herrick kept suggesting the idea until late that year. Wilson kept to his position, enticing as the invitation must have been. All in all, despite Herrick's knowledge that the change of administrations in Washington had doomed his diplomatic career and that he would soon be of the "ex-order," which, he wrote to Page, would have no place for Democrats, only for involuntarily retired Republicans, relations between the ambassador in France and the Democratic president were cordial.[7]

Wilson permitted Herrick to remain as long as he did in part because the president and Colonel House realized that the ambassador represented American interests satisfactorily, but principally because he and the colonel could find no suitable Democrat for the position after Wilson's high-strung campaign manager, Frank McCombs, refused it. Wilson thought that the New York progressive banker, George Foster Peabody, who had recommended a New York politico, Frederic R. Coudert, would himself be suitable. Neither Peabody nor Coudert received an offer, possibly because New York by that time had more than its share of diplomatic appointees. The president seemed to consider Paris a fit place of exile for troublemakers, for after McCombs's refusal was reasonably certain Wilson mentioned George Harvey. Aware of the latter's increasing animosity toward the president, House suggested that they wait to see what the editor said in the next issue of the *North American Review*, and by January 1914 Harvey had written himself out of the post. House raised the name of his friend Hugh Wallace. Wilson once had considered Wallace a good Western candidate, but now concluded that he would be an unwise choice because he had lived so long in the East that he could no longer be considered an appointment from his native state of Washington.[8]

Herrick remained in Paris. He endeavored to secure an advantageous commercial treaty between the United States and France, besides working on the Mexican question and Bryan's peace treaties. The French government at first opposed the United States on Mexico but gradually came to support it. As for the peace treaties, the French immediately accepted the idea. Herrick repeatedly told the department of French trade discrimination against the United States. Receiving no reply he told House while the latter was visiting in Paris in June 1914 that a new treaty was imperative. He persuaded the French to request one and was ready to suggest personnel, including former Counselor John Bassett Moore, for the treaty-making commission Wilson should appoint. House told Wilson of this, and the president passed the information to the secretary of state who until that time seemed unaware of Herrick's communications.[9]

During his visit House had informed the ambassador that the president was pleased with his work and too busy to appoint a successor, but Herrick knew before the colonel left who that individual would be. On June 11, the same day House wrote Wilson praising the ambassador, Herrick communicated to the department that William Graves Sharp was persona grata to the French government. Bryan and other Democratic leaders feared that Herrick might use any increasing prestige to return to political prominence, and they had used House's absence from the United States to secure an appointment of their choosing.[10]

Sharp was totally without diplomatic experience. Page wrote that Sharp was living proof of the fact that "in whatever obscurity a man may be, he is hardly safe from an Ambassadorial appointment." A wealthy Democrat, like his predecessor Herrick a native of Ohio, he had no qualifications other than that he had once served in the House of Representatives as ranking member of the committee on foreign affairs. He had made a fortune in pig iron, chemicals, and charcoal, and built the Lake Superior Iron and Chemical Company. Although he opposed Bryan in 1896, his support of the income tax gained him the reputation of a progressive. He had served in the House since 1908. A "level headed, plain, unassuming American of the Middle West type," he had been offered, then denied, the embassy in Russia, because along with other members of his House committee he had voted against the renewal of the Russian-American commercial treaty in 1911. France provided an alternative to Russia.[11]

In the long run it might have been better if the Democrats had left the more talented Republican Herrick in Paris, as they had left the apolitical Maurice F. Egan in the legation in Copenhagen. Herrick announced he would present his letter of recall on August 3, 1914, an interesting date. The outbreak of war caused him to remain at his post until December. He supervised the major part of the early wartime work—assuming belligerent embassies' interests, aiding stranded Americans, assisting in transfer of embassy staffs. He won more affection from the French. The arrival of Sharp in early September created embarrassment. It was not customary for a former ambassador to be present when a new appointee assumed his post, although Herrick had faced a similar arrangement when his predecessor Robert Bacon was still in Paris when he arrived. Herrick's tactful behavior increased the admiration that Americans abroad held for him, possibly to the detriment of his successor's reputation. House later reported that Sharp was a constant talker and self-advertiser who spoke hardly a paragraph without criticizing Herrick. He distrusted his subordinates because they were Republicans and insisted on seeing all outgoing letters and telegrams, yet each day he spent hours greeting Americans and newspapermen, refusing to be interrupted for more important embassy business. In sharp contrast to Gerard he insisted on his right to be the sole American diplomatic representative visiting the foreign office or other ministries and used his first secretary of embassy, Robert Woods Bliss, as a mere interpreter. Bliss was one of the most able of the first secretaries in all the European missions, as well as one of the richest (he owned the Washington mansion of Dumbarton Oaks), and he was to have a long and distinguished career in the department.

In 1913–14 American domestic politics had to be taken into account in all European capitals. The other major capital of Germandom at that time, Vienna, was in President Wilson's mind almost as ill served as Berlin. Wilson thought as little of his ambassador to Austria-Hungary, Frederic Courtland Penfield, as he did of Gerard. A legal resident of Pennsylvania, Penfield maintained a house and office in New York City, where he visited frequently with Democratic politicians including Colonel House. He was a graduate of Russell's Military School of New Haven and had studied abroad before his appointment as vice-consul general at London in 1885 and consul general and diplomatic agent at Cairo from 1893 to 1897. The author of several able books on economic and international subjects, including *Present Day Egypt* (1899) and *East of Suez* (1907), he had received many decorations and was a fellow of the Royal Geographic Society, officer of the French Legion of Honor, and a member of the French Academy. He married wealth in the person of the ultra-Catholic Mrs. Anna Weightmann Walker of Philadelphia in 1908. Like Gerard he made no secret of ambassadorial ambitions. According to Harvey, "From the day on which the proceeds of the . . . quinine monopoly were drawn upon to the extent of fifty thousand dollars in aid of Mr. Bryan's canvass in 1908, there was never a question in any informed mind of the under-lying cause of enthusiastic endeavor on the part of the . . . family in the interest of true Democracy. An embassy was the desideratum." A heavy contributor to Wilson's campaign (according to one corre-spondent, to the amount of $90,000, but according to Penfield's some-what heated reply, only $12,000), he was one of the earliest callers on the president-elect after election day and a frequent caller thereafter at House's lodgings.[12]

In Wilson's initial calculations the foreign experience of Penfield was a strong point in his favor. Penfield received Moore's endorse-ment; the counselor wrote Wilson that Penfield had made a good rec-ord in Egypt and deserved an important post. Not everyone who knew Penfield agreed. McAdoo told Wilson that he was "not big enough for anything." Wilson hesitated, and designated him for Greece, and of-fered the Vienna post to the talented Maurice F. Egan, minister to Denmark since 1907. Egan's letter declining Vienna may have been the decisive factor in the subsequent choice. The minister to Denmark had consulted the Austro-Hungarian minister in Copenhagen, Count László Széchényi, who enthusiastically assured him that Egan's arrival in Vienna would be so welcome that the count and his wife would themselves help with the expenses. But the Danish foreign minister, Schlefeldt, had been minister in Vienna and warned Egan to remain in Copenhagen because the Austrian capital was expensive. Egan weighed the advice and then sent Wilson an amusing letter and a "regretful" cable: "Warmest thanks; most desirable honor; not suffi-ciently well off to accept." Egan wrote Page later, "If I were an Am-bassador, I think I should be carried raving mad to an almshouse!" Penfield had no need to suffer such a fate and, like Egan, was Catholic, an attribute thought desirable for an ambassador in Vienna.[13]

Penfield found the embassy offices and personnel conventional, and wrote Moore that several employees were horrified that he intended to be ambassador "in every sense." He determined to show his staff how to work and spent full days in the office, welcoming every American caller. He dismissed an Austrian "yokel" who, as doorkeeper, spoke no English and allegedly in the past had admitted no Americans.[14]

Ambassador Penfield was conceited to a fault. After a meeting Jo-seph C. Grew commented that one could say of him what usually was said of Wilson's minister to the Netherlands, Henry van Dyke, that he was one of the few men who could strut sitting down. Penfield never lost his fondness for boasting. He told Constantin Dumba, the unfortunate Austrian ambassador in Washington who was expelled in 1916, that Wilson had offered the German post, but that he, Penfield, had turned it down (the president denied this). He wrote House in 1913 that his and his wife's religion would be helpful in the "most coveted" Vienna position and wrote later that he coveted France more and suggested Sharp's removal. He boasted to House of the "rockbottom and confidential information" he gave the department and later told Grew that he had received a warning of the outbreak of war and cabled it to the department. If he did, the department missed it; there is no record of any such dispatch in the files. Most of Penfield's dispatches before the war dealt with such matters as a cholera epidemic in the Balkans, obscenity in intercepted mail, and the illness of the aged emperor.[15]

Political considerations involved rewarding rival factions within the Democratic party, and this was the basis for Wilson's selection of two Virginians to embassies in southern Europe—Joseph Willard to Spain and Thomas Nelson Page to Italy. "Slim" Willard was the owner of railroads, hotels, and notably the "new Willard" on Pennsylvania Avenue in Washington, in 1913–14 one of the leading hostelries in the capital. He was a generous contributor to Wilson's campaign. He represented the progressive group among Wilson supporters in Virginia; his friends, including a former governor of Virginia, Representative Andrew J. Montague, claimed him to have been "an original Wilson man." (By early 1913 it was apparent that if all the original Wilson men had supported their candidate in 1912 there would have been no need for an election, as Wilson could have won by acclamation.)[16]

Thomas N. Page's sallies into politics were tangential to literary pursuits. Page was the leader of the Virginia Democratic machine, which had supported Oscar Underwood for some thirty ballots at the convention of 1912, but he had seen the light and taken a prominent seat on the Wilson bandwagon. He managed to become chairman of the reception committee for the inauguration. He was not as wealthy as Willard but his writings were well known.[17]

The two members of the Virginia Democracy, Willard and Thomas Page, actively sought their appointments. Willard wrote friends asking assistance, among them the speaker of the Virginia House of Delegates, Richard E. Byrd, father of the famous rear admiral. Willard's business partner, Thomas B. Love, kept him informed of Bryan's whereabouts. From the beginning there was rivalry between the two groups in the Virginia party for an appointment, and Representative Montague, fearful as were many local politicians that the squabble would result in appointment of neither man, wrote Wilson endorsing Willard for Rome or Brussels and urging the president not to let Page edge him out. Montague did not oppose Page, he claimed, "regardless of his merits or demerits, and however attentuated . . . his associations with Virginia" and however "negligible" may have been his interest and activity in Wilson's campaign. Montague talked to Bryan and reported that while "exact words gave no definite assurance," Willard was certain to receive a "substantial diplomatic appointment." Bryan asked for a promise that the rich Virginian "would not run an establishment so elaborate and expensive as to contradict democratic ideas and embarrass poorer men." Willard answered that he and his family had lived "here and abroad, from time to time" in various cities, always without ostentation and display and entirely democratically; to do otherwise would contradict his past life and be "offensive to . . . taste and inclination." Montague gave Willard's reply directly to Bryan to assure that it would not be placed in department files. Bryan and Wilson were satisfied. Willard received an appointment first to Belgium and then, because Gerard threatened to reject the Madrid appointment, to Spain. Shortly afterward the United States and Spanish governments raised their legations to embassy rank, so Willard, named minister in late July 1913, became an ambassador on September 11.[18]

House later would remark that of all ambassadors in wartime Europe, Willard possessed the quickest intelligence, grasping details of a supposedly complicated diplomatic code almost before House had finished explaining it. Perhaps this was a reflection on the lack of intelligence of the other ambassadors to whom House explained the code. House's codes were, by most accounts, ridiculously simple. In the months before the war the ambassador sent the department few reports relating to Spanish internal affairs, and those he did send showed far less knowledge of the country than did those of his predecessor, Henry B. Ide, who as George Harvey wrote, "was fully acquainted with the language and customs of Spain." During the first year Ambassador Willard was occupied with the need to find a suitable embassy building, the demands of Spanish society arising from the change in the chancery's status, and the arrangement of his personal affairs in the United States and Spain. Willard's daughter Belle became engaged to Kermit Roosevelt in January 1914 and after some delay in locating Kermit's father, who was exploring in South America, the two young people were married on June 11, 1914, in the chapel of the British embassy in Madrid. Shortly thereafter Willard went on leave to the United States, where he was when hostilities began in Europe. During the first days of the World War the ambassador's Pierce-Arrow, which his chauffeur had driven to Paris for repairs, became a major concern. Willard and his business partner attempted to secure war-risk insurance on it, with little success.[19]

Meanwhile Thomas Page had arranged for Rome. His friends, most of them college professors and men of letters, at first sought his appointment to succeed Whitelaw Reid at the Court of St. James's, a position for which they considered the author of "Marse Chan" admirably suited. Among his endorsers were such individuals as the publisher of most of Page's local color short stories and novels, Charles Scribner of New York; the rector of the University of Virginia, Armistead C. Gordon; the chairman of the House committee on foreign affairs, Henry D. Flood; and Senator John Sharp Williams of Mississippi. The struggle between Willard's and Page's followers distressed members of both Virginia political camps who feared President Wilson's displeasure. Precautions were taken. Byrd among others endorsed Willard but denied opposing Page. The latter remained carefully aloof from any seeming effort to secure an appointment, in accord with the ancient American tradition that the office must seek the man. Page wrote Gordon that he had put every man engaged in the contest on the reception committee for the inauguration, including even Willard and Montague, and that a failure to receive any post would not bother him as he had never set his heart on an appointment anyway.[20]

Privately Page was busy seeing Colonel House about Rome, where his cousin George Page lived and was the director of the Banca Commerciale Italiana. The wife of the first secretary of embassy there, Mrs. Post Wheeler, wrote many years later that Page was in Rome in 1912 "building his social fences . . . going about commonly with one of his books under his arm" in preparation for the ambassadorship. There was, incidentally, never any chance that he would receive the London post that his admirers thought he deserved. Harvey told House in January 1913 that Thomas Page "would merely walk through the part and leave no impression." Page told House early in March that he would prefer Italy to France, but when he added that he would prefer London over either, House broke in with the remark that the London post was to be offered another man. Page seems not to have given London another thought. House, however, had been suitably impressed. House believed strongly in the American tradition of modesty, although his detractors later would contend that he was hardly its exemplar. To his diary House confessed his favorable opinion of Page, together (he lived, he knew, in an imperfect world) with some criticism. He believed Page to be "clean, cultured, and a gentleman" worthy of an appointment but not a big one. And so in a "covert way" the colonel told Page he would go abroad. A few days later House informed Page that the post of destiny was Rome but warned him, because Page had "no political sense whatever," to avoid the president, who suspected Page's "reactionary tendencies"—for the wrong word might destroy his chances.[21]

Thomas N. Page was "an agreeable man and evidently intelligent," with "a delightful Virginia accent"; so thought First Secretary Grew in Berlin. Page took up the study of French and Italian, admitting to Walter Hines Page in London (the two men were unrelated, Walter Page being a North Carolinian) that his early study of language had suffered from the "exactions of the plough-handle and the pen." His reception in Rome proved favorable, as unlike many Americans of his day he was friendly to the Italian people. He admired the royal family, describing the not altogether talented Victor Emmanuel as "a wise, sane, sound man, and one of the most notable whom I have ever known in my life." From early conversation with the king he learned that the Balkan troubles—the first and second Balkan wars—were not to be taken lightly, that there might well be further more serious fighting. This information he discovered in October 1913 and wrote of it "confidentially" to Walter Page. It did not occur to him to transmit this prophecy, as he described it, to the department.

Like his colleague in London, Thomas Page wrote long letters to his family and friends filled with news of embassy business and "right burdensome" social events. During his first year he spent much time in house hunting, for the Roman embassy had gained an unsavory reputation as a meeting place for "immodest looking women," at least if one can credit Post Wheeler's account written from a vantage of many years and many injuries from the diplomatic service, most of them inflicted in Rome in 1912–13. Ambassador Page insisted on a house with a garden, and such an establishment was difficult to find. His eventual choice was an apartment without a garden in the Palazzo del Drago, formerly occupied by Ambassadors Henry White and Lloyd C. Griscom. Despite its association with a title and its high rental, it was far from palatial. Accustomed to gracious Southern living, Page complained of the fireplaces that "all of them bunched together could be put in the big open fireplace in our library at home." He wrote Walter Page that he intended to take up with the authorities in Washington the question of permanent and suitable lodgings for American envoys. His voice in this regard was by that time one among many.[22]

Thomas Page's major accomplishment before the war was to secure the Italian government's consent to participation in the Panama-Pacific Exposition in San Francisco in 1915. He understood (remarkable for a Southerner) the Italian displeasure over the threatened American immigration legislation which might distinguish between the northern and southern Italians, a barrier to the government's agreement to participate.

It was in the matter of the San Francisco Exposition that Page met Ira Nelson Morris, whom the administration had sent to Rome early in 1914 to secure Italian participation. Morris gave parties at which members of the local smart set received gold wrist watches and other prizes of solid silver. He maintained his own press bureau so that he could seize credit for any success that seemed to come his way. Page complained to President Wilson that Morris damaged American dignity, and he boasted of his own forbearance and refusal to attend Morris's parties. This letter to Wilson was his lengthiest communication with a government official before the war. The ambassador believed correctly that Morris wanted his post and was trying to have him transferred to France. He wrote somewhat snappishly, "I am not going to Paris." As it turned out, there was no need for worry. House knew firsthand of Morris's desire and thought Morris "would be an absurd appointment, as anyone would know after meeting him." The Chicago meatpacking heir Morris, married to a Rothschild, received an appointment to Sweden later in 1914, a reward, as mentioned, for having established a proadministration newspaper in his home city.[23]

There should be some account of appointments by the Wilson administration to Russia and Turkey, the two Eastern diplomatic posts of importance in the Europe of that time. After the Pindell fiasco (Senator Jim Ham Lewis's purported recommendation, President Wilson's denial, and then the offer of the Russian post to the Joliet newspaperman, the Senate's nomination, and Pindell's prearranged rejection of the post), the important St. Petersburg embassy remained without an ambassador until the late summer of 1914. The slow and ponderous mobilization of the Russian army in July 1914 forced the other major nations of Europe into a mobilization race and helped bring on the World War. A suitable American envoy in the Russian capital might have appreciated this development in advance. Perhaps a skilled American envoy could have done something—anything would have been better than what happened—to stop it. Consider, however, the individuals mentioned within the Wilson administration for appointment to Russia. House and Norman Hapgood had considered Rudolph Spreckels, who turned down Berlin, but agreed that Spreckels was "too opinionated, too dictatorial, and altogether too uncertain" for a diplomatic post. There was talk in June 1914 of the appointment of John W. Garrett, then ambassador to Argentina, who had announced the impossibility of his return to Buenos Aires because of the illness of his wife. President Wilson was enthusiastic about appointing the able Garrett to Russia and instructed him to extend his vacation so as to arrange for the appointment, which never materialized.[24] The eventual appointment of the San Francisco banker, George T. Marye, came far too late. Marye did not arrive in St. Petersburg until October 24, although he had been nominated and confirmed several weeks earlier.

Marye proved no great reward for the Russians' patience. He was "a tiny little man without any weight whatsoever." Grew wrote unkindly: "It has . . . been said . . . that one can imagine him in his pyjamas regarding himself in the mirror and saying to himself in an awed whisper, 'Ambassador, Ambassador'!"[25] His assets were his wealth and his friendship with Bryan. In the absence of an ambassador the first secretary of embassy, Charles S. Wilson, who had been with the diplomatic service since 1901 and spent seven of those years in Eastern Europe, served as chargé d'affaires.

Religious and ethnic considerations aided in selection of the Democratic appointment in Turkey, Henry Morgenthau. The German-born Morgenthau was opposed to having any position made a distinctly Jewish appointment. Above all he disliked the idea that Turkey was the only country where a Jew would be received as American ambassador.[26] Upon the urging of Senator James O'Gorman and of President Wilson, Rabbi Stephen S. Wise of New York induced Morgenthau to reconsider his refusal of the Turkish post. Wise convinced the New York financier (whom Ray Stannard Baker later described as "a curious combination of naive simplicity and of cleverness that amounts to cunning, combined with many fine qualities of vision and ideals of public service") that he could best serve his coreligionists if he went to Constantinople. Flattered, Morgenthau agreed. In the event he actually was able to use the post to advance Jewish interests. Among other efforts in Constantinople he assisted a scholar who was seeking to prove that Christopher Columbus was of Jewish ancestry.[27]

As with Penfield and Marye, vanity was Morgenthau's flaw. "Business is business," he wrote, "and details are the substance of larger concerns. Therefore, I promptly acquainted myself with the records of the embassy for several years preceding [no mean task, for former Ambassador William W. Rockhill had written frequent long reports], and took absolute charge of its functions, as I was in duty bound to do. The mysteries faded instantly." He considered the members of the diplomatic corps in Constantinople personal foes and decided to "impress his adversaries by mystifying them," refusing to call on the other ambassadors in the capital until they called on him. Felix Frankfurter, who knew Morgenthau well, later commented that he at first had assumed Morgenthau's incoherent, rhetorical speech "just the froth of the man," until, he said, he realized that with Morgenthau "the froth was the man."[28]

These were the American ambassadors who were serving in the most important posts in Europe during the outbreak of war. With the exception of Herrick they were all amateurs, all Democrats, for the most part wealthy, for the most part involved in the American domestic political scene. The Department of State and the chief executive of the United States had provided them with almost no instructions before they assumed their posts. They were to use their ingenuity to ascertain what they were supposed to do, and when they should do it.

Suppose, however, that they had sent back urgent messages. What might have happened to serious results of ambassadorial activity forwarded to Washington? The order of dissemination of information within the department changed frequently, depending upon the personnel. Important dispatches from Europe arriving in Washington could have been silently placed in filing cabinets. There they would have remained, unreflected upon, perhaps unread, until historians discovered those relics of diplomacy many years later.

# 8

# Ministers and Secretaries

The diplomatic service before the First World War contained three tiers, or rungs, of officials, whose prestige diminished as one descended. First were the ambassadors, who, whatever their quirks and inexperience, were men of national prominence, selected for political importance and, though to a much lesser extent, administrative judgment, natural intelligence, and social grace. They were men of wealth. Ambassadors were paid so little that they had to reach into their own or others' pockets to maintain diplomatic establishments. Second were the ministers. A legation did not offer the prestige of an ambassadorship and in most cases entailed less important work. President Wilson and Secretary of State Bryan could distribute these posts to less talented men—politicians or friends whose preelection activities or connections deserved recognition. Ministers also faced many problems. Secretaries of embassy and legation were the third tier of American diplomatic representation. They were essential guides for the amateur envoys Wilson appointed. They received such meager wages that wealth was the single requisite for appointment; almost all other qualifications were secondary.

Responsibility for handling diplomatic crises—more specifically the crisis of August 1914—fell equally on ambassadors, ministers, and diplomatic secretaries without regard to talent or wealth. In some cases the least qualified individuals were those upon whom the heaviest burdens fell. It was a matter of chance.

Typical of the ministers appointed by President Wilson were the men chosen for the two smaller posts of Eastern Europe in 1914—the Balkans (a single legation represented the American government to Bulgaria, Rumania, and Serbia, with headquarters in Bucharest) and Greece. Few Americans outside Chicago, and probably few within, had heard of Charles J. Vopicka, who became the minister for Bulgaria-Rumania-Serbia. He had come from Bohemia to the United States when he was twenty-three, having put himself through business college in Prague by singing in church choirs. He had little flair for politics. His only attempt for office, as a candidate for representative in Congress in 1904, proved unsuccessful. He was much better at business. He had been in the country a short time when he joined a fellow immigrant in establishing the Bohemian Brewing Company, later named the Atlas Brewing Company. His name carried weight with Chicago's Slavic population, among whom he was purported to have a large following, and Secretary Bryan had this following in mind in June 1913 when he recommended Vopicka for Bucharest. Bryan wanted to recognize all the nationalities he could, and Chicago had a large East European bloc. The secretary heard that the Chicago brewer was a "man of literary tastes." He had reservations about Vopicka's business endeavors. He did not know if the literary reputation, actually slight except perhaps among readers of Slavic language newspapers, sufficed to compensate for the nature of the business. The president agreed that it would be well to recognize the Slavs and the state of Illinois, and suggested that Bryan investigate. The secretary told Wilson in early August that Jim Ham Lewis assured him that Vopicka had resigned as head of the brewery. Moreover, Vopicka allegedly did not drink, and the administration was "in a position . . . to deny that the Minister . . . is officially connected with that business."[1]

Vopicka in Bucharest assumed the post vacated by John B. Jackson, who had been with the diplomatic service either as a secretary or a minister since 1890 and had served as minister to Greece, Persia, and Cuba before going to Rumania in 1911. Many Democrats, including George Harvey and John Bassett Moore, thought Jackson's record called for consideration. At Jackson's request Moore inquired of the president, who replied that Jackson would "in all likelihood be retired," for Wilson felt "more and more keenly the necessity of being represented at foreign courts by men who easily catch and instinctively themselves occupy our own point of view with regard to public measures."[2] Jackson did not meet these requirements.

From the outset Vopicka exhibited few of the qualities of a diplomat. On the way to his post he stopped in his native Prague, and his presence created such enthusiasm that the State Department, upon Ambassador Frederic Penfield's urgent request, cabled the minister to make no more speeches in the Austrian empire.[3] Vopicka proceeded to Bucharest, where he thought his reception was good. Unknown to him, he made a poor impression—as much by his lack of manners as by his indiscretions. Henry Morgenthau, not altogether a sophisticated envoy, believed Vopicka "the funniest man for the post, so conceited and so poorly bred; no culture at all" and soon was joining Ambassador Penfield in recounting the minister's gaucheries. Among other incidents, Vopicka told King Ferdinand of Bulgaria of his friendship with King Charles of Rumania and King Peter of Serbia, assuring the Bulgarian monarch that "if he wanted any adjustment of matters, he could call on him." Queen Eleanora of Bulgaria invited Vopicka to accompany her on a visit to a hospital, and the minister replied by messenger that "he would call her up on the phone and let her know"; whereupon the queen announced she had become indisposed. Vopicka erased this latter error by agreeing to become vice-president of a society the queen had organized to aid some 140,000 refugees of the Second Balkan War and by appealing to Slavic-Americans for funds. The appeal brought $75,000, a sum that seems to have revived Eleanora's health. The minister spent much of his first year arranging for the queen to visit the United States, but in the face of increasing national tensions the State Department discouraged the plan.[4]

The American legation in Athens was as poorly served as Bucharest. A former Massachusetts populist, George Fred Williams, received a temporary appointment in 1913, replacing Jacob G. Schurman, who had understood enough of the Balkan imbroglio to write a book predicting a holocaust. In the summer of 1914 Williams, in a burst of Byronic enthusiasm, took leave of his legation to assist the struggle for Albanian independence. The department in Washington was so startled that it could do little more than relieve Williams formally and explain to reporters that, after all, the appointment had been for a year. The *New York Times* announced sarcastically that the New Englander "with the blood in his veins of both Puritan and German robber barons and a mentality in which metaphysics was in constant conflict with Christian orthodoxy" might have been the victim of "Greek malaria."[5]

The situation in the remaining legations in Europe improved little as one moved westward. One observer referred to Pleasant Stovall, President Wilson's appointment to Switzerland, where the legation had to perform important intermediary functions after August 1914, as a complete nonentity. One of the president's boyhood friends, Stovall was a native of Georgia, founder and editor of the *Savannah Press* and author of a life of the Southern politician, Robert Toombs. He had been active in Georgia's Democratic politics and received the appointment as a personal and regional as well as political favor. He established his headquarters in Bern, the first time a minister had done so (previous residences had been in Lucerne or Geneva), and found his early experience in the Swiss capital delightful. Fortunately the work was easy. Edward M. House later reported that Stovall was slow of comprehension, and there was other testimony to the minister's ineptitude.[6]

Another friend of the president, Thomas H. Birch of New Jersey, a former carriage manufacturer and colonel in the state's national guard who had served as Governor Wilson's aide-de-camp, became minister to Portugal. For Birch the mission was a second choice. The president, having trouble filling the Persian post, offered it to Birch, but the New Jersey colonel, brokenhearted over what he considered a slight, "not as good an appointment as he had a right to expect," turned it down despite Bryan's effort to convince him that Persia was "really a desirable place" to which the secretary of state himself would like to go. In the meantime the State Department secured an agrément from the Portuguese government for the Indiana author Meredith Nicholson. After consideration the Hoosier decided he had "little sympathy with those southern peoples" and that prolonged absence from the United States might interfere with the contemplation he found essential to literary pursuits. Birch received the Portuguese appointment at secondhand. (The eventual appointment to Persia, John L. Caldwell of Kansas, was reportedly a source of disgust to his colleagues: he had the table manners of a cannibal. What the Persians thought of Caldwell is unknown.)[7]

Minister Birch did not know that there was distinction of rank among missions and had cards made with an embossed gold eagle and stationery engraved "American Embassy, Lisbon." Questioned by department officials, he answered that he had had the items produced so he could give them to New Jersey acquaintances. Third Assistant Secretary Dudley F. Malone, who perhaps had forgotten his own encounter in the matter of cardprinting, told Birch he had "changed the Legation to Portugal into an Embassy with a stroke of the pen. It took an Act of Congress to do it in Madrid." After arriving at his new post the minister created a stir with his first appearance by dressing in the uniform of a New Jersey colonel.[8]

Maurice Egan was the only envoy to retain his post from the administration of Theodore Roosevelt through that of Wilson, and his presence in Copenhagen enhanced the American image in that relatively unimportant part of Europe. The urbane Egan, a former professor of English literature at the University of Notre Dame and the Catholic University of America, had received his appointment in 1907 because he was apolitical. Copenhagen demanded such a minister, and no large amount of money. Egan performed conscientiously, as well as his increasing ill health permitted.[9]

Albert G. Schmedeman of Wisconsin, minister to Norway, had no higher recommendation for his post than Norwegian ancestry, but that was enough for the Wilson administration. A director of the Bank of Wisconsin, he spent most of his first year in Christiania conducting an international conference over the commercial jurisdiction of Spitzbergen. He showed more knowledge of that affair than did department officials, who seemed hardly to understand what was going on in this minor dispute involving two soon-to-be belligerents, Germany and Russia.[10]

The Swedish post remained vacant until after the outbreak of war, when Ira Morris finally secured his desired appointment. Morris was distinguished principally by his great wealth (his father had made a fortune in meat-packing, and the son had augmented this inheritance by marrying Constance Lily Rothschild). His appointment added little to American prestige abroad, although Morris possessed a good education, was traveled, had written several books, had studied international law, and in addition had produced the proadministration newspaper in Chicago.[11]

But it was the Wilson administration's good fortune to have made talented appointments to The Hague and Brussels. At the time of Henry van Dyke's and Brand Whitlock's appointments there was no indication that these two individuals were qualified for diplomacy. Both men had as their highest qualification the "plain living and high thinking" that accompanied a type of literary talent admired early in this century.

Van Dyke was a noted Congregational minister, much admired for his sparkling sermons. He had left a New York pastorate for a professorship of English literature at Princeton. A writer of short stories with a high moral tone, he won national fame with publication of a short story that attracted a generation of his countrymen entitled "The Other Wise Man." Despite the fact that he had been on the wrong side in Wilson's quarrel with the faculty and trustees of Princeton, he admired Wilson's principles, and in 1913 the new president of the United States, backed by his daugher Jessie and by House, agreed that he was ideal for the Netherlands. Aware of van Dyke's notable flaws—vanity and extreme sensitivity—Wilson tolerated them because of the high-mindedness.[12]

Van Dyke had two aims when he accepted the Netherlands post: he intended to initiate a Third Hague Peace Conference, and he wanted to study Dutch imperial policies in the East Indies. Bryan endorsed with enthusiasm the former aim, which had the backing of Andrew Carnegie. The secretary of state showed some geographic ignorance about the East Indian matter. Van Dyke worked hard to achieve both goals. The minister found the legation a much greater chore than he anticipated, certainly not "one of elegant leisure," and occasional visits to Luxembourg, to which he also was accredited, and acceptance of invitations to preach from Dutch pulpits and to Y.M.C.A. groups, increased his workload. The war shattered his hope for a Third Hague Peace Conference.[13]

Unlike van Dyke, who received his appointment soon after Wilson's inauguration for reasons unrelated to politics, the four-time mayor of Toledo, Whitlock, waited several months for appointment to Brussels and for political reasons came close to losing it. President Wilson was unconvinced that the mayor was a loyal supporter of the administration. Although Whitlock had greeted the president's inaugural address and Bryan's appointment with letters of enthusiastic approval, there was some reason to doubt his sincerity. He had avoided voting for Wilson in 1912 by taking a trip to Europe, ostensibly to study municipal government, in truth to put himself out of reach. But he had tired of municipal office and wanted some small post in Europe where he might devote more time to writing novels, his avocation. Governor James Cox and Newton D. Baker pleaded his case and urged William Dean Howells to write Wilson. Howells finally did so somewhat unwillingly as he had not voted for Wilson either and did not intend to do so in future elections.[14]

Whitlock increased his own difficulties by a stubborn refusal to apply for office, on the ground that he had never sought favor and would not do so. At one time the president considered Whitlock for Sweden. By June of 1913, Whitlock was convinced that he had little chance of an appointment anywhere. Baker's influence in the autumn of that year probably changed Wilson's mind. In October, Whitlock was startled to receive a letter from Theodore Marburg, then minister to Belgium, who had received the State Department's request to secure the agrément, welcoming Whitlock to the post.[15]

Whitlock spoke excellent French and upon arrival in Brussels he learned the local dialect quickly. He found life in Belgium agreeable, the matter of a diplomatic uniform an amusing diversion, and despite some initial fear regarding expenses he was able to secure a modestly furnished house in the diplomatic quarter. Shortly before the outbreak of the war he rented a house near the sea where he began work on *J. Hardin & Son*, one of four novels he had in mind.[16] Immersed in this leisurely existence he offered no sign that within a few weeks he would be reckoned one of the most important individuals in the president's diplomatic service.

As for the lower ranks of the service in 1913–14, they could ill provide the amateur ambassadors and ministers with the assistance so sorely needed. In the months before the war no chief of an American mission in Europe, not even of the largest embassy, could boast of a staff of more than three diplomatic secretaries. There were, of course, clerks and stenographers. An embassy such as Constantinople might have two or three translators. Sometimes there was a military attaché, usually assigned to more than one post, and in some places a naval attaché. Commercial attachés could have relieved much of the work in the embassies in Europe and they might well have provided invaluable sources of information. They were not appointed until 1915 and after. Everything rested with the diplomatic secretaries.

In most cases in Europe the diplomatic secretaries, "the eyes and ears of the department of state," were men of some experience, ability, and professional sense. Unfortunately they represented a wealthy elite distrusted by the administration in Washington. They received meager compensation, rarely more than $2,500 yearly. The government paid none of their expenses except transportation (excluding vacations and leaves). Social and living expenses were large. It cost these men, most of whom were too young to have saved any money, between $5,000 and $12,000 yearly for living expenses alone. For social expenses, the preserving of social amenities, a first or second secretary of a large embassy such as London, Paris, or Berlin would pay out much more.[17]

An inadequate merit system assured that none of the underlings could rise above the rank of first secretary of embassy unless appointed in a regular manner. If he should enter the ministerial or ambassadorial ranks he lost his diplomatic service classification. The merit system begun by Elihu Root and Wilbur J. Carr had proved successful in the consular service, and a member of that branch could rise to the post of consul general, roughly comparable to a minister of legation. Congressmen were wary of permitting similar advancement for secretaries of the diplomatic service. The value of the service was not understood during the years before the World War, and attempts to make promotions automatic raised the charge of unconstitutionality, since the president possessed the right of appointment of ministers and ambassadors. Some service personnel also feared that a merit system would corrupt their small professional club. Occupational security in 1913–14 lay in the executive orders of two Republican presidents, Roosevelt and Taft, and in the decision of Wilson to abide by the orders. Secretaries of legation and embassy lived in fear that their careers might end, if not in the abolition of the executive orders, then in transfer to the employ of an incompetent or cantankerous chief or to some remote, unattractive place. At the same time the ministers and ambassadors complained of the impermanence of their small staffs and of the chance that the already thin ranks might be depleted with little warning.[18]

It was possible to argue that if wealth was the sine qua non of admission to the diplomatic service, and if that wealth annoyed the leaders of the more recently appointed Wilson administration, at least diplomatic secretaries had to take examinations and hence must be of some competence in their jobs. According to executive orders in 1905 and

1909, admission to the service demanded an average grade of 80 percent in written and oral examinations administered by a board composed (according to the order of 1909 as amended September 17, 1913) of the third assistant secretary of state, the solicitor, the chiefs of the diplomatic and appointments bureaus, and an examiner appointed by the civil service commission. Candidates had to demonstrate written proficiency in a language other than English—after 1909, French, German, or Spanish—and knowledge of international law, diplomatic usage, United States history, commerce, and government, and the modern history of Europe, Latin America, and the Far East. The oral examination determined more elusive qualities necessary for diplomacy—alertness, knowledge of contemporary affairs, general education, command of spoken English. The examinations were held when vacancies occurred in the service. As they were designated by the president from a list prepared in the department, applicants had to watch the newspapers for dates and times.

To all appearance it was a rigorous examination. The department gave an applicant no reading list, only a sample copy of the examination. Very few men took the examination, and most of those who did failed. To pass the examination did not guarantee appointment to a mission; it indicated eligibility for two years, and if the time elapsed without appointment the aspirant had to repeat the entire process. Between 1905 and 1909 the examination had been easier, and knowledge of a foreign language had not been taken seriously, but by 1913 the requirements were of such difficulty that only 27.7 percent passed, and 60 percent of those qualifying received appointments; 42.8 percent passed in 1914, and 77.7 percent of these men reached diplomatic posts. Each year fewer men took the examination, with the result that the percentage of individuals passing it rose.[19]

Although the method of appointment seemed reasonable, it was not yet effective by 1913–14. The average tenure of first secretaries of European legations and embassies in 1913 was eleven years (for some secretaries the figure included consular experience), and most of these men thus had entered before the examination system. Joseph C. Grew, whom his recent biographer has called "the model professional diplomat of his generation," entered by presidential appointment; Theodore Roosevelt recognized the young Harvard graduate's prowess in killing an Amoy tiger. Post Wheeler, in Rome in 1913, had joined after examination, but he admitted the help of senatorial friends. Other men who took and passed the examination could often cite similar encouragement.[20]

Appointment was to a post, and language proficiency did not determine where a secretary might go. Grew and wife both spoke fluent German and were posted to Berlin. But Page's assistant in London in 1914, Irwin Laughlin, despite the ambassador's assertion that this "ornament to the service" was a master of several languages including German, had spoken so little of that tongue when stationed in Berlin in 1909 that the ever-critical Grew considered him a liability to the embassy staff. The secretary of legation at The Hague at the time of van Dyke's arrival, James G. Bailey, spoke no German, French, or Dutch; his previous appointments had been to Spanish-speaking countries. When Wheeler became first secretary in St. Petersburg in 1910, his Russian was insecure—so much so that his "translation" of a collection of Russian fairy tales (he apparently spent embassy funds to hire translators) raised amused eyebrows on the part of Ambassador William W. Rockhill and Second Secretary of Embassy John V. A. MacMurray, and malicious colleagues later spoke of plagiarism.[21]

The secretaries were constantly transferred, and if by chance they could speak the language in one locale they might not make themselves understood in the next. Movement from one capital to another kept secretaries from becoming too attached to one nation's policy. Secretaries in Europe in July 1914 had served in an average of three or four chanceries before appointment to their posts of that year. Marshall Langhorne, whom Grew considered more incompetent than Laughlin, entered the consular service in 1901 and had been in four consulates before taking the diplomatic examination in 1906, traveled from Norway to three Latin American posts, then returned to Europe as first secretary at The Hague in 1914. Laughlin's career involved Japan in 1904–5, and after appointment as secretary of embassy there, Bangkok, Peking, St. Petersburg, Athens, Paris, Berlin, and Constantinople. With good reason American diplomats complained of the peripatetic tenure of their staffs. Staff members always felt uneasy, as transfers were matters of personal whim of superiors or, more often, politics.[22]

For the secretaries there was always hope. Appointment to the rank of chief of mission was a desideratum for every officer of the diplomatic service. Most secretaries looked to the time when a ministerial or ambassadorial post might be a matter of merit rather than politics. Presidents Roosevelt and Taft had promoted diplomatic secretaries to the rank of minister; a third of Taft's ministers had been diplomatic secretaries with an average of nine years of diplomatic experience. Most of these officials had been in Latin America, the target of dollar diplomacy. With the end of the latter policy and the election of a Democratic administration, the career ministers (with exception of Henry P. Fletcher) lost their jobs. During President Wilson's first two years the only career men offered ministerial posts were MacMurray, who rejected Siam because he thought acceptance under a Democrat would be tantamount to ending his career when the Republicans regained office, and the first secretary of the Tokyo embassy in 1913, Arthur Bailly-Blanchard, who accepted Haiti. A longtime officer of the diplomatic service who had spent most of his career in Paris, Bailly-Blanchard asked to return to the French capital as he found Tokyo not to his liking. Bryan refused because other men he considered more deserving were available, so he suggested Haiti, not exactly a prize, but certainly a diplomatic hot spot.[23]

Diplomatic service officers were a youthful group, and their youth kept alive their hope. The average age of first secretaries in Europe in 1914 was thirty-eight, and second and third secretaries were younger, for the lack of a future in the service caused men to leave for jobs in business or law. The majority of these well-educated, rich young men had attended preparatory schools or were educated by tutors. Some had gone to Eton, or the Ecole des Sciences Politiques in Paris. Most were graduates of the Ivy League colleges of the East Coast. Of the sixteen first secretaries in Europe in July 1914, six were Harvard graduates, and two came from Yale. Paris's Robert Woods Bliss, Berlin's Grew, Italy's Peter Augustus Jay, and Russia's Charles Wilson, all first secretaries of embassy, were Harvard men. Of twenty-nine secretaries of all ranks, ten were not from the Ivy League.[24]

The group made no secret of its elitist sympathies. Grew sought Harvard men for the Berlin embassy, or better, individuals who, like himself, had also attended Groton. With the Harvard alumnus William

Phillips as third assistant secretary of state, Berlin secured nine Harvard graduates for the embassy during the war, four of them from Groton.[25]

Social grace was important for a diplomatic secretary, as was a wife who was charming and an exemplary hostess. Ambassador Walter H. Page noted the Laughlins' skill in entertaining. Social activity was a preoccupation of secretaries in Berlin and St. Petersburg. Mrs. Grew was the former Alice de Vernadois Perry, a descendant of the Commodore. The Grews found Berlin a social desert, for the kaiser had banned the tango and the one-step from diplomatic functions, making Berlin "a sleepy and uninteresting capital."[26] Secretaries sometimes were bachelors, and then there was trouble. Page suggested the transfer of Third Secretary of Embassy Hallett Johnson because the young man seemed too immature for the social life demanded of him, and Phillips, who knew London social life, concurred. Later Phillips inquired about Elbridge Gerry Greene, who replaced Johnson, because "a young man is open to many temptations and to having his head turned by the fair ladies." The bachelor MacMurray when in St. Petersburg had become so irritated by the almost nightly round of entertainments that he had sought a department position in Washington, an avenue open to him largely because of his social standing and friendship with prominent officials.[27]

To their credit, most of the diplomatic secretaries abhorred inefficiency and were endowed with a spirit of service. They possessed managerial skill and sought to organize chanceries along the lines of business corporations—perhaps those of their fathers, for nearly every secretary came from a home where the father or grandfather had gained wealth through hard work and efficiency. Grew and MacMurray placed great stress on use of the typewriter, so that communications were handled more rapidly than under the old system, which involved hours of laborious hand copying. In St. Petersburg Grew had suggested the use of carbons, only to be turned down. Under the direction of Rockhill and MacMurray the St. Petersburg embassy reformed its filing system, adopting a method similar to that in the department after 1911.[28]

An embassy might be entitled to as many as three secretaries, and the ranking of secretaries then followed—along with a crude but effective division of labor. The junior or third secretary would be in charge of office work, the next in rank researched and digested reports, and the first secretary was administrative overseer and the chief of mission's counselor who might deal, as did Grew and Bliss, with the local foreign office. The ambassador dealt directly with the minister of foreign affairs of the country and with the head of state if necessary. In the ambassador's absence the first secretary might be chargé d'affaires, in which case he received an increment in salary.[29]

Despite the desire for efficiency, for a proper division of labor, the work day was flexible; a diplomatic officer never knew when he might be called upon to handle some emergency, however trivial. An eight-to-five workday was a virtual impossibility. Hugh Gibson later described a diplomatic post as "a great deal like a fire-engine house. You never can tell when an alarm may be turned in." In general it was the custom to follow the workday prevailing in the local capital (in London the day did not begin until 10:00 A.M.), but as it was common practice to house the chief of mission and his offices in the same building, some officer or clerk was usually on hand earlier.[30]

Service gossip tended to "relieve the monotony of life." There was a miasma of gossip that lightened the secretaries' labor, whatever the incidence of crisis or humdrum. In a group so bound by educational and social background, as well as by profession, it is not surprising that gossip, dealing mainly with diplomatic personnel and their wives, occupied an inordinate amount of the diplomatic secretaries' time. Page commented that nothing could occur in his embassy, "a small whispering gallery," that was not known immediately in the American establishments of every European capital. News came to the embassy by "the rear door" that he could secure in no other way—especially through the department under Bryan. The ambassador claimed he "could find out in a day what any given Secretary in any given capital thinks of his new and of his old Ambassador; and what any given Ambassador thinks of his secretaries."[31]

The secretaries were aware of events in Washington, for they probably had served terms in department offices, especially in the information and regional divisions, and whether at home or abroad all the secretaries seem to have been inveterate letter writers. Nor were they scrupulous about confidential information. Grew knew of James Gerard's appointment before either his superior, Ambassador John G. A. Leishman, or Gerard found out. Grew had intercepted a cable "to be decoded by the ambassador" and, not finding any notice that he as first secretary could not decode it, did so before passing it to Leishman. He immediately informed Second Secretary Willing Spencer, his colleague on vacation. From another of Grew's letters Secretary of Embassy Charles S. Wilson learned that Henry M. Pindell was intended to be only a stopgap for Charles Crane, and the first secretary in Berlin also spread word of MacMurray's refusal of Siam. He frequently wrote other secretaries requesting information to add to his personal store.[32]

Politics in the narrow sense was not often a subject of secretarial gossip, except as it concerned appointments. Most secretaries in 1913–14, having received their appointment from Republican presidents and their recommendation from Republican congressmen, were of that party. It was more from fear of losing place that they distrusted the new administration. They were especially unsure of President Wilson's attitude toward the diplomatic service after he removed the career men from ministerial posts, and they had less regard for Bryan, who had recommended most of the ministerial replacements. In urging Peter Jay's appointment to a good post when it appeared that the young descendant of the nation's early secretary of foreign affairs was to be removed from his duties as a special agent at Cairo (a combined diplomatic and consular position, unfortunately not under civil service regulations), Ambassador Page noted that the secretaries were like navy men, apolitical.[33] Again, chagrin over the change of party did not arise from political hostility; had the Democrats assured service officers that their tenure would be regarded as it had been during the Taft regime, loyalty to Wilson and Bryan would have been unquestionable.

Gossip among officers of the diplomatic service in 1913–14 turned upon their appointments, the talents or quirks of new and old chiefs, and especially the situation in the American embassy in Rome under Thomas Page's predecessor, Ambassador Thomas J. O'Brien. The "Wheeler-Benson incident" provides insight into the pettiness of much legation and embassy activity before the Great War.

It was a complex business. Post Wheeler, appointed first secretary of embassy in 1912, had arrived in Rome with some ill will. He believed that his transfer from St. Petersburg, where he had served with Rockhill and MacMurray and then with Ambassador Curtis Guild, was unwarranted. His experiences in St. Petersburg had been unpleasant. Coming from Tokyo, he had alienated MacMurray, who described Wheeler as "a small man playing big," officious, rude, lacking in linguistic and managerial skills (both of which MacMurray prided himself upon possessing to an unusual degree). Rockhill ordinarily secluded himself in his private office with his work on an edition of Chinese treaties, but came to share his second secretary's dislike of Wheeler. The latter and his wife, the author Hallie Erminie Rives, were social climbers, and perhaps Wheeler was among that minority of service officers whom Hugh Gibson later described as cookie pushers, cranks, and freaks who deserved to be removed. The Wheelers made themselves unpopular in St. Petersburg, and as MacMurray wrote many letters, word of this got back not only to the department but to every legation and embassy. MacMurray had accepted a position in Washington in the department in 1911, after having endured months during which First Secretary Wheeler did not speak to him. Guild then replaced Rockhill, had no less trouble with Wheeler, and recommended his transfer. The arrival of Alexander Benson as second secretary sparked another feud, and Benson, according to Wheeler's account, pledged himself to the harassment of "the PW's."

This was the background. After Wheeler departed St. Petersburg for Rome, Benson presumably by chance followed him to Rome as second secretary. Ambassador O'Brien was soon aware that the feeling between the Rome embassy's first and second secretaries was becoming incendiary.[34]

Then the gossip began. Some of the stories concerned Mrs. Wheeler and her ancestry (among other libels, her maiden name, Rives, that of a distinguished Virginia family, was said to have been falsely assumed). There was her husband's purported plagiarism at government expense in publication of the Russian folktales. More serious was the charge that Wheeler had taken advantage of the tariff exemption accorded diplomats to sell the Rome embassy's gasoline at a profit. Little or no evidence lay behind this accusation, but many persons in other cities besides Rome were willing to believe it. Matters reached such a point that the department recalled both Wheeler and Benson to Washington "to give cause why . . . resignation should not be accepted." They reported their respective stories to Malone and to Secretary of State Bryan. Wheeler was sure the gasoline charge had been trumped up by Benson and that if anyone was stealing gasoline it was Ambassador O'Brien.[35]

Neither Malone nor Bryan proved friendly to Wheeler. Neither believed the gasoline charge, and Malone's report maintained that the charge was not the main cause for complaint against the first secretary; he was simply a troublemaker. Wheeler was convinced that a plot existed within the department, led by MacMurray, to drum him out of the service, and he hired investigators and a lawyer to plead his case and spent money for telegrams to embassy personnel with whom he had served, requesting them to telegraph the president regarding his honesty and amiability. A surprising number of telegrams went to Washington. There was actually little need for them; shortly after the secretaries' departure for Washington, Ambassador O'Brien telegraphed the department that there was no foundation for the most serious charges on either side. He asked that neither secretary be permitted to return to Rome but did not suggest their expulsion from the service, although he later wrote Malone that Wheeler was absolutely self-centered and a tremendous self-advertiser, disloyal, remiss in his work, appearing at the embassy for only two hours each day.[36]

When Thomas Page arrived in Rome he found the embassy still alive with gossip about the two secretaries. Acquainted with the rumors by courtesy of a young clerk in Rome, Harold Sherwood Spencer, brother of Willing Spencer, another victim of Wheeler's wrath while they were in St. Petersburg, Page also requested the secretaries' transfer.[37]

Malone's report to the secretary of state and to the president hinted that there might have been some truth to Wheeler's charge that there was a plan in the department for his removal. In fairness to Wheeler, Malone pointed out that if the department had known of the friction between Wheeler and Benson, it should not have sent both men to Rome. If the department did not know, Malone went on, it had only itself to blame. Malone recommended that Benson be reprimanded and transferred, and Wheeler dismissed, because every ambassador with whom the latter had served had thought him unfit for the service. President Wilson had little use for Wheeler, whom he had known from Princeton days, but the telegrams he received convinced him that removal was unwise. The president was especially impressed by one letter in Wheeler's behalf by a Methodist bishop. Wheeler was transferred to Tokyo where, despite the president's express wish that he retire from the service at the end of six months, he remained until the end of the war. Benson was reprimanded and exiled to Latin America. Grew, who knew all about the matter in his distant Berlin post, wrote tellingly that it was "not Phillips' fault" that Wheeler had not been removed from the service, an indication that there was some private communication concerning the matter between the Harvard secretary of embassy and Malone's Harvard replacement as third assistant secretary of state.[38]

Removal of two secretaries from a major embassy required a shake-up in European embassy staffs. Arthur Hugh Frazier went from Vienna to Rome to serve as first secretary ad interim, leaving the embassy in Vienna understaffed during the early months of Penfield's tenure. Although Page wanted to keep Frazier in Rome, he shortly was transferred to Paris, where Herrick was begging for assistance. Wheeler's permanent replacement was Peter Jay, who until that time had shown little promise of becoming a first-rate diplomatic officer, and U. Grant-Smith, a diplomat of experience, replaced Frazier in Vienna.[39] The entire incident illuminates the preoccupations of a service made up of wealthy young men.

# 9

# Summer 1914

It is now easy to see that in 1914 an era came to an end and another began. With half a century and more of retrospect we can look back on that year which in its very invocation carries the meaning of catastrophe, a time when the world shifted and went an unexpected way from which there would be no turning back. We can discern the long train of crises and disasters that has led down to our present time.

Having studied the end of an era and the beginning of another, the historian wonders what might have been done, how far back it would have been necessary to go, to have saved the peoples of Europe and the world from the troubles into which they were about to enter in 1914. One has the feeling that in preceding years the choices were large, the opportunities abounding for European and world peace. If only the leaders of the European chancelleries had seized the moments, indeed any moment. The organization of foreign affairs in the last years of the nineteenth century would have made the task fairly easy. The 1880s and 1890s, whatever their problems, were a time when foreign policy was conducted by a few people in a few places called foreign offices, places not frequented by the uninitiated. In those bad old days it was possible for Foreign Minister Théophile Delcassé of France to make a treaty and give a copy to the president of the Republic and then lock his own copy in the safe at the Quai d'Orsay and say nothing about the terms of the treaty to the Chamber of Deputies. The existence of some sort of treaty was known to members of the Chamber and to those Frenchmen who read their newspapers carefully. It did not occur to very many people to protest to Delcassé, to inquire about the treaty's terms. In such a time when there had not been the intrusion of public opinion into diplomacy or such a public fascination with diplomacy as later accompanied the diplomacies of all the great nations of the world, the Continent and the world might have been set on the road to peace.

In the years before 1914 the putative leaders of Europe unfortunately proved incapable of moving the Continent toward peace. They were preoccupied with their national and personal concerns. They did not want to give up anything. The peace of Europe did not seem in danger; there had been no great European war since the final defeat of Napoleon in 1815.

Might not Americans have taken an initiative for peace? An intriguing possibility lay here. President Woodrow Wilson was accustomed to tell his countrymen that they comprised all peoples and therefore understood all peoples. Although the president may have been talking politically, there was truth in what he said. Many of the people of the United States, especially in the eastern cities but throughout broad portions of the country, had come from Europe, and their combined heritages provided a foundation for more understanding of Europe, surely, than was present in the individual nations of the Continent.

But it was unlikely that the people of the United States, despite the advantage of their broadly European ancestry, could have served as a mediating force for peace in 1914—a force that would have given the diplomacies of the several European nations time to cool down and reconsider. There was the long tradition of national isolation and the extraordinary ignorance, popular and official, of recent world politics, especially the politics of Europe after 1888, which had produced by 1914 a national inability to do anything important in international affairs. In the crucial years before the World War the American people were dreaming. Even after the war began they did not cease to dream. In 1917 intervention was a piece of emotionalism and not the result of careful calculation. The pervasive nationalism of Americans thereafter proved impossible to manage. To mobilize American opinion for war was easy, but to mobilize it for peace proved far more difficult than President Wilson imagined, and in the fiery test of 1917–18 nationalism rather than internationalism gripped the people. In some ways in 1917–18 the president tried to oppose American nationalism. At the same time he was urging Americans to new patriotic exertion. In the end, in 1919–20, when he was championing the League of Nations, he discovered that his own people would not back him.

It is saddening to observe the proud, wishful mood of Americans in the years before the war. Few Americans thought that a great war was possible. It was an era of talk about impending war without any large conviction that war would come. American writers, even politicians, indulged in the speculation, as did Europeans. Not long after he left the State Department in 1913, Francis Mairs Huntington-Wilson published a novel entitled *Stultitia*, an allegory prophesying war. Perhaps he was in a pessimistic mood regarding the future of American foreign policy without him. The novel was not a best-seller. Better known were the articles by the former diplomat Lewis Einstein predicting conflict between the great powers of Europe and urging increased attention to problems across the Atlantic. Ambassador Walter H. Page, writing to his eldest son from London in December 1913, related how the British spoke constantly of "danger and the probability of war" and the need for preparedness. Nearly every American journal carried articles describing the Balkan situation and deploring the armaments race. But that generation thought the prospect of war "an absurdity— 'it would cost too much'; 'the international bankers would never permit it'; 'the Socialist parties in Europe would call a general strike.'"[1] Talk of peace was far more common. With a fascination not bestowed upon martial matters the prewar generation beheld the peace movement, led in the United States by such men as William Jennings Bryan and Andrew Carnegie. The secretary of state wrote in 1913 that he believed there would be no more war in his lifetime, and he devoted most of his office hours in the summer of 1914 to preparation, completion, and signing of his cooling-off treaties. It troubled him that the governments of Germany and Austria-Hungary showed no willingness to sign. In the Netherlands the work of peace occupied the most important part of the agenda of Henry van Dyke, who between preaching and fishing busied himself with plans for the Third Hague Peace Conference which, he was assured in June 1914, would meet in 1916, rather than in 1915 as he had planned. It was the Americans, not the Europeans, who had asked for a delay.[2]

Increased militarism in Europe and an alarming increase in the stockpile of armaments on the part of all European powers led President Wilson to permit his adviser, Edward M. House, to go to Europe in the summer of 1914 to pursue the Great Adventure. The trip easily came to nothing. House reveled in his new acquaintance with the great and near-great of Europe. In mid-June he wrote that the British looked only to Ascot and garden parties and that the war spirit was not dominant in France, only in Germany, where the one thought was "to advance industrially and glorify war." As the tour progressed the president believed the mission successful, as did House. He missed the colonel; Wilson's last letters to the absent House reveal a note of impatience that he finish the peacemaking.[3]

In the summer of 1914 the president's attention was not on international affairs. The president was a troubled man, for his wife Ellen, to whom he was devoted, was dying from Bright's disease. Although she had rallied in the early summer, by late July and early August signs of imminent death were visible to the doctor, if not to the anguished husband.

In the State Department it was business as usual. As the days went by in the quiet, almost idyllic summer of 1914, and the Packards, Pierce-Arrows, and ubiquitous Fords passed back and forth in front of the State, War, and Navy Building housing the Department of State, it was difficult to discern any difference between that summer and, say, the summer of 1913. All summers of the era seemed to run confusedly together, and the business of American diplomacy, as of American politics, ran along in an orderly way. If an observer had looked up the long run of stone steps toward the doors of State, War, and Navy, he could be assured that inside that great neoclassical pile the work of the department was going its way. The spittoons would be in their corners, and the black messengers would be carrying messages from one swinging-door office to another. Inside the offices the dignitaries of the department would be functioning, with their wooden "in" and "out" boxes filling up or emptying as the day brought cables from this place or that.

In the office of the secretary, looking out on the Washington monument, in that office with the grandfather's clock and the great sweep of Brussels carpet and the walls hung with portraits and paintings selected by his wife, sat the plebeian secretary from Nebraska, thinking and talking more of domestic politics than of diplomacy. If he thought of the latter it was in regard to those conciliation treaties. The controversy surrounding Bryan's summer trips on the Chautauqua circuit had died down, and in this summer he was away nearly every weekend to some neighboring state to tell listeners about peace and temperance and the good life. He seldom went farther than two hundred miles from Washington; the expense and time would have been scarcely worth the pay he received, which was perhaps two hundred dollars a speech. During weekdays he arrived at his office at about 7:30 A.M., and if his work could not be described as strenuous it was no less conscientious than that of his colleagues.[4]

Many of the department's officials and clerical assistants were on vacation. The secretary left town on Friday afternoons; Robert Lansing was vacationing in New York; First Assistant John Osborne was away as usual and not expected back until mid-August; Alvey Adee was on another bicycle tour of Europe. Adee had requested his usual two-month vacation with pay early in May and had asked that it be extended one month without salary. The president, when Bryan consulted him, knew of "nothing to prevent his going," so the second assistant was away until well after the outbreak of war.[5] In late July, William Phillips wrote to Counselor Robert Lansing that he and the solicitor, Cone Johnson, were carrying most of the burden. Fortunately for these two inexperienced men, Lansing was available for consultation at his vacation site, where he daily received department flimsies. If legal technicalities got too complicated Phillips would write or telegraph Lansing who would send down advice. Most of Lansing's legal advice went to the delegates at the conference over Spitzbergen, then meeting in Norway under the direction of Minister Albert G. Schmedeman, a novice in diplomacy who wrote frequent, barely comprehensible cables. Apparently Bryan knew little about the contention over the northern islands where a few Americans had mining interests. Perhaps other members of the department considered the archipelago not of sufficient importance to occupy the secretary. Bryan's initials appeared rarely on dispatches relating to the conference. In Europe, Adee became a conference delegate when the chief American representative, William Miller Collier, onetime minister to Spain, suffered a nervous breakdown. It was Adee's only stint as a delegate to an international conference, and he found the duty irksome because of his deafness. He planned to ask the department for a three-week extension of leave for more cycling once the conference finished. His concise, optimistic reports scarcely noted the increasing animosity between German and Russian representatives at the meeting, which adjourned on July 30 when war between the two nations was imminent.[6]

For a long time Mexican problems had been uppermost in the minds of Americans if and when they bothered to consider foreign affairs, but even matters there had calmed with the retirement of Victoriano Huerta and the meeting of the A.B.C. powers at Niagara Falls. The Panama Canal tolls controversy with England had reached a satisfactory conclusion in mid-June. In that warm, drowsy summer news of the Austrian archduke's assassination on June 28 seemed a minor event. The two offices of the department that dealt with European affairs, the division of West European affairs and the division of Near Eastern affairs, had no comment. Department policy was to remain uninvolved in European matters, and after many years of the Eastern Question the division of Near Eastern affairs seemed to bear this always in mind.

No warning of the assassination's importance came from the European capitals to cause alarm. American ambassadors and ministers in Europe, including Frederic Penfield, James Gerard, Charles Vopicka, and Walter Page, considered the matter of little consequence. American envoys attended local ceremonies honoring the deceased archduke and his wife, who also had been killed, and Penfield in Vienna bore Wilson's and Bryan's condolences to Emperor Francis Joseph. Beyond that the matter seemed another Balkan assassination. Few persons connected it with the reports of House and other observers that there was jingoism in Germany, with the uneasiness expressed by Sir Edward Grey and Sir William Tyrrell over the matter, with the Albanian escapade of the minister in Greece, George Fred Williams, with Penfield's reports of the calling up of Austrian veterans in reserve units, with the refusal of Germany and Austria-Hungary to sign cooling-off treaties.[7]

For Americans in the European capitals the summer was scarcely less quiet than in Washington. The ambassadors and ministers were on vacation or planning to go on vacation. Page left London in mid-July for a country place within commuting distance of the embassy where he could rest and play golf after the social and diplomatic season, but, he wrote Wilson, there was so little diplomatic business, despite the problem of "that infernal near-Eastern country," Serbia, that proximity seemed unnecessary. Myron T. Herrick was preparing to leave

130

Paris for good early in August, to make room for his successor, William G. Sharp, and Parisian newspapers were filled with comment on his departure. When news of the assassination reached Germany, Gerard, not yet on vacation, was spending time away from Berlin, practicing his shooting and watching military maneuvers with the kaiser. Late in July the ambassador pronounced Berlin "as quiet as a grave." Only a few days before, on July 18, he had telegraphed Bryan that there could be no hope of German agreement to a conciliation treaty so long as the kaiser's regime held power. Meanwhile his first secretary, Joseph C. Grew, in the United States for six weeks during June and July, returned to Berlin on July 27 to find embassy business progressing in the quiet fashion that Gerard and Grew together had made possible.[8]

Everywhere in Europe, American chanceries were peaceful. Thomas Page left the Italian capital for an extended vacation, visited with the American ambassador in London, and traveled northward to Scotland where he remained until forced to return to Rome. The marriage of Ambassador Joseph Willard's daughter to the son of former-President Roosevelt left that envoy with little to worry about except the care of his automobile, which he sent to Paris for repairs early in July, after which he departed with his family for the United States, where he remained until early August. Ambassadors Henry Morgenthau and Penfield requested leaves; they planned to bid farewell to their embassies in late summer.[9]

The embassy in Russia and the legation in Sweden were without chiefs of mission. Aside from Schmedeman and van Dyke the remaining American envoys were relaxing.

Brand Whitlock walked in the sunlight at his rented estate near the sea where he worked on his novel. Like Walter Page he was close enough to the capital to return in an emergency; his secretary, Hugh Gibson, together with a single clerk, remained on duty in Brussels. The minister and his family took long walks and viewed an aerial exhibition—"monoplanes soaring and circling on high, like immense and graceful birds." To the horror of the family a woman skydiver whom they were watching was killed when her parachute failed. Whitlock's journal was only showing a misplaced sense of foreboding when, a few days before the invasion of Belgium, he described this tragedy and the storm which brought a gloomy end to a perfect summer day.[10]

In Switzerland at the height of the tourist season (it was a joke that summer that nearly every American tourist, not yet required to carry a passport, bore a letter of introduction to European society signed by the secretary of state) Pleasant Stovall attended horse shows with the Austrian, French, German, and Russian envoys, all of whom chatted about the Balkan disaster but assured him there would be no war.[11]

Vopicka attended horse races with the royal families.[12]

Van Dyke and Morgenthau wrote privately of rumors of war following the assassination but did not inform the department.[13]

Such was the scene before the guns of August. The events beginning July 24 caught department officials and American representatives in Europe almost completely unaware. Living closer to the controversy than any other American ambassador, Penfield reported in a letter of July 13, which the department received on July 30, of the situation in Austria-Hungary following the assassination. The event had shaken the populace, he wrote, because Austrians felt that the Archduke Charles was too inexperienced at the age of twenty-seven and perhaps incapable of handling policy in event of the emperor's death. He remarked that the archduke's wife, Zita, the Bourbon princess of Parma, was charming and the imperial couple's domestic life praiseworthy. The ambassador in Vienna said nothing of a possible conflict, though somewhat later he told Grew that a highly placed source, a lady, had told him of the inevitability of war between Austria and Serbia several days before hostilities began.[14]

Only the vice-consul general in Budapest, Frank Mallett, seems to have had insight about the state of affairs in the Austro-Hungarian empire. The Maine-born Mallett was no large figure in the consular service, though in past years his Budapest dispatches had won acclaim from Secretary Philander Knox and from Wilbur Carr. He had entered the consular service as a clerk in Budapest in 1904, after education in private schools in the United States and Europe and a brief attempt at a consular clerkship in Cologne. Mallett had many personal problems, most of them related to women and finances. In 1913–14 he was in trouble with the consular bureau because of complaints on both

132

counts—reports which Carr dismissed as indiscretions on the part of an otherwise fine officer.[15] But it was Mallett who on July 13, 1914, wrote the earliest dispatch announcing the inevitability of war between Austria and Serbia. He had noted the Austrian mobilization on the Serbian frontier and the commandeering of horses by the Austrian army.[16]

Mallett's key dispatch went to the United States by ordinary post. To have sent it by cable would have drawn a rebuke from the department, the warning so frequently given to ministers and consuls whose telegrams were long. Mallett's letter contained about 150 words. The men in the cable and telegraph room downstairs at the department objected to long messages because of the time it took to decipher them; besides, each word cut into the consular service's budget.[17]

Mallett's letter reached the department on July 27, the day after the chargé d'affaires in Russia, Charles Wilson, telegraphed the certainty of Russian intervention in an Austro-Serbian conflict. That same day Penfield reported, also by telegram, that a conflict was certain. The ambassador in Vienna noted that Austrian troops had been moving southward for several days, a fact that had not impressed him before.[18]

It is interesting to observe what became of Mallett. Not long after his letter predicting war, he left on vacation. He wanted to tour the Balkans, he told his superiors. After war broke out he requested permission from the consul general in Budapest, William Coffin, to go to St. Petersburg under auspices of the Hungarian Red Cross to consult regarding prisoners of war. Arrested by the Russian police in St. Petersburg as an enemy agent (Carr reprimanded Coffin for giving his vice-consul permission to go to Russia), Mallett received short shrift from the novice Ambassador George T. Marye. By the time he departed the Russian capital he was in ill favor all around. His financial situation in Budapest banks was startling, as he had been using consular funds to pay his debts. After dismissing him from the service in December 1914, the department could not easily locate him (he turned up in Christiania). He later carried on a long plea for readmission to the service and drifted into paranoia. His prescience about affairs in Austria-Hungary may well have been related to his financial connections—a telling commentary on American political reportage from Eastern Europe in 1914.[19]

After July 27, 1914, telegrams from the European embassies, legations, and consulates deluged the department, by now in disorder because of the staff's inability to keep up. Reporters hovered in the doorways of the offices, hoping to glimpse the datelines of yellow cables and dispatches with the red and blue tags indicating importance. On August 1, Bryan, as usual unfriendly to reporters, announced that news of the European situation would henceforth be given to newspapers through channels and banished the journalists.[20]

The chance of a warning had irretrievably passed; the crisis was in course. Information poured into Washington so rapidly that the department verged on chaos. The contradictory testimony contained in the dispatches indicated a similar breakdown within the European embassies and legations. The able chargé in St. Petersburg, overworked and harassed by an excited Russian populace which a few days later sacked the German embassy, stressed the inevitability of Russian entrance, while Ambassador Gerard reported from Berlin that although he was postponing his vacation until August 12 he was certain that "matters will be arranged without general European war." Penfield believed the conflict would be limited to the Balkans. Herrick regarded the situation as "the gravest in history" and civilization "threatened by demoralization which would follow a general conflagration."[21]

Myron T. Herrick's telegram, received at 7:30 P.M. on July 28, asked Wilson to use his good offices. Bryan wired Walter Page a few hours later to ask if Herrick's suggestion would be taken in London. Page telegraphed his doubts; Lord Grey had asked if the same offer of mediation was going out to other capitals.

The United States did not make a similar offer in other capitals, and perhaps that was the president's mistake. Colonel House offered his services as a mediator after returning on July 29, as he thought his acquaintance with European leaders would carry weight. Grey suggested a conference in which the United States would act as mediator; Wilson hesitated, did not consult department officials, then decided to do nothing rather than violate the long-standing policy of nonintervention in European affairs. By August 4, when the president again considered mediation, shown in a message drafted and addressed to the Russian government, matters were out of hand. The last hope that war could be avoided through American intervention was lost.[22]

Confusion reigned as declarations of war accumulated. Lansing returned to the counselor's office only a few days before the events, but upon his return Phillips left on vacation. Both the first and third assistant secretaries had to be recalled for the duration of the emergency. As for the second secretary, Adee, he departed Christiania as soon as the Spitzbergen Conference adjourned on July 30. For several days he could not be found and his relatives expressed concern. He turned up in the Copenhagen legation (without his bicycle, lost in Paris). There he found that Minister Maurice Egan was on leave and Secretary of Legation Alexander Magruder was virtually alone. Adee cheerfully took charge of diplomatic business and wrote his grandniece that "in companionship with about 60,000 American tourists" he was trying to get away.[23]

Throughout the week of the grand calamity, July 28–August 3, telegrams arrived—dozens upon dozens of messages. Tens of thousands of tourists were caught on the Continent or afraid of being caught—most of them without passports, many without funds. Friends and relatives, especially those with connections in the department, clamored. Embassies, legations, consulates flooded the department with the latest declarations of war, mobilization, and neutrality, also demanding assistance and advice for Americans in Europe. Bryan and his assistants, together with Carr, in touch with consulates crucial in handling monetary aspects of the crisis, remained at their desks until late each night, studying each telegram, trying to make sense out of contradictory requests and reports, all pessimistic. "Was it safe for two ladies to travel from China to Paris by way of St. Petersburg?" It was risky, and that was the substance of the reply. "Could the department locate a certain individual of great means and importance somewhere in central Europe?" It would try.[24]

Only a few hours after Gerard telegraphed his opinion that the Russian mobilization of July 30 made general war inevitable, Bryan permitted himself the respite of viewing, together with his Sunday School class, a motion picture depicting the Biblical story of Joseph and his brothers. Later the secretary of state found time to recommend that some too explicit scenes in the film be deleted before distribution to American audiences. For the first time in his wife's memory Bryan did not attend church on Sunday, August 2—he was at his desk in the department the entire day. All the while the secretary's letters to Wilson dealt largely with the Mexican situation.[25]

A special problem encountered by American diplomats was the need to issue passports to thousands of citizens. By August 1, several days after requests began pouring into the telegraph room, Bryan addressed a circular to American ambassadors and ministers in Europe authorizing them to issue passports to citizens who asked and to use typewritten forms of their making if official blanks were not available. This permission was after the fact, for Gibson wrote in his diary the same evening that his legation, to which Whitlock had returned a few days before, was doing "a land-office business," turning out "by the dozen" passports for which there were no forms.[26]

The problem of assisting Americans seemed slow in reaching solution, but the work of the department in securing money and credits for those persons who had been stranded abroad was remarkably swift. Within ten days of the first declarations of war the department established an agency under Carr. Including shipments of gold within the first two weeks of war, $2,750,000 was appropriated for emergency relief, and by September 1914 over 30,000 requests had been processed from travelers and relatives in the United States. Such work necessitated an increase of personnel, and Carr received twelve clerks. Within a fortnight personnel had increased by one hundred fifty—further evidence that the department could mobilize for an emergency.[27]

The assumption by American embassies and legations of representation for belligerents in enemy capitals, a complex matter, occurred in every capital within a few days, although not until August 17 did Bryan issue instructions. The envoys repeatedly requested permission and instructions but replies did not come soon enough from the overworked secretary. The harried counselor and solicitor were preoccupied with a declaration of neutrality. Diplomats went ahead on their own. Chargé Wilson in St. Petersburg was under duress because of destruction of the German embassy and fear that the same would happen to the Austrian chancery unless Americans took action. The chargé asked permission to raise the American flag over the Austrian residence to protect the lives and property of persons inside and was told he could do so, although he was not allowed to use force, as he suggested, to prevent the commandeering of German and Austrian embassy automobiles by the Russian government.[28] Whitlock was embarrassed in Brussels by the request of the German minister that he assume the work of the invader's embassy, after he already had agreed to take over French interests. The Ohioan suggested to the German, and to Bryan, that another neutral legation handle the situation, and the German minister, equally embarrassed, agreed; but the secretary of state informed Whitlock that he was to refuse no request, regardless of origin.[29]

The war thus caught the department both at home and abroad "asleep at the wheel"—although it is questionable whether European foreign offices, presumably more sophisticated, better staffed and organized, were better prepared. The British foreign office, so admired by Americans but understaffed and racked by internal conflicts, was not. Gibson's laconic comment on July 28, "Well, the roof has fallen in," showed some farsightedness, compared with a remark by the Austrian minister in Switzerland to Minister Stovall, "Well, it will be just a little war."[30]

The war was to bring great changes to the department in its Washington offices and representation abroad. Confusion in understaffed embassies and legations in late July and early August 1914 led President Wilson to propose a reform of the diplomatic service. The Stone-Flood Bill, introduced in May 1914 by Senator William J. Stone and Representative Henry D. Flood, would never have passed congressional or presidential scrutiny in December of that year had not events overridden the politicians. The act was not perfect, but it did put the diplomatic service on the same merit footing as the consular service. Because of the tremendous increase in department work—according to Chief Clerk Benjamin Davis, 400 percent during the first six weeks of war—workers within the department more than doubled. The increase in embassy and legation personnel was greater. If the war did not stop the political appointment of ambassadors and ministers, it did call attention to the worst features of such a system and perhaps made Wilson and his successors more conscious of selections. Several former career men were rehired for the emergency and assisted in larger embassies. Some former diplomats were among those caught in Europe in late July; they volunteered their services. Diplomatic secretaries such as Irwin Laughlin, Grew, Gibson, Hoffman Phillip, Hugh Wilson, and

Robert Woods Bliss, gained experience which led to their promotion within a few years. The war proved the need for increased pay and larger quarters for officials overseas. It was no coincidence that the next decade saw legislation reorganizing and reforming the diplomatic and consular services, and the purchase of American embassies and consulates, although diplomats continued to be underpaid for another generation and more, until another war.[31]

It was not lack of talented personnel that caused unpreparedness for events such as those of early August 1914. Inexperienced and untrained, at least for that sort of crisis, many members of the diplomatic and consular services later proved that they possessed ability. For the American diplomatic establishment the unfortunate point about the crisis was that the makers and administrators of foreign policy could not have made use of more diplomatic talent at an earlier date. Carr unwittingly put his finger on the problem. After his first day of work on the relief board, established under his direction on August 7, 1914, he wrote happily in his diary: "I worked hard until 1:40 A.M. Home. This diary and to bed. A great day. One feels alive once more."[32] It is a commentary on the department's lack of seriousness regarding world problems, especially those in Europe, that only the onset of what was to be the greatest war in modern history could bring relief from the routine.

# Notes

## CHAPTER TWO

1. Hugh Wilson, *Education of a Diplomat* (New York City: Longmans, Green, 1938), p. 32; *Register of the Department of State*, 1913, passim.

2. *United States Government Manual, 1975–76*, pp. 347–61.

3. Graham H. Stuart, *American Diplomatic and Consular Practice*, 2nd ed. (New York: Appleton-Century-Crofts, 1952), pp. 18–23.

4. Ibid., p. 21; Stuart, *The Department of State: A History of Its Organization, Procedure, and Personnel* (New York: Macmillan, 1949), p. 201; *Register of the Department of State*, 1908, passim.

5. Worthington C. Ford, ed., *The Writings of John Quincy Adams*, 7 vols. (New York: Macmillan, 1916), 6:354, requoted from Stuart, *Department of State*, p. 54.

6. Katherine E. Crane, *Mr. Carr of State: Forty-Seven Years in the Department of State* (New York: St. Martin's Press, 1960), pp. 10–11.

7. Stuart, *Department of State*, pp. 54, 58; "Entrance into Department of State," autobiographical file, n.d., John Bassett Moore Papers, Library of Congress, Washington, D.C.; Milton O. Gustafson, ed., *The National Archives and Foreign Relations Research* (Athens: Ohio University Press, 1974), pp. 3–8.

8. Francis Mairs Huntington-Wilson, *Memoirs of an Ex-Diplomat* (Boston: B. Humphries, 1945), p. 170. Huntington-Wilson did not hyphenate his name until after the World War.

9. Ibid., p. 159.

10. Stuart, *Department of State*, pp. 67–69, 77–78.

11. Ibid., pp. 142–46; Lewis D. Einstein, *A Diplomat Looks Back* (New Haven: Yale University Press, 1968), p. 26.

12. Stuart, *Diplomatic and Consular Practice*, p. 23; Robert H. Ferrell, *George C. Marshall*, in Samuel Flagg Bemis and Robert H. Ferrell, eds., *The American Secretaries of State and Their Diplomacy*, 18 vols. (New York: Cooper Square, 1927–70), 15:42–45.

13. Stuart, *Department of State*, pp. 90–91, 119, 131.

14. Ibid., p. 130.

15. "Entrance into Department of State," Moore Papers; *Dictionary of American Biography*, "Adee, Alvey Augustus"; John A. DeNovo, "The

Enigmatic Alvey A. Adee and American Foreign Relations, 1870–1924,"
*Prologue*, 7 (Summer 1975), 69–80.

16. Quoted without citation in Tyler Dennett, *John Hay: From Poetry to Politics* (New York: Dodd, Mead, 1934), pp. 201, 440.

17. Clipping from *The Healthy Home*, May 1913, in Adee Family Papers, Library of Congress, Washington, D.C.; Stuart, *Diplomatic and Consular Practice*, p. 63; Huntington-Wilson, *Memoirs*, p. 154. Adee was a perfectionist in literary matters, and he also had a sense of humor; it is unfortunate that his frequently amusing notations are about all that remain as a record of his life. Although he kept a diary he never wrote of department affairs and arranged for the diary and all his other papers to be destroyed after his death.

18. Crane, *Mr. Carr*, pp. 41–43; clipping from *Boston Transcript*, date illegible, scrapbook in Adee Family Papers.

19. Huntington-Wilson, *Memoirs*, p. 154.

20. "Semper Paratus Adee" was one of the nicknames Hay had for his favorite colleague (William Roscoe Thayer, *The Life and Letters of John Hay*, 2 vols. [Boston: Houghton Mifflin, 1915], 2:187). Information on workload within the department is in National Civil Service Reform League, *Report on the Foreign Service* (New York: National Civil Service Reform League, 1919), pp. 175, 195–97; Stuart, *Department of State*, p. 212; Crane, *Mr. Carr*, p. 141.

21. Huntington-Wilson, *Memoirs*, p. 153.

22. Department of State, "Outline of the Organization and Work of the Department of State, 1911," 111.08/10. Citations followed by file numbers refer to the unpublished records of the State Department, deposited in the National Archives, Washington, D.C.

23. Huntington-Wilson, *Memoirs*, p. 157; see also the reminiscences of Nelson Trusler Johnson, Transcript of Interviews of 1954, p. 27, Oral History Research Office, Columbia University.

24. Crane, *Mr. Carr*, pp. 50–51; Philip C. Jessup, *Elihu Root*, 2 vols. (New York: Dodd, Mead, 1938), 2:104.

25. Stuart, *Diplomatic and Consular Practice*, p. 91; Root to Roosevelt, Nov. 29, 1905, requoted from Jessup, *Elihu Root*, 2:104.

26. Crane, *Mr. Carr*, passim.

27. Stuart, *Department of State*, p. 205.

28. Ibid.; Crane, *Mr. Carr*, pp. 54–55, 148. Civil service examiners assisted in the preparation and administration of examinations for the diplomatic and consular services, but neither of the services ever was under the direct supervision of the civil service commission. Nor is the latter-day (since 1924) foreign service.

29. Huntington-Wilson, *Memoirs*, pp. 155–56; Crane, *Mr. Carr*, pp. 109, 119, 131–32.

30. Crane, *Mr. Carr*, p. 181. There were extenuating circumstances.

Carr's first wife, the former Mary Eugenia Crane, was an invalid from shortly after their marriage in 1897 until her death in 1911 (ibid., pp. 16–17). Carr, with his low salary, was responsible for her care.

31. Ibid., pp. 7, 127.
32. Requoted from ibid., p. 122.
33. Ibid., pp. 116–18, 139.
34. Huntington-Wilson, *Memoirs*, pp. 46–47.
35. Ibid., pp. 48, 144, 155–56.
36. Ibid., pp. 155–60, 166–70.
37. Copies of the plans for reorganization, dated July, August, September, 1906, are in the Francis Mairs Huntington-Wilson Papers (microfilm), Ursinus College Library, Collegeville, Pa. The date of submission of the plans to Root was October 29, 1906.
38. Jessup, *Elihu Root*, 1:457–58.
39. Archibald Wellington Butt, *Taft and Roosevelt: The Intimate Letters of Archie Butt*, 2 vols. (Garden City, N.Y.: Doubleday, Doran, 1930), 2:770–71.
40. Jessup, *Elihu Root*, 2:112; Griscom to Huntington-Wilson, March 30, 1906, Huntington-Wilson Papers; Reminiscences of William Phillips, Oral History Research Office, Columbia University, p. 30.
41. Huntington-Wilson, *Memoirs*, pp. 161, 165; Reminiscences of William Phillips, p. 29. Phillips gave Huntington-Wilson credit for the system of regional divisions but maintained he and Heintzleman had "worked it out" (ibid., p. 30).
42. Huntington-Wilson, *Memoirs*, pp. 162, 173.
43. Ibid., p. 177.
44. Ibid., p. 178.
45. T. Bentley Mott, *Twenty Years as a Military Attaché* (New York: Oxford University Press, 1937), p. 172.
46. Huntington-Wilson, *Memoirs*, p. 232; Wilson, *Education of a Diplomat*, p. 10. President Taft's remark is requoted from Butt, *Intimate Letters of Archie Butt*, 1:371.
47. Knox's alleged domination of the department is confirmed in a letter from Taft to Knox, October 9, 1909, Philander C. Knox Papers, Library of Congress, Washington, D.C. The information regarding the Tariff Act is in Stuart, *Department of State*, pp. 212–13.
48. Huntington-Wilson, *Memoirs*, pp. 190–91, 201; Department of State, "Outline, 1911," 111.08/10, pp. 27–28; Stuart, *Department of State*, p. 213; Anderson to Knox, December 13, 1910, Huntington-Wilson to Knox, January 7, 1912, draft letter, Huntington-Wilson to the secretary of the treasury, January 1912, Knox Papers; Wilson to Moore, April 18, 1913, Woodrow Wilson Papers, Library of Congress, Washington, D.C.
49. *Register of the Department of State*, 1909–1912.

50. Department of State, "Outline, 1911," 111.08/10, pp. 70–72; Huntington-Wilson, *Memoirs*, pp. 179–80, 184. Department translators of the five official languages—French, German, Spanish, Italian, and Portuguese—were responsible not only for department mail and foreign-language newspaper and magazine articles, but for all correspondence in foreign languages received at the White House. The translators, usually two, with a single clerk, occasionally had to translate other languages. Department of State, "Outline, 1911," 111.08/10, p. 82.

51. Department of State, "Outline, 1911," 111.08/10, p. 28; *Register of the Department of State*, 1909–1913.

52. Stuart, *Department of State*, p. 217; departmental order, September 12, 1912, 111.26/19.

53. Huntington-Wilson, *Memoirs*, p. 193.

54. Stuart, *Department of State*, pp. 218–19; Crane, *Mr. Carr*, pp. 137–38.

55. Stuart, *Department of State*, p. 219; *Register of the Department of State*, 1909–1913.

56. Department of State, "Outline, 1911," 111.08/10, pp. 69–70.

57. Ibid., pp. 43–44.

## CHAPTER THREE

1. Arthur S. Link, *Wilson: The Road to the White House* (Princeton: Princeton University Press, 1947), pp. 96–97, 317–18.

2. Ibid., pp. 448–65; Paolo E. Coletta, *William Jennings Bryan: Progressive Politician and Moral Statesman, 1909–1915* (Lincoln: University of Nebraska Press, 1969), pp. 81, 86–87.

3. Coletta, *Bryan: Moral Statesman*, pp. 211–12; Paolo E. Coletta, "Bryan, Anti-Imperialism, and Missionary Diplomacy," *Nebraska History*, 44 (September 1963), 167–87; House to Wilson, February 1, 1913, copy in the Edward M. House Collection, Yale University Library.

4. Bryan to Wilson, December 25, 1912, Wilson Papers; Wilson to Bryan, January 16, 1913, William Jennings Bryan Papers, Library of Congress, Washington, D.C. Beginning in August 1913 *The Commoner* was published monthly rather than weekly, with the secretary's brother Charles as associate editor. It brought Bryan over $5,000 yearly. Coletta, *Bryan: Moral Statesman*, pp. 107–8.

5. House diary, January 30, 1913, House Collection.

6. "Bryan and the Cabinet," *American Review of Reviews*, 47 (January 1913), 27.

7. *New York Times*, February 2, 1913.

8. House diary, February 19, 1913; Bryan to Wilson, February 26, 1913, Wilson Papers.

9. William Jennings Bryan and Mary B. Bryan, *Memoirs* (Philadelphia: John C. Winston, 1925), pp. 343–44; Coletta, *Bryan: Moral Statesman*, pp. 91–92.

10. Remarks of Bryan upon introduction to personnel of the Department of State, March 5, 1913, Bryan Papers; Crane, *Mr. Carr*, p. 149; diary of Wilbur J. Carr, February 19, 1913, in W. J. Carr Papers, Library of Congress, Washington, D.C.

11. Bryan and Bryan, *Memoirs*, p. 354; Coletta, *Bryan: Moral Statesman*, p. 100; William Phillips, *Ventures in Diplomacy* (Boston: Beacon Press, 1953), pp. 63–64.

12. Huntington-Wilson, *Memoirs*, p. 192.

13. Carr diary, Apr. 11, 1913, McNeir to Moore, April 14, 1913, Moore Papers; autobiographical file, August 1941, ibid.

14. Memorandum by Moore, August 27, 1913, Moore Papers.

15. Coletta, *Bryan: Moral Statesman*, p. 110; autobiographical file, Moore Papers.

16. Carr diary, April 1, 12, 1913; Crane, *Mr. Carr*, pp. 155–56. Phillips later declared that Bryan opposed all civil service regulations (Reminiscences of William Phillips, p. 68).

17. Bryan to Wilson, July 31, 1913, Bryan letterbooks, Bryan Papers; House diary, April 12, 18, 1913; Crane, *Mr. Carr*, p. 156.

18. Requoted from Paolo E. Coletta, *William Jennings Bryan: Political Evangelist, 1860–1908* (Lincoln: University of Nebraska Press, 1964), p. 372.

19. Memorandum by Moore, July 17, 1913, Moore Papers; *Register of the Department of State*, 1913.

20. Arthur S. Link, *Wilson: The New Freedom* (Princeton: Princeton University Press, 1956), p. 105; Bryan to Wilson, May 24, 1913, Wilson Papers.

21. Bryan to Wilson, February 20, 1914, Bryan letterbooks, Bryan Papers. The Swedish post did not go to the Connecticut man; neither did it go to Arkansas, but to an Illinois meatpacker of Jewish descent, Ira Nelson Morris. He had demonstrated loyalty to the administration in 1914 by establishment of a pro–Wilson-Bryan newspaper. Bryan to Wilson, April 16, 1914, ibid., Wilson to Bryan, April 30, 1914, William Jennings Bryan–Woodrow Wilson Correspondence (microfilm), National Archives, Washington, D.C.

22. Bryan to Wilson, September 25, 1913, Wilson Papers; Coletta, *Bryan: Moral Statesman*, p. 115.

23. George Harvey, "The Diplomats of Democracy," *North American Review*, 199 (February 1914), 169–72; "Diplomatic Appointments of W. J. Bryan," undated and unsigned memorandum, House Collection.

24. House diary, March 7, 8, 1913.

25. Reminiscences of William Phillips, pp. 57–58.

26. Coletta, *Bryan: Political Evangelist*, p. 318. Bryan's ignorance of the simplest details of world affairs seemed invincible. Ambassador Whitelaw Reid was embarrassed that Bryan upon meeting Sir Edward Grey was unaware of the foreign secretary's position and asked if Grey had any connection with the British government (Reid to Roosevelt, July 17, 1906, quoted in ibid., p. 367).

27. Coletta, *Bryan: Political Evangelist*, p. 364; Ray Stannard Baker, memorandum of interview with Henry van Dyke, November 12, 1925, R. S. Baker Papers, Library of Congress, Washington, D.C.; W. J. Bryan, *The Old World and Its Ways* (St. Louis: Thompson Publishing Company, 1907), pp. 215–22.

28. Carr diary, March 9, 1913.

29. Richard Megargee, "The Diplomacy of John Bassett Moore: Realism in American Foreign Policy" (Ph.D. thesis, Northwestern University, 1963), p. 171; memorandum by Moore, October 21, 1913, Moore Papers.

30. Memoranda by Moore, June 29, July 16, October 23, 1913, Moore Papers.

31. Carr diary, April 18, 1914.

32. Ibid., April 1, 10, 23, 24, July 11, 1913; memoranda by Moore, July 16, November 19, 1913, Moore Papers.

33. Coletta, *Bryan: Moral Statesman*, p. 112; Stuart, *Diplomatic and Consular Practice*, pp. 26–27.

34. Burton J. Hendrick, *The Life and Letters of Walter Hines Page*, 3 vols. (Garden City, N.Y.: Doubleday, Page, 1923–25), 1:194, 223–25; diary of Joseph C. Grew, July 14, 1915, in J. C. Grew Papers, Houghton Library, Harvard, Cambridge, Mass.; Phillips, *Ventures in Diplomacy*, p. 64; Huntington-Wilson, *Memoirs*, p. 246.

35. Coletta, *Bryan: Moral Statesman*, pp. 108–9; *New York Times*, March 12, 1913.

36. Arthur W. Dunn, *From Harrison to Harding: A Personal Narrative Covering a Third of a Century, 1888–1921*, 2 vols. (New York: G. P. Putnam's Sons, 1922), 2:227.

37. *New York Times*, March 12, 1913.

38. Bryan to Wilson, July 30, 1913, Wilson to Bryan, July 31, 1913 (copy), Wilson Papers; Carr diary, May 28, 1913; Vincent Starrett, *Born in a Bookshop* (Norman: University of Oklahoma Press, 1965), pp. 146–47.

39. Bryan and Bryan, *Memoirs*, pp. 187–89, 352; Charles Morrow Wilson, *The Commoner: William Jennings Bryan* (Garden City, N.Y.: Doubleday, 1970), p. 330.

40. Link, *Wilson: The New Freedom*, pp. 111–12; *New York Times*,

October 17, 1913; "The Bryan Scandal," *Nation*, 97 (September 18, 1913), 257.

41. Merle E. Curti, *Bryan and World Peace*, Smith College Studies in History, 16 (1931), 150–51; handwritten copy of peace plan as submitted to Wilson, April 1913, Bryan Papers; statement by the secretary of state on April 24, 1913, on presenting the president's peace plan to the representatives of foreign governments resident in Washington, Department of State, *Foreign Relations of the United States, 1913* (Washington, D.C., 1920), pp. 8–9.

42. Hendrick, *Walter Hines Page*, 1:226, 235.

## CHAPTER FOUR

1. Ray Stannard Baker, interview with D. F. Houston, February 1, 1928, R. S. Baker Papers, Library of Congress, Washington, D.C.

2. Wilson to Page, June 7, 1899, Wilson to Shaw, June 8, 1899, Link et al., eds., *The Papers of Woodrow Wilson* (Princeton: Princeton University Press, 1966–), 11:126–27.

3. House diary, July 3, 1913.

4. Letters and clippings, Bryan file, 1913, Wilson Papers; Coletta, *Bryan: Moral Statesman*, pp. 107–8.

5. Charles Seymour, ed., *The Intimate Papers of Colonel House*, 4 vols. (Boston: Houghton Mifflin, 1926–28), 1:176; James Burris Angell to Wilson, November 12, 1887, Wilson to Angell, November 15, 1887, Link et al., eds., *Papers of Woodrow Wilson*, 5:628–30; Link, *Wilson: The New Freedom*, pp. 105–6.

6. Wilson to MacMurray, December 21, 1905, Link et al., eds., *Papers of Woodrow Wilson*, 16:570; MacMurray to Wilson, August 15, 1913 (copy), MacMurray to his mother, August 19, 1913, John V. A. MacMurray Papers, John Foster Dulles Library, Princeton, N.J.

7. House diary, November 2, 1912; Ray Stannard Baker, *Woodrow Wilson: Life and Letters*, 8 vols. (Garden City, N.Y.: Doubleday, Doran, 1927–39), 4:23–25, 42; Wilson to Bryan, February 14, 1913, Bryan Papers.

8. Josephus Daniels, *The Wilson Era: Years of Peace, 1910–1917* (Chapel Hill: University of North Carolina Press, 1944), pp. 149–50; House diary, February 1, 21, 1913.

9. Bryan to Wilson, June 28, 1913, Wilson Papers; Wilson to Bryan, May 21, July 1, August 8, 1913, Bryan-Wilson Correspondence; Wilson to Bryan, May 22, 1914, Bryan Papers.

10. *New York World*, December 22, 1912, requoted from Link, *Wilson: The New Freedom*, p. 6.

11. Moore to T. L. Hunter, April 22, 1936, Moore Papers.

12. Harvey, "Diplomats of Democracy," pp. 163–64.

13. Seymour, *House Papers*, 1 : 97; House diary, November 16, December 18, 19, 23, 1912, January 15, February 22, 26, March 26, April 1, June 25, 1913; *New York Times*, March 24, 1913; Wilson to McCombs, August 6, 1913 (copy), Wilson Papers.

14. E. Wilson to Mary Margaret Fine, March 18, 1913, cited in Arthur Walworth, *Woodrow Wilson*, 2 vols., 2nd ed., rev. (Boston: Houghton Mifflin, 1965), 1 : 346–47, n. 5.

15. Huntington-Wilson, *Memoirs*, pp. 204–7.

16. Link, *Wilson: The New Freedom*, pp. 103–4; Wilson to Bryan, September 24, 1913, Bryan-Wilson correspondence; Bryan to Wilson, September 25, 1913, Wilson Papers; "Mr. Pindell of Peoria," *Literary Digest*, 47 (November 22, 1913), 992; House diary, December 14, 1916; copies of telegrams: Bryan to American embassy, St. Petersburg, November 13, 1913, C. S. Wilson to Bryan, November 14, 20, December 6, 1913, Bryan to American embassy, St. Petersburg, December 8, 1913, C. S. Wilson to Bryan, December 9, 1913, Moore Papers; Pindell to Wilson, January 27, 28, 1914, Wilson to Pindell, February 2, 1914 (copy), Pindell to Wilson, February 5, 1914, Wilson to Pindell, February 10, 1914 (copy), Wilson Papers; memorandum by Moore, February 3, 1914, with clipping, "Pindell Resigns as Ambassador," from *Washington Evening Star*, February 2, 1914, Moore Papers; House diary, January 24, 31, February 13, April 3, 4, 1913; Crane to Wilson, April 8, 1913, Wilson Papers; Wilson to Bryan, June 25, 1913, Wilson to Bryan, January 16, February 11(?), 1913, Bryan Papers.

17. Link, *Wilson: The New Freedom*, p. 102; House diary, March 25, 1913; *Dictionary of American Biography*, "Guthrie, George Wilkins."

18. Rockhill to Wilson, December 18, 1912, Wilson Papers; diary of W. W. Rockhill, March 14, May 3, 1913, W. W. Rockhill Papers, Houghton Library, Harvard University; Rockhill to Bryan, May 3, 1913 (copy), Bryan to Rockhill, August 27, 1913; ibid.; memorandum by Moore, June 8, 1913, Moore Papers; Felix Frankfurter, *Felix Frankfurter Reminisces: Recorded in Talks with Dr. Harlan B. Phillips* (New York: Reynal, 1960), p. 148; R. S. Baker, interview with Morgenthau, November 1, 1927, Baker Papers; Wilson to Bryan, August 11, 1913, Bryan-Wilson correspondence; Stephen Wise to Morgenthau, August 7, 1913, Henry Morgenthau Papers, Library of Congress, Washington, D.C.; Wilson to J. A. O'Gorman, August 11, 1913 (photostat), Morgenthau file, Wilson Papers.

19. Reminiscences of William Phillips, p. 69; memorandum by Moore, July 25, 1913, "Moore's Memoirs," p. 490, in E. M. Borchard file, Moore Papers; Carr diary, February 17, 1914; memorandum by Moore, July 22, 1913, Moore Papers; Frankfurter, *Felix Frankfurter Reminisces*, pp. 67–69.

20. Telegram, Wilson to Bryan, April 29, 1913, 811.52/71a; Coletta, *Bryan: Moral Statesman*, pp. 214–16; Stuart, *Diplomatic and Consular*

*Practice*, p. 7; memorandum by Moore of conversation with Senator O'Gorman, March 4, 1916, Borchard file, Moore Papers.

21. Moore to his wife, July 11, 1915, requoted from "Moore's Memoirs," p. 527, Moore Papers.

22. Reminiscences of William Phillips, p. 62; Reminiscences of James W. Gerard, transcript of interviews of 1949–50, p. 33, Oral History Research Office, Columbia University.

23. Phillips, *Ventures in Diplomacy*, p. 67; House diary, September 1, 2, 1913; Reminiscences of William Phillips, pp. 61–62; House diary, November 25, December 9, 1913.

24. Seymour, *House Papers*, 1:178–79; House diary, December 12, 14, 1913, May 13, 1914; Phillips, *Ventures in Diplomacy*, p. 63.

25. House diary, April 3, 1913.

26. Seymour, *House Papers*, 1:180; W. Straight to Fletcher, November 11, 1913, April 6, 11, 18, 1914, Fletcher to Boaz W. Long, March 31, 1914 (copy), Henry P. Fletcher Papers, Library of Congress, Washington, D.C.; House diary, January 5, 1913.

27. House to Wilson, June 8, 14, 1913 (copies), House diary, June 12, November 28, 1913, March 25, April 29, May 8, 30, 1914; Phillips to House, March 24, 1914, House to Phillips, March 26, 1914 (copy), House Collection.

28. House to Wilson, August 25, 1914, Wilson Papers.

29. House to Page, January 4, 1914, Walter Hines Page Papers, Houghton Library, Harvard University; House to Fletcher, January 29, 1914, Fletcher Papers.

30. Page to Wilson, July 9, 1913, photostat in Wilson file, W. H. Page Papers; Seymour, *House Papers,* 1:238–39, 247; Link, *Wilson: The New Freedom*, pp. 314–18; House diary, April 8, 10, 18; diary of Walter Page, December 24, 1913; House to Page, February 26, 1914, W. H. Page Papers; Page to House, April 27, 1914, House Collection.

31. Page to Wilson, July 9, 1913, photostat in W. H. Page Papers; House diary, June 24, 1914.

32. Seymour, *House Papers*, 1:194, 247–75; House diary, June 24, July 20, 1914; House to Wilson, June 11, 26, July 3, 4, 1914, Wilson Papers; James W. Gerard, *My First Eighty-Three Years in America* (Garden City, N.Y.: Doubleday, 1951), p. 193.

## CHAPTER FIVE

1. Rockhill to MacMurray, April 11, 1913, MacMurray Papers; Constantin Dumba, *Memoirs of a Diplomat*, trans. Ian F. D. Morrow (Boston: Little, Brown, 1932), p. 174; *International Encyclopedia of the Social Sciences*,

"Moore, John Bassett"; *Register of the Department of State*, 1913; Megargee, "The Diplomacy of John Bassett Moore," pp. 23, 36, 152.

2. Autobiographical file, August 1941, Moore Papers; Bryan to Wilson, March 15, 17, 1913, Wilson Papers.

3. Moore to Bryan, March 13, 1913, Bryan to Wilson, March 15, 1913, Wilson Papers; Moore to Borchard, March 20, 1913 (copy), Borchard to Moore, March 21, 1913, Moore Papers.

4. Wilson to Moore, March 17, 1913 (photocopy), autobiographical file, August 1941, Moore Papers.

5. Moore to Wilson, April 10, 1913, Wilson Papers; Wilson to Moore, April 12, 1913 (photocopy), autobiographical file, August 1941, Moore Papers; Moore to Wilson, April 14, 1913, Wilson Papers.

6. Bryan to Wilson, April 15, 1913, Wilson Papers; Wilson to Moore, April 16, 1913 (photocopy), Moore Papers; Moore to Wilson, April 18, 1913, Wilson Papers; Wilson to Moore, April 21, 1913 (photocopy), Moore Papers.

7. Megargee, "The Diplomacy of John Bassett Moore," pp. 161–62, 177; memorandum by Moore of conversation with Henry P. Fletcher, January 21, 1920, "Moore's Memoirs," pp. 486–87, Borchard file, Moore Papers.

8. Moore to Sir William Haggard, July 12, 1913 (copy), "The Cosmos Club in 1913," in "Moore's Memoirs," p. 479, Moore Papers.

9. Memoranda for the secretary of state, May 14, August 22, 1913, draft copies, Moore Papers; Frankfurter, *Felix Frankfurter Reminisces*, pp. 67–68; Moore to Wilson, October 28, 1913 (copy), Moore Papers.

10. Memorandum by Moore on rumors of resignation, quoting from letter to his wife, August 8, 1913, Moore Papers.

11. Dumba to Moore, August 13, 1913, Moore to Dumba, August 14, 1913 (copy), ibid.

12. Huntington-Wilson to Moore, September 7, 1913, Moore to Huntington-Wilson, September 13, 1913 (draft copy); Moore to G. L. Rives, September 13, 1913 (copy), Moore Papers.

13. Clippings, *Philadelphia Star*, November 17, 1913, *New York Tribune*, November 18, 1913, draft letter of resignation with corrections, November 1913, Moore Papers.

14. House diary, January 27, 30, 1914; Moore to Bryan, February 2, 1914, Bryan Papers; Moore to Wilson, February 2, 1914 (copy), Wilson Papers; draft copies of resignation, February 1914, Moore Papers; Carr diary, February 17, 1914; Moore to Dearing, February 23, 1914 (copy), clippings, *New York Times*, March 5, 1914, *New York Tribune*, March 14, 1914, Moore Papers.

15. Moore to Van Dyne, March 18, 1914 (copy), Moore Papers.

16. Carr diary, February 17, 1914; Mary B. Bryan journal, May 1, 1913, requoted from Coletta, *Bryan: Moral Statesman*, p. 110.

17. Daniel M. Smith, *Robert Lansing and American Neutrality* (Berkeley:

University of California Press, 1958), passim; *Register of the Department of State*, 1915; Coudert to Wilson, January 7, 1913 (copy), Coudert to Scott, January 7, 1913, Scott to Coudert, January 21, 1913 (copy), J. M. Carlisle to Lansing, January 25, 1913, Purcell to O'Gorman, February 7, 1913 (copy), Robert Lansing Papers, Library of Congress, Washington, D.C.

18. Smith, *Robert Lansing*, pp. 2–3; Lansing to A. M. Innes, January 14, 1914 (copy), Lansing Papers.

19. Carr diary, April 22, October 29, 1914; Crane, *Mr. Carr*, p. 180.

20. Phillips, *Ventures in Diplomacy*, p. 73; Alexander DeConde, *The American Secretary of State: An Interpretation* (New York: Praeger, 1962), p. 99.

21. Huntington-Wilson, *Memoirs*, pp. 248–50; Huntington-Wilson to Bryan, March 16, 1913, Bryan to Wilson, March 16, 1913, Huntington-Wilson to Wilson, March 19, 1913, Wilson Papers; Wilson to Huntington-Wilson, March 20, 1913, Huntington-Wilson Papers; House diary, March 20, 1913. The former first assistant would have been astonished had he known how little stir his resignation caused within and without the department (see Carr diary, March 21, 1913; clippings in Department of State, Confidential Publications, 1895–1929, R. G. 59, National Archives, Washington, D.C.). In 1918, Huntington-Wilson, by then divorced from his beautiful and politically influential wife, sought a position in the wartime government. President Wilson wrote Newton D. Baker that "he behaved in a way which I thought very silly when he was in the State Department and it was a great relief to me when he left the service, but he is all right in his way" (January 9, 1918 [copy], Wilson Papers).

22. Autobiographical file, Moore Papers.

23. Daniels, *Years of Peace*, pp. 149–50; *Register of the Department of State*, 1915; *New York Times*, March 23, 1913, Bryan to Osborne, November 7, 1908, March 24, 1909, Wilson to Osborne, September 1, 1911, John E. Osborne Papers, Wyoming State Archives and Historical Department, Cheyenne.

24. Carr diary, May 8, 1913, January 21, 27, February 10, 16, 1914; obituary, *New York Times*, April 25, 1943.

25. *New York Times*, April 1, 1913, February 17, 1914; Crane, *Mr. Carr*, pp. 46–47; Adee to Moore, February 3, 1913, Moore to Adee, February 6, 1913 (copy), Moore to Adee, October 20, 1913 (original, with notations), Moore Papers.

26. Obituary, *New York Times*, October 5, 1950; House diary, February 21, 28, March 11, 20, 25, August 24, October 14, 1913; R. S. Baker, interview with Malone, November 1, 1927, Baker Papers.

27. Crane, *Mr. Carr*, p. 147; memoranda by Moore, June 8, August 7, 1913, Moore Papers. House thought that Malone had a "fine conception of what our Consular Service should be like" (House to Page, September 10,

1913, W. H. Page Papers); House diary, August 9, 1913; R. S. Baker, interview with Malone, November 1, 1927, Baker Papers.

28. John Reddy, "The Most Unforgettable Character I've Met," *Reader's Digest*, 59 (August 1956), 87.

29. Memoranda by Moore, June 8, August 13, 1913, Moore Papers.

30. Memorandum by Moore, August 7, 1913, ibid., House diary, August 10, 1913; *Register of the Department of State*, 1914.

31. *New York Times*, March 5, 1914; reminiscences of William Phillips, pp. 44–45; Carr diary, November 3, 1914; Phillips, *Ventures in Diplomacy*, pp. 3–16, 33–34, 45–46, 59; Phillips to Moore, September 8, 1913, Moore Papers.

32. House diary, November 11, 25, 1913; Moore to Phillips, December 14, 1913 (copy), Phillips to Moore, December 16, 1913, Moore Papers; Phillips to House, December 17, 1913, House Collection; Wilson to Page, January 6, 1914, Page-Wilson file, W. H. Page Papers; Page to House, August 28, 1913, House Collection; Phillips to Page, March 27, 1914, W. H. Page Papers; Wilson to Bryan, January 8, 1914, Bryan Papers.

33. Phillips, *Ventures in Diplomacy*, pp. 60–62; House to Page, January 24, 1914, W. H. Page Papers.

34. Phillips, *Ventures in Diplomacy*, p. 62. Phillips was astonished that he would be asked to assist Bryan, "who detested Republicans in general" (ibid.).

35. Phillips to Page, March 21, 27, April 30, 1914, Laughlin to Page, May 6, 1914, W. H. Page Papers; Phillips, *Ventures in Diplomacy*, pp. 64–65; Phillips to House, March 30, 1914, House Collection.

36. Reminiscences of William Phillips, p. 38. In May 1914, Phillips reported to the colonel that he was "terrifically busy" and found it difficult to imagine he was accomplishing anything (Phillips to House, May 14, 1914, House Collection).

37. Phillips, *Ventures in Diplomacy*, p. 63; House diary, May 8, 11, September 5, 1914; Dean Acheson, *Present at the Creation* (New York: Norton, 1969), p. 11.

38. Wilson to Bryan, February 14, 1914, Bryan Papers; Whitlock to N. Baker, February 4, 1913 (copy), Brand Whitlock Papers, Library of Congress, Washington, D.C.; Bryan to Wilson, June 2, 1913, Wilson Papers; Bryan to Moore, July 19, 1913, Moore Papers.

39. Carr diary, January 22, 1914 (Carr found him "positive, accurate in estimate of men, and more searching in exams than Osborne"); Louis G. Geiger, *Joseph W. Folk of Missouri* (Columbia: University of Missouri Press, 1953), passim; Wilson to Moore, June 25, 1913 (copy), Moore to Wilson, June 26, 1913, Bryan to Wilson, June 28, 1913, Wilson to Bryan, July 1, 1913 (copy), Wilson Papers; Moore to Bryan, July 29, 1913 (copy), Moore papers; *Register of the Department of State*, 1913, 1914.

40. T. W. Gregory, requoted from Ernest R. May, "Bryan and the World War, 1914–1915" (Ph.D. thesis, University of California, Los Angeles, 1951), p. 31; House to McCombs, June 12, 1912 (copy), House Collection; *Register of the Department of State*, 1915.

41. *Register of the Department of State*, 1915; May, "Bryan and the World War," p. 134, n.26; Carr diary, August 16, 1918; Crane, *Mr. Carr*, p. 235.

42. *The Commoner*, April 25, 1913; Page to House, December 20, 1913, House Collection.

43. Carr to Joseph E. Willard, January 30, 1914, Joseph E. Willard Family Papers, Library of Congress, Washington, D.C.; Carr diary, January 8, February 10, April 17, May 17, November 17, 1914.

44. Crane, *Mr. Carr*, pp. 158–59, 163; Carr diary, May 7, June 29, 1914.

45. Telegrams, Doyle to Rose, April 26, 1913 (copy), Rose to Doyle, April 26, 1913 (copy), Moore Papers; Bryan to Wilson, April 26, 1913, Wilson Papers.

46. E. T. Williams to Bryan, March 18, 1913, Department of State, *Foreign Relations, 1913*, pp. 96–98; Ernest R. May, "American Policy and Japan's Entrance into World War I," *Mississippi Valley Historical Review*, 40 (1953), 283.

47. Lewis to Bryan, July 13, 1913, Wilson Papers; obituary, *New York Times*, October 23, 1928. Senator Lewis's career, Moore noted, was "one of the grotesque features of American politics, his chief assets being popular manners and resplendent red whiskers"; Lewis was not noted for recommendations of good men, and Putney was decidedly untalented (memorandum by Moore, November 16, 1913, Moore to Dearing, February 23, 1914 [draft, not sent], Moore Papers).

48. Bryan originally intended James to be a foreign trade adviser, as it was one of the few positions not under civil service regulations (Bryan to Wilson, July 26, 1913, Bryan-Wilson correspondence); Flournoy to Moore, March 6, 1914, Moore Papers.

49. Carr diary, May 23, 1913; memorandum by Moore, December 23, 1913, Moore Papers. For other comments on Rose see Crane, *Mr. Carr*, p. 162.

50. Memorandum by Moore, August 27, 1913, Moore Papers.

51. *Register of the Department of State*, 1912, 1913, 1914; Moore to Dearing, February 23, 1914 (draft, not sent), Moore Papers.

52. Department orders: June 28, 1913, 111.08/45, October 16, 1913, 119.2/64, June 4, 1914, 119.2/76.

53. May, "Bryan and the World War," pp. 41–43; department order, March 6, 1914, 116.6/8; memorandum, chief clerk to chiefs of bureaus and divisions, June 8, 1911, 116.6/1; *New York Times*, March 13, 1913.

54. Department orders: March 10, 1913, 111.08/43; April 25, 1913, Octo-

ber 8, 1913 (signed by Moore as acting secretary), copies in Moore Papers.
55. Carr diary, April 28, 1914.


## CHAPTER SIX

1. Waldo H. Heinrichs, *American Ambassador: Joseph C. Grew and the Development of the United States Diplomatic Tradition* (Boston: Little, Brown, 1966), p. 12; R. U. Johnson to Wilson, April 2, 1913, Wilson Papers.

2. Ross Gregory, *Walter Hines Page: Ambassador to the Court of St. James's* (Lexington: University of Kentucky Press, 1970), pp. 1–22, passim; Wilson to Page, October 30, 1885, June 7, 1899, June 7, 1911, August 21, 1911, Page to Wilson, election day, 1912 (copy), W. H. Page Papers.

3. Page to Wilson, December 30, 1912, Wilson Papers; Hendrick, *Walter Hines Page*, 1:118–19.

4. Baker, Wilson, 4:27–28; House diary, January 16, 17, March 18, 20, 1913; Seymour, *House Papers*, 1:180–81.

5. W. H. Page, "The Consecutive Story: The Ambassadorship," in W. H. Page Papers; House diary, March 26, 1913.

6. Wilson to Page, March 28, April 2, 1913, Page-Wilson file, W. H. Page Papers; Seymour, *House Papers*, 1:181; R. S. Baker, *Wilson*, 4:28.

7. Seymour, *House Papers*, 1:182; "The Ambassadorship," W. H. Page Papers; Hendrick, *Walter Hines Page*, 1:133–35.

8. Page to Wilson, April 7, June 5, 1914, Page-Wilson file, W. H. Page Papers.

9. Katherine Page to Arthur Page, September 20, 1913, Page to Wilson, June 5, 1914, Page-Wilson file, ibid.

10. Wilson to Page, May 18, 1914, Page to Wilson, June 5, 1914, ibid.; House diary, May 8, 1914.

11. Page to House, August 28, 1913, January 30, February 13, 1914, House Collection; Seymour, *House Papers*, 1:136, 233–35; House diary, May 8, 1914; Page to Wilson, October 25, 1913 (draft), June 5, 1914 (draft), W. H. Page Papers.

12. Page to Wilson, June 5, 1914 (draft), Page to Wilson, June 5, 1914, Wilson to Page, June 19, 1914, Page to Wilson, July 5, 1914, Page-Wilson file, House to Page, August 17, September 4, October 3, 1914, W. H. Page Papers. Two letters from House to Page in 1916 indicate that Page knew who his benefactor was and that House by that time was not attempting to conceal Dodge's identity. "I have not yet seen Arthur but will in a few days. Cleve Dodge was in yesterday. He wants to know if it is time for him to get busy again. Will you not let me know this so I may speak to him?" (House to Page, March 10, 1916, ibid.). "Your note of March 27th comes to me this morning.

I called up 'our good and high friend' and he is sending me a check payable to Arthur for ten. He says if this is not enough to please be frank and let him know since it has been a long time between drinks" (House to Page, April 18, 1916; see also strong hint in letter, House to Page, April 19, 1914, ibid., that Dodge was willing to make such an arrangement).

13. Page to John ? (name illegible), November 27, 1917, ibid.; House diary, July 7, 1914.

14. *Register of the Department of State*, 1913; Hendrick, *Walter Hines Page*, 1:157.

15. Hendrick, *Walter Hines Page*, 1:159–60; Page to A. Page, July 13, 1913, Page to Robert Page, December 22, 1913, Page to Leila Page, December 25, 1913, W. H. Page Papers.

16. Hendrick, *Walter Hines Page*, 1:166.

17. Page to E. A. Alderman, Christmas, 1913 (copy), W. H. Page Papers; Page to House, January 2, September 22, 1914, House Collection; Gregory, *Walter Hines Page*, pp. 44–46.

18. Page to House, August 25, September 24, November 23, 1913, January 8 (?), February 13, 1914, House Collection; Hendrick, *Walter Hines Page*, 1:194, 212, 235–36; House diary, January 29, 1914; Page to Wilson, December 21, 1913, Page-Wilson file, W. H. Page Papers.

19. Hendrick, *Walter Hines Page*, 1:189–90, 219, 285–86; Page to Wilson, June 8, 1913, Wilson Papers; Wilson to Page, March 7, 1914, Page-Wilson file, W. H. Page Papers.

20. House diary, May 8, July 12, 20, 1914.

21. Link, *Wilson: The New Freedom*, pp. 101–2, n.27; Gerard, *My First Eighty-Three Years*, pp. 163–65, 167.

22. Gerard, *My First Eighty-Three Years*, pp. 3–34, passim, 122–23, 154–55. An agent of Gerard, Thomas D. McCarthy, wrote to Bryan in May 1914, thanking the department for its quick restoration of the confiscated Cinco Minas property. Not surprisingly, the department deposited the money in a German bank (McCarthy to Bryan, May 18, 1914, Bryan-Wilson Correspondence).

23. Reminiscences of James W. Gerard, pp. 29, 33; House diary, October 22, December 10, 1912, January 17, February 13, April 6, 20, 1913; Seymour, *House Papers*, 1:183–84; Gerard, *My First Eighty-Three Years*, p. 168; McCombs to Wilson, March 10, 1913, Wilson Papers; Harvey, "The Diplomats of Democracy," pp. 164–65.

24. Winslow to House, June 10, 1913 (letter and cable), House to Winslow, June 11, 1913 (copy), Winslow to House, June 17, 1913 (cable), House Collection; Gerard, *My First Eighty-Three Years*, pp. 68, 169–70; Gerard to Wilson, June 30, 1913 (telegram), Wilson Papers; Winslow to House, June 27, 1913 (cable), House Collection.

25. Gerard, *My Four Years in Germany*, p. 20; Page to House, September

13, 1913, House Collection; Heinrichs, *American Ambassador*, p. 15; Gerard, *My First Eighty-Three Years*, pp. 247–48.

26. Statement of allotment of appropriations for foreign missions compiled by John E. Osborne for Bryan, transmitted to Wilson, February 16, 1914, Wilson Papers; Gerard, *My First Eighty-Three Years*, pp. 174, 207; Seymour, *House Papers*, 1:186–87; House diary, August 28, 1913, Grew to his mother, October 12, 1913, Grew Papers.

27. Grew diary, January 10, 1914, May 29, July 23, 1915, Grew to family, undated and unsent fragment of letter, Grew Papers; Heinrichs, *American Ambassador*, p. 24.

## CHAPTER SEVEN

1. House to Wilson, June 11, 1914, Wilson Papers.

2. *Register of the Department of State*, 1914; *Dictionary of American Biography*, "Herrick, Myron Timothy"; Mott, *Twenty Years as a Military Attaché*, pp. 323–24; Mott, *Myron T. Herrick, Friend of France* (Garden City, N.Y.: Doubleday, Doran, 1929), pp. 95–96.

3. Mott, *Myron T. Herrick*, p. 106.

4. Ibid., pp. 98–100; Mott, *Twenty Years as a Military Attaché*, pp. 324–25; House diary, June 12, 1913; Allan Nevins, ed., *The Letters and Journal of Brand Whitlock*, 2 vols. (New York: Appleton-Century, 1936), 1:175.

5. Mott, *Twenty Years as a Military Attaché*, p. 325, n.1.

6. Herrick to Knox, February 7, 1913, Knox Papers; Herrick to Huntington-Wilson, February 7, 1913, Huntington-Wilson Papers; Herrick to House, January 20, 1913 (forwarded to Wilson), Wilson Papers.

7. Herrick to Wilson, July 15, August 13, September 30, December 2, 1913, Wilson to Herrick, July 25, August 16, 18, 22, October 14, 1913 (copies), Wilson Papers.

8. House diary, December 29, 31, 1912, January 11, March 25, 1913; Bryan to Wilson, March 23, August 8, 1913, Wilson Papers; House diary, May 10, November 29, 1913, January 21, April 28, 1914.

9. House to Wilson, June 11, 1914 (copy), House Collection; letter forwarded to Bryan, June 22, 1914, stamped by secretary of state, July 1, 1914, Bryan-Wilson Correspondence; House diary, June 8, 1914.

10. Herrick to secretary of state, June 11, 1914, personnel files, records of the Department of State, National Archives, Washington, D.C.; May, "Bryan and the World War," pp. 36–37.

11. Page diary, October 12, 1914, W. H. Page Papers; House diary, March 11, 1915; House to Wallace, July 7, 1914, Bryan to Wilson, n.d., Wilson Papers.

12. *Dictionary of American Biography*, "Penfield, Frederic Courtland"; clipping from *St. Louis Star*, July 2, 1913, in Henry van Dyke Papers, John Foster Dulles Library, Princeton, N.J.; Harvey, "The Diplomats of Democracy," p. 165; House diary, December 23, 1913; Link, *Wilson: The New Freedom*, p. 1.

13. Moore to Wilson, February 26, 1913, Wilson Papers; House diary, March 20, 1913; memorandum by Moore for M. Shand, June 6, 1913, Moore Papers; Wilson to Egan, June 10, 1913 (telegram), Egan to Wilson, June 14, 1913 (telegram), Wilson Papers, Egan to Wilson, June 13, 1913, Bryan-Wilson Correspondence; Egan to Page, February 8, 1916, W. H. Page Papers.

14. Penfield to secretary of state, March 5, 1914 (copy), Wilson Papers; Penfield to Moore, October 12, 1913, Moore Papers.

15. Grew diary, March 28, 1914; House diary, July 23, December 23, 1913, April 15, 1916; Penfield to House, August 1, 1916, House Collection; Grew diary, May 7, 1915; Penfield to Department of State, October 4, 1913, 158.632/105, October 7, 1913, 158.632/106, October 9, 1913, 863.1157/34, April 23, 1914, 863.001F85/3.

16. *Dictionary of American Biography*, "Willard, Joseph Edward"; clippings, Willard Family Papers, Library of Congress, Washington, D.C.

17. *Dictionary of American Biography*, "Page, Thomas Nelson"; W. C. Eustis to T. N. Page, Thomas Nelson Page Papers, Duke University Library.

18. R. Byrd to Wilson, March 12, 1913 (copy), R. Byrd to Willard, March 12, 1913, Willard Family Papers; Montague to Wilson, March 10, 1913, Wilson Papers; Wilson to Bryan, April 8, 1913, Bryan-Wilson Correspondence; Montague to Willard, April 9, 16, 1913, Willard to Bryan, April 14, 1913 (copy), Willard Family Papers.

19. House diary, April 11, 1915; Willard to Department of State, December 27, 1913, 852.00/157, March 28, 1914, 852.00/159; Ide to Department of State, January 16, 1912, 852.00/150, April 22, 1912, 852.00/51, July 30, 1912, 852.00/152; Harvey, "The Diplomats of Democracy," p. 164; Bryan to Wilson, February 7, 1914, Bryan letterbooks, Bryan Papers; Willard to secretary of state, April 18, 1914 (copy), Willard Family Papers; Willard to Marquis de Valdeiglesias (copy of invitation), Willard Family Papers; Willard to Department of State, March 2, 1914, acknowledging grant of ten-day leave for daughter's wedding, March 12, 1914, requesting ten-day extension, July 2, 1914, acknowledging grant of leave of absence, State Department personnel files, National Archives; G. B. Fernald to M. Jules Berthelot, July 10, 1914, Love to T. G. Tabb, August 7, 1914, Love to Alfriend, August 7, 1914, Alfriend to Love, August 8, 10, 1914, Love to Willard, August 13, 1914, Willard Family Papers.

20. Scribner to T. N. Page, February 6, April 2, 1913, Gordon to T. N. Page, March 7, 1913, T. N. Page to Gordon, March 17, April 7, 1913

(copies), Flood to T. N. Page, March 8, 1913, J. S. Williams to Wilson, March 14, 1913 (several copies), R. Byrd to T. N. Page, March 14, 1913, T. N. Page to J. S. Williams, March 15, 1913 (copy), T. N. Page to Ruth Page, March 7, 1913, T. N. Page Papers.

21. G. B. Page to T. N. Page, July 19, 1913, T. N. Page Papers; Post Wheeler and Hallie Erminie Rives, *Dome of Many-Coloured Glass* (Garden City, N.Y.: Doubleday, 1955), p. 462; House diary, January 16, March 11, March 20, April 1, 12, 1913; Seymour, *House Papers,* 2:183.

22. Grew diary, April 18, 1915; T. N. Page to Rosewell and Ruth Page, October 5, 23, 1913, May 20, 1914, T. N. Page Papers; T. N. Page to W. H. Page, October 18, 1913, W. H. Page Papers; Wheeler and Rives, *Dome of Many-Coloured Glass*, p. 468; T. N. Page to Wilson, January 1, 1914, Wilson Papers; Lloyd C. Griscom, *Diplomatically Speaking* (Boston: Little, Brown, 1940), pp. 278–79; T. N. Page to Rosewell and Ruth Page, January 6, 1914, T. N. Page Papers; T. N. Page to Page, October 18, 1913, W. H. Page Papers.

23. Ira Nelson Morris, *From an American Legation* (New York: Knopf, 1923), p. 5; T. N. Page to Rosewell and Ruth Page, March 8, 1914; T. N. Page to Wilson, March 20, 1914 (copy), T. N. Page Papers; House diary, April 25, 1914; T. N. Page to Rosewell Page, February 10, 1914; T. N. Page Papers.

24. Phillips to Bryan, June 11, 1914, Wilson Papers; Wilson to Bryan, June 12, 24, 1914, Bryan Papers.

25. Grew diary, March 28, 1915; Page diary, October 12, 1914.

26. Frankfurter, *Felix Frankfurter Reminisces*, p. 152; memorandum by Moore, June 8, 1913, Moore Papers; Seymour, *House Papers*, 1:96; House diary, December 18, 1912, Feb. 18, 1913.

27. Wise to Morgenthau, August 7, 1913, Morgenthau Papers; R. S. Baker, memorandum of interview with Morgenthau, November 1, 1927, Baker Papers; Straus to Morgenthau, March 12, 1914, Morgenthau to Straus, May 27, 1914 (copy), Morgenthau to L. Marshall, June 23, 1914 (copy), Morgenthau Papers; Henry Morgenthau, *All in a Lifetime* (Garden City, N.Y.: Doubleday, Page, 1922), pp. 159–61, chap. 10, passim.

28. Morgenthau, *All in a Lifetime*, pp. 178–79, 183–81; Frankfurter, *Felix Frankfurter Reminisces*, p. 146.

## CHAPTER EIGHT

1. *Dictionary of American Biography*, "Vopicka, Charles Joseph"; Bryan to Wilson, June 7, 1913, Wilson Papers; Wilson to Bryan, June 9, 1913, Bryan Papers; Bryan to Wilson, August 12, 1913, Wilson Papers; Link, *Wilson: The New Freedom*, p. 106, n.40.

2. *Register of the Department of State*, 1913; Harvey, "The Diplomats of Democracy," p. 163; Jackson to Moore, June 23, 1913, Moore to Jackson, July 17, 26, 1913 (copies), Wilson to Moore, July 22, 1913 (photocopy), Moore Papers.

3. Charles J. Vopicka, *Secrets of the Balkans: Seven Years of a Diplomatist's Life in the Storm Center of Europe* (Chicago: Rand McNally, 1921), pp. 19–20.

4. Ibid., pp. 20, 22; Morgenthau diary, January 14, February 11, 1914; Vopicka, *Secrets of the Balkans*, pp. 26–28.

5. Schurman to Wilson, February 17, 1913, Wilson Papers; *New York Times*, June 27, June 29, 1914.

6. Phillips diary, November 14, 1917; Stovall to Baker, June 1, 1925, Baker Papers; *Dictionary of American Biography*, "Stovall, Pleasant Alexander"; Pleasant Stovall, *Switzerland and the World War* (Savannah, Ga.: Mason, 1939), passim; House diary, March 30, 1915; Phillips diary, January 7, October 18, December 12, 1917.

7. *Register of the Department of State*, 1915; Bryan to Wilson, June 9, 1913, Wilson Papers; secretary of legation, Lisbon, to secretary of state, June 17, 1913, 123.N52/4; Nicholson to Whitlock, June 30, 1913, Whitlock Papers; "Diplomatic Appointments of W. J. Bryan," House Collection.

8. Carr diary, November 7, 1913; Harvey, "The Diplomats of Democracy," pp. 162–63.

9. *Register of the Department of State*, 1915; Maurice Francis Egan, *Recollections of a Happy Life* (New York: George H. Doran, 1924), passim.

10. *Register of the Department of State*, 1915; department file on Spitzbergen, 850d.00.

11. *Who Was Who in America, 1897–1942: A Companion Volume to Who's Who in America*, p. 868.

12. *Register of the Department of State*, 1915; van Dyke to Wilson, June 6, 1913, Wilson Papers; House diary, March 25, 1913; Wilson to Bryan, February 14, 1914, Bryan-Wilson Correspondence.

13. R. S. Baker, memorandum of interview with van Dyke, November 12, 1925, Baker Papers; van Dyke to M. S. Burt, July 13, 1914, van Dyke to G. Warburton, April 15, 1914 (copies), van Dyke papers; department file on Third Hague Peace Conference, 500.A3.

14. Whitlock to Nicholson, March 21, 1913 (copy), Whitlock to Bryan, March 6, 1913 (copy), Whitlock to Baker, March 22, 1913 (copy), Cox to Whitlock, February 24, 1913, Wilson to Cox, September 17, 1913 (copy), Howells to Whitlock, March 19, 24, 1913, Whitlock Papers; Jack Tager, *The Intellectual as Reformer: Brand Whitlock and the Progressive Movement* (Cleveland: Press of Case Western Reserve University, 1968), pp. 148–50; Robert M. Crunden, *Hero in Spite of Himself: Brand Whitlock in Art, Politics, and War* (New York: Knopf, 1969), pp. 229–35.

15. Tager, *The Intellectual as Reformer*, pp. 148–50; Wilson to Bryan, August 9, 1913, Bryan-Wilson Correspondence; Wilson to Bryan, August 11, 1913, Bryan Papers; Whitlock to A. J. Nock, June 14, 1913 (copy), Cox to Wilson, September 19, 1913 (copy), Marburg to Whitlock, October 14, 1913, Whitlock to Baker, October 15, 1913 (copy), Whitlock Papers.

16. Nevins, ed., *Brand Whitlock*, 1:175–76; Whitlock to R. B. Jewett, April 9, 1914 (copy), Whitlock Papers; Crunden, *Hero in Spite of Himself*, pp. 239–48.

17. Material on numbers of personnel in embassies and legations obtained from *Register of the Department of State*, 1913, 1914; William Barnes and John Heath Morgan, *The Foreign Service of the United States: Origins, Development, and Functions* (Washington: Government Printing Office, 1961), p. xi; J. Rives Childs, *American Foreign Service* (New York: Henry Holt, 1948), pp. 10–11. For diverse attitudes toward democracy in the diplomatic service, see George F. Kennan, foreword to Lewis D. Einstein, *A Diplomat Looks Back* (New Haven: Yale University Press, 1968), pp. xi–xii, and Stovall, *Switzerland*, pp. 165–66.

18. Warren E. Ilchman, *Professional Diplomacy in the United States, 1779–1939: A Study in Administrative History* (Chicago: University of Chicago Press, 1961), chap. 3, especially pp. 104–11.

19. Ibid.; Huntington-Wilson, *Memoirs*, pp. 158–59; Ilchman, *Professional Diplomacy*, pp. 91, 134. Thirty-six candidates took the examination in 1913, and the number greatly decreased in 1914 and 1915 (ibid.).

20. Heinrichs, *American Ambassador*, p. 14; Joseph C. Grew, *Turbulent Era: A Diplomatic Record of Forty Years, 1904–1945*, 2 vols. (Boston: Houghton Mifflin, 1952), 1:12–14.

21. Heinrichs, *American Ambassador*, p. 14; Grew to his mother, March 27, 1910, Grew to Penfield, November 16, 1915 (copies), Grew Papers; van Dyke to Burlingame, December 23, 1913 (copy), van Dyke Papers; *Register of the Department of State*, 1914; diary of J.V.A. MacMurray, March 17, 1911, MacMurray Papers.

22. *Register of the Department of State*, 1913, 1914; Grew to A. H. Frazier, December 8, 1913 (copy), Grew Papers.

23. *Register of the Department of State*, 1912, 1913, 1914; Ilchman, *Professional Diplomacy*, pp. 82, 111.

24. *Register of the Department of State*, 1914; Heinrichs, *American Ambassador*, p. 97.

25. Heinrichs, *American Ambassador*, p. 22.

26. Page to Wilson, July 5, 1914, Wilson Papers; Heinrichs, *American Ambassador*, pp. 9, 14; Grew to his mother, November 26, 1913, Grew Papers.

27. Page to Malone, June 20, 1913, Page to Bryan, January 4, 1914,

Wilson Papers; Phillips to House, June 10, 1914, House Collection.

28. Heinrichs, *American Ambassador*, p. 13.

29. Testimony of J. Butler Wright, January 15, 1924, Committee on Foreign Affairs, *Foreign Service of the United States, Hearings on H. R. 17 and H. R. 6357*, 68th Cong., 1st sess., 1924, p. 46.

30. Testimony of Hugh Gibson, January 15, 1924, ibid., p. 48.

31. Grew to MacMurray, November 9, 1910 (copy), Grew Papers; Heinrichs, *American Ambassador*, p. 16; Page to Wilson, December 21, 1913 (copy), W. H. Page Papers.

32. Grew to W. Spencer, June 26, 1913, Grew to C. S. Wilson, October 16, November 6, 1913, Grew to Bell, May 30, 1913, Grew to A. H. Frazier, October 11, 1913 (copies), Grew Papers.

33. Page to Bryan, August 18, 1913 (copy), W. H. Page Papers; Bryan to Wilson, August 8, 1913, Wilson Papers; Page to Malone, September 25, 1913 (copy), W. H. Page Papers.

34. MacMurray to his mother, January 25, July 24, October 15, 1910, MacMurray Papers; Gibson's testimony, January 15, 1924, *Foreign Service Hearings*, p. 40; Guild to MacMurray, December 30, 1911, MacMurray Papers; Guild to Knox, January 24, 1912, Knox Papers; Wheeler and Rives, *Dome of Many-Coloured Glass*, pp. 411–12, 465–66.

35. O'Brien to secretary of state, September 16, 1913, 123/W56/76; Wheeler and Rives, *Dome of Many-Coloured Glass*, pp. 469–71, 475–76, 484–88; Bryan to American Embassy, Paris, August 19, 1913, to be relayed to Rome, 123.W56/69B; Bryan to O'Brien, September 11, 1913, 123.W56/71; Bryan to Benson, September 29, 1913, 123.B44/36A; Grew to U. Grant-Smith, September 19, 1913, Grew to A. H. Frazier, October 11, 1913 (copies), Grew Papers; Carr diary, November 13, 1913.

36. Malone's report on the situation in the embassy in Rome, n.d., 123.B44/41; Wheeler to Department of State, n.d., stamped by secretary, December 2, 1913, 123.W56/82; twenty-six telegrams and letters, Wheeler file, Bryan to Wilson, November 25, 1913, Wilson Papers; O'Brien to secretary of state, September 16, 1913, 123.W56/77; unsigned memorandum to Malone, October 13, 1913, 123.B44/41.

37. T. N. Page to Rosewell and Ruth Page, October 5, 1913; H. S. Spencer to T. N. Page, July 27, 31, 1913, T. N. Page to Spencer, August 22, 1913 (copy), T. N. Page to Bryan, August 7, 1913 (copy), T. N. Page to Malone, August 30, 1913 (copy), T. N. Page to M. Shand, August 30, 1913 (copy), T. N. Page Papers; T. N. Page to secretary of state, September 27, 1913, 123.W56/75.

38. Malone's report, 123.B44/41; Wheeler and Rives, *Dome of Many-Coloured Glass*, pp. 390–91, 432; Bryan to Wilson, November 25, 1913, Wilson Papers; Wilson to Bryan, November 28, 1913, 123.B44/41; Wilson

to Bryan, March 17, 21, 1914 (carbons), Wilson Papers; Grew to A. B. Ruddock, June 2, 1914 (copy), Grew Papers.

39. *Register of the Department of State,* 1914.


## CHAPTER NINE

1. Huntington-Wilson, *Memoirs*, pp. 245–46; Kennan, foreword to Einstein, *A Diplomat Looks Back*, pp. vii–ix; Hendrick, *Walter Hines Page*, 1 : 161–62; Wilson, *Education of a Diplomat*, pp. 2–3.

2. W. J. Bryan, "Our Foreign Policy," *The Independent*, 76 (October 9, 1913), p. 73; Henry van Dyke, *Fighting for Peace* (New York: Charles Scribner's Sons, 1917), pp. 27–29; Circular, Bryan to diplomatic officers of the United States accredited to governments which took part in the Second International Peace Conference at The Hague, June 22, 1914, *Foreign Relations, 1914*, pp. 10–11.

3. House to Bryan, June 13, 1914 (copy), House Collection; House to Wilson, May 29, June 3, 17, 1914, Wilson Papers; Bryan to House, June 28, 1914, Wilson to House, June 26, July 9, 1914 (copies), House Collection.

4. Bryan's Chautauqua schedule for June 1914 indicates twenty lectures in twelve days, in Pennsylvania, New Jersey, and Virginia (Paul M. Pearson to Bryan, February 2, 1914, Bryan Papers).

5. Phillips to Lansing, July 21, 1914, Lansing Papers; Bryan to Wilson, June 10, 1914 (Wilson's reply noted), May 9, 1914 (Wilson's reply noted), Wilson Papers.

6. Phillips to Lansing, July 2, 1914, 850d.00/305, Lansing to Phillips, June 30, 1914, 850d.00/310, Schmedeman to Bryan, June 26, 1914, 850d.00/302, June 27, 1914, 850d.00/305, Bryan to Schmedeman (prepared by Phillips), June 29, 1914, 850d.00/304, June 30, 1914, 850d.00/310, Bryan to Adee, June 24, 1914, with attached, Adee to Bryan, June 26, 1914, 850d.00/292; George Sheppard Hunsberger, "The Diplomatic Career of Alvey Augustus Adee with Special Reference to the Boxer Rebellion" (M.A. thesis, American University, 1953), p. 58; Adee to Bryan, July 2, 1914, 850d.00/312; Schmedeman to Bryan, July 30, 1914, *Foreign Relations, 1914*, p. 981.

7. Reminiscences of DeWitt Clinton Poole, p. 59, Transcript of Interviews of 1952, Oral History Research Office, Columbia University; House to Wilson, May 29, 1914, Wilson Papers; House diary, July 11, 20, 1914.

8. Page to Wilson, June 8, July 5, 12, 1914, Page-Wilson correspondence, Wilson Papers; Page to Arthur Page, July 26, 1914, W. H. Page Papers; *New York Times*, July 21, 1914; Gerard to House, July 7, 1914, House Collection; Seymour, *House Papers*, 1 : 270; Heinrichs, *American Ambassador*, p. 19.

9. T. N. Page to Rosewell and Ruth Page, July 18, 1914, T. N. Page Papers; Department of State to Willard, July 2, 1914, Morgenthau to Department of State, July 10, 1914, Penfield to Department of State, May 23, 1914, personnel files, Department of State, National Archives, Washington, D.C.

10. Journal of Brand Whitlock, July 20, 21, 1914, in Whitlock Papers.

11. *New York Times*, June 21, 1914; Stovall, *Switzerland*, pp. 17–24.

12. Vopicka, *Secrets of the Balkans*, p. 28.

13. J. M. Schiff to Morgenthau, July 2, 1914, Morgenthau diary, July 27, 1914, Morgenthau Papers; van Dyke, *Fighting for Peace*, pp. 29, 39–40, 44–45.

14. Penfield to Bryan, July 13, 1914, *Foreign Relations, 1914, Supplement*, pp. 22–23, Grew diary, May 7, 1915.

15. *Register of the Department of State*, 1914; J. E. Dunning to Department of State, May 3, 1913, 125.2433/24; complaint against Mallett by Marie Duhaut, May 23, 1913, 125.2433/25, Mallett's reply, July 25, 1913, 125.2433/30; complaint against Mallett by Mary Almasy, September 20, 1913, 125.2433/32, by Marie Duhaut, August 5, 1913, 125/2433/36; Hengstler to Carr, November 22, 1913, 125/2433/39, Carr to Hengstler, December 19, 1913, 125.2433/41.

16. Mallett to Bryan, July 13, 1914, *Foreign Relations, 1914, Supplement*, p. 16.

17. E. T. Williams to MacMurray, June 3, 1914, MacMurray Papers. Williams urged MacMurray to condense telegrams because of "grumbling down stairs." See the description of the State Department code room before the World War in Herbert O. Yardley, *The American Black Chamber* (Indianapolis: Bobbs-Merrill, 1931), pp. 17–26.

18. C. S. Wilson to Bryan, July 26, 1914, *Foreign Relations, 1914, Supplement*, p. 15; Penfield to Bryan, July 27, 1914, ibid., p. 18.

19. Mallett to Bryan, July 13, 1914, 125.2433/43, December 2, 1914, 125.2433/47, Marye to Bryan, December 2, 1914, 125.2433/48, Bryan to Marye, December 8, 1914, 125.2433/50, Mallett to Bryan, n.d., 125.2433/67, Schmedeman to Bryan, February 10, 1915, 125.2433/59, February 18, 1915, 125.2433/63, Coffin to Bryan, March 16, 1915, 125.2433/66, L. Dreyfus to Carr, August 18, 1915, 125.2433/143, Mallett to Carr, October 20, 1917, 125.2433/170.

20. May, "Bryan and the World War," p. 20.

21. C. S. Wilson to Bryan, July 28, 1914, *Foreign Relations, 1914, Supplement*, p. 17; Gerard to Bryan, July 27, 1914, ibid., p. 16, Penfield to Bryan, July 27, 1914, Herrick to Bryan, July 28, 1914, ibid., p. 18.

22. Ibid., pp. 18–19, Bryan to Page, July 28, 1914, ibid., p. 19, Page to Bryan, July 31, 1914, ibid., pp. 24–25; Page to Wilson, July 29, 1914, House to Wilson, July 31, August 1, 1914, Bryan to American Embassy, St.

Petersburg, August 4, 1914 (not sent), Wilson Papers. See discussion in Link, *Wilson: The Struggle for Neutrality, 1914–1915* (Princeton, N.J.: Princeton University Press, 1960), pp. 5–6.

23. Magruder to Department of State, August 3, 1914, 111.13/3; Adee to C. E. Tyler, August 3, 6, 1914, G. S. Hunsberger, "Alvey Augustus Adee," p. 58.

24. A. W. Mackintosh to Department of State, July 27, 1914, Bryan to Mackintosh, July 29, 1914, 763.72/7. File 763.72, which deals with the outbreak of war in Europe, includes numerous telegrams and letters and references to messages requesting similar information.

25. Unsigned acknowledgment of Bryan's endorsement of film, August 7, 1914, Wilson to Bryan, August 25, 1914 (copy), Bryan to Wilson, July 31, 1914 (three letters), Wilson Papers; May, "Bryan and the World War," pp. 17, 21.

26. Bryan to ambassadors and ministers in European countries, August 1, 1914, *Foreign Relations, 1914, Supplement*, p. 721; Hugh Gibson, *A Journal from Our Legation in Belgium* (Garden City, N.Y.: Doubleday, Page, 1917), p. 6.

27. Crane, *Mr. Carr*, pp. 164–67; Bryan and Bryan, *Memoirs*, pp. 415–16; Lansing to Wilson, August 1, 1914 requesting additional funds, appended draft of joint resolution appropriating "amount . . . ample for any reasonable development of the situation," Wilson Papers; Bryan to Page, August 6, 1914, W. H. Page Papers; Stuart, *Department of State*, pp. 243–44.

28. Bryan to American diplomatic and consular officers, August 17, 1914, *Foreign Relations, 1914, Supplement*, pp. 740–41, C. S. Wilson to Bryan, August 7, 8, 12, 1914, ibid., pp. 736–38.

29. Whitlock to Bryan, August 4, 1914, Bryan to Whitlock, August 5, 1914, ibid., pp. 735–36.

30. See Zara Steiner, *The Foreign Office and Foreign Policy* (Cambridge, Eng.: Cambridge University Press, 1969), pp. 121–71, passim; Gibson, *Journal*, p. 6; Stovall, *Switzerland*, p. 21.

31. Ilchman, *Professional Diplomacy*, pp. 127–28; Stuart, *Department of State*, pp. 243–44; diplomatic lists in *Register of the Department of State*, 1914, 1915, 1916. "The European war came upon the United States in 1914 as a surprise chiefly because the Department of State through inadequate equipment had been unable to gather information and interpret it in a manner which would reveal the hidden purposes of the governments by which hostilities were precipitated" (Lansing to John Jacob Rogers in support of diplomatic reform proposed by Representative Rogers, January 21, 1920, reprinted in *Foreign Service Hearings*, p. 30).

32. Carr diary, August 7, 1914; Crane, *Mr. Carr*, p. 165.

# Essay on Sources

## PRIMARY MATERIALS

### Government Records, Unpublished and Published

The unpublished records of the Department of State, located in the National Archives, Washington, D.C., are for the early years of this century open to all qualified researchers. Exceptions are the personnel files of diplomatic and consular officers, but even for these there are summaries of contents of the correspondence in the card catalogue of the department files and in the summary volumes known as the purport books. I was permitted to see personnel files for the years before 1920; in only one instance had items, of a strictly confidential nature, been removed.

According to the numerical filing system then in use, material on the administration of the State Department at home and abroad includes files numbered 110 through 130. For the early years, 1909–14, this collection is very thin and indicates the informality with which administrative work was conducted in the relatively small department before the World War. Especially valuable, however, is an "Outline of the Organization and Work of the Department of State, 1911," 111.08/10, prepared by direction of Secretary Philander C. Knox.

Department correspondence incident to the outbreak of war, 763.72, is on microfilm, as is much of the correspondence concerning specific countries and their relations with the United States during this period. The department's card catalogue and the purport books again provide a guide to documents. The Division of Information, *Confidential Publications, 1895–1929*, Record Group 59, contains newspaper clippings relating to appointments, resignations, and important decisions on foreign policy. *Reports of Bureau Officers* for 1908–14 contains useful information. Essential for statistical and biographical material is the *Register of the Department of State*, published annually, including the table of organization of each year's department, lists of personnel, biographies and salaries, executive orders relating to the diplomatic and consular services, and sample examinations for admission to the services. I consulted the *Register* for the years 1906–16; the *Register* for 1913 includes biographical material on diplomatic officers, consuls-general, consuls, consular assistants, interpreters, and student interpreters who died or retired from the services after January 1, 1906.

*Foreign Relations of the United States*, published annually, includes the most important documents relating to policy. I consulted volumes for 1912 through 1914. The World War prompted annual supplements including documents pertinent to the war. *Foreign Relations, 1914, Supplement*, besides listing official positions of principal persons mentioned in the correspondence, was of use as a guide to unpublished material in the archives relating to the outbreak of war. Material concerning the unpreparedness of the department prior to the war is in House of Representatives, *Foreign Affairs Committee Hearings on Bill to Reorganize Service*, 63rd Congress, 2nd Session, and *Foreign Service of the United States, Hearings on H. R. 17 and H. R. 6357*, 68th Congress, 1st Session. These hearings, both of which are on microfiche, include statements by the secretaries of state and diplomatic personnel concerning the importance of passage of the Stone-Flood Act and the Rogers Act, respectively.

### *Personal Papers, Oral History*

The papers of President Woodrow Wilson in the manuscripts division of the Library of Congress are a huge collection; most valuable for my study were the executive files, Series Four, arranged according to topic or person. Series Three consists of the presidential letterbooks. Colonel Edward M. House's and many of Walter Hines Page's letters to Wilson, together with much department correspondence with the president, are among the personal correspondence, Series Two, arranged chronologically. Carbons of Wilson's replies to letters, usually too brief to be of use, often are included. The Ray Stannard Baker Papers, also at the Library of Congress, complement the Wilson collection and include Baker's correspondence and transcripts of interviews with individuals important in the administration.

The Library of Congress holds the most important collection of William Jennings Bryan papers. Letterbooks include secretarial correspondence, but the collection for 1913–14 is largely devoid of personal material. The manuscript by Grace Bryan Hargreaves, an interesting memoir by Bryan's daughter, is in this collection. A recent addition to the papers comprises Bryan's and Wilson's correspondence for 1913–15, mainly relating to diplomatic and consular appointments, but it contains few items not in other collections. The National Archives has the Bryan-Wilson official correspondence for Bryan's secretaryship on four reels of microfilm, the first two of which relate to the period covered in this study.

In the Library of Congress, and second only to the Wilson Papers in importance, are the papers of John Bassett Moore, some 100,000 items, well-organized and filed. Within these papers are an autobiographical file, and also "Moore's Memoirs," the latter in the collection by Moore's protégé, Edwin M. Borchard, of material written by and about Moore. The collection for the 1913–14 period is exceptionally rich, filled with Moore's long memoranda of department events and personalities. Boxes 91–93 relate to Moore's activities as counselor and reveal that Moore frequently disregarded the department's filing arrangement, retaining in his personal records material properly belonging in the department archives.

The papers of Wilbur J. Carr, in the Library of Congress, include an important handwritten diary, at some points difficult to decipher, valuable for Carr's comments on department personnel as well as a revelation of his personality. At the library too are the papers of: the Adee family, a small collection that has little personal correspondence but an interesting scrapbook of clippings; Robert Lansing, scant for the prewar period (the desk diary begins after the outbreak of war); Chandler P. Anderson, of small worth for 1913–14; Henry P. Fletcher, containing several letters revealing House's influence on appointments; Philander C. Knox, little not already common knowledge; Henry Morgenthau, a diary for 1913–14 that shows signs of careful editing; Brand Whitlock, personal correspondence as well as a journal; the Joseph E. Willard family, not yet catalogued in detail but arranged chronologically, containing material mainly on Willard's business matters and a few letters indicating desire for a diplomatic appointment.

The Edward M. House Collection at the Yale University Library comprises not only the Colonel's diary, which recounts almost verbatim important conversations with Wilson, Phillips, and Bryan, but also correspondence filed alphabetically by correspondent, as well as chronologically. House's diary and letters show more clearly than department materials or the Wilson papers the extent of the colonel's influence on department administration in 1913–14.

The Houghton Library at Harvard houses the papers of Walter Hines Page. Divided into two major sections relating to Page's American and English sojourns, and into several minor ones, the collection provides insights into the personalities of Page, Wilson, House, Phillips, and other department personnel. The long-winded Page never seemed to realize when his descriptions were probably boring the reader—however valuable they may be to researchers. The Page-Wilson Correspondence, 1913–18, four volumes of photocopies of letters between the two men, is in both the Wilson and the Page papers.

At Harvard are the papers of Joseph C. Grew, including his diary and numerous letters to diplomatic personnel, 1909–15; William E. Phillips, containing portions of journals of 1917; William W. Rockhill, several telling letters about his resignation and replacement; and William Dean Howells, whose manuscripts were researched for correspondence with Brand Whitlock and Wilson, with little success.

The Francis Mairs Huntington-Wilson Papers are on four reels of microfilm, available through interlibrary loan from Ursinus College, Collegeville, Pennsylvania. They verify material in his memoirs, notably reorganization of the department between 1906 and 1913, and contain a journal of later date, which provides a fascinating glimpse into his first marriage and its effect on his career.

Thomas Nelson Page's papers are in the manuscript department of the William R. Perkins Library at Duke University. Three boxes of correspondence of 1913 and one for 1914–15 include many letters about activities as chairman of the inaugural committee and the originals of letters from Rome to his brother and sister-in-law. The latter correspondence approaches in detail Walter H. Page's description of embassy life in London.

The John Foster Dulles Library at Princeton holds the papers of Henry van Dyke, poorly organized, of some use in showing van Dyke's efforts relating to the proposed Third Hague Peace Conference and other international conferences. The papers also include the manuscript of Tertius van Dyke's biography of his father.

An important collection, also at the Dulles Library, is that of the career diplomat John Van Antwerp MacMurray, who kept a diary and copied large portions of it in frequent letters to his mother. His material dating from 1905 to 1914 was invaluable. These papers are well-arranged and easily used.

The director of manuscripts of the Wyoming State Historical Division kindly assisted in locating and copying letters from the John E. Osborne Collection in Cheyenne. The collection includes several letters from Bryan, mostly relating to personal matters, and is not very helpful as an indication of Osborne's work in the department in 1913–14.

I was informed by the librarians of the collections concerned that the papers of Hugh Gibson at the Hoover Institution on War, Revolution, and Peace, Stanford University, the papers of Hugh R. Wilson at the Herbert Hoover Presidential Library in West Branch, Iowa, the papers of Frederic Courtland Penfield, in the Historical Society of Pennsylvania collections, the papers of Albert Schmedeman, at the State Historical Society of Wisconsin, Madison, the papers of Joseph W. Folk at the University of Missouri, and the papers of Myron T. Herrick, at Case Western Reserve University, Cleveland, contain little of importance for the years 1913–14 concerning department or diplomatic affairs. The papers of Paul Reinsch, also in the State Historical Society of Wisconsin, have been thoroughly explored by Noel Pugach in a fine doctoral dissertation, "Progress, Prosperity and the Open Door: The Ideas and Career of Paul S. Reinsch" (University of Wisconsin, 1967).

Seen at the Oral History Research Office at Columbia University were reminiscences of Perrin C. Galpin (1956), James W. Gerard (1949–50), Lloyd C. Griscom (1951), Nelson Trusler Johnson (1951–54), William Phillips (1951), and DeWitt Clinton Poole (1952), all of which contain information on prewar diplomatic practices and Secretary Bryan's department. The reminiscences of Gerard, Griscom, and Phillips supplement or repeat material in their memoirs.

## Essay on Sources

### Published Diaries, Letters, Memoirs, Personal Accounts

Participants in the Great War, regardless of their importance, often recalled their experiences in published memoirs, letters, and autobiographies. Hugh Gibson was one of the first to publish, with *A Journal from Our Legation in Belgium* (Garden City, N.Y.: Doubleday, Page, 1917). Gibson's diary says little about prewar activities; he arrived in Brussels in the summer of 1914. Ambassador James W. Gerard, forced to leave Berlin when the United States entered the war, produced *My Four Years in Germany* (New York: George H. Doran, 1917), an unreliable account later made into a motion picture by Warner Brothers, in which Halbert Brown took the part of the ambassador. Gerard wrote another contemporary account, *Face to Face with Kaiserism* (New York: George H. Doran, 1918). He included large sections of these books in his memoir, *My First Eighty-Three Years in America* (Garden City, N.Y.: Doubleday, 1951), which is best on his early life as a lawyer and judge and more modest concerning his part in diplomacy than are his earlier books.

Henry van Dyke wrote a series of articles describing the activities of his legation at war's outbreak, which were published in *Scribner's Magazine* for September, October and November 1917. These were brought together in book form, *Fighting for Peace* (New York: Charles Scribner's Sons, 1917). Maurice Francis Egan's equally prowar book is *Ten Years near the German Frontier: A Retrospect and a Warning* (New York: George H. Doran, 1919), but his more complete memoir, *Recollections of a Happy Life* (New York: George H. Doran, 1924), is a better account. Henry Morgenthau described his appointment and activities in Constantinople in florid style, *Ambassador Morgenthau's Story* (Garden City, N.Y.: Doubleday, Page, 1919), and *All in a Life-Time* (Garden City, N.Y.: Doubleday, Page, 1922), both more valuable to the student of political than of diplomatic or administrative history. Brand Whitlock's *Belgium: A Personal Narrative* (New York: D. Appleton, 1919) is a war memoir relating events beginning in 1915. Thomas Nelson Page, *Italy and the World War* (New York: Charles Scribner's Sons, 1924) is a history, not a personal account. Charles J. Vopicka emphasizes the importance of his Slavic ancestry in *Secrets of the Balkans: Seven Years of a Diplomatist's Life in the Storm Center of Europe* (Chicago: Rand McNally, 1921).

From the "other side" came Johann H. von Bernstorff, *My Three Years in America* (New York: Charles Scribner's Sons, 1920), noting the former ambassador's admiration for House and his appreciation of Bryan's sincerity. By this time American political leaders of the Wilson era had begun publication of their memoirs. Champ Clark, *My Quarter Century of American Politics*, 2 vols. (New York: Harper, 1920) is biased against Bryan. Joseph P. Tumulty, *Woodrow Wilson as I Know Him* (Garden City, N.Y.: Doubleday, Page, 1921) is unreliable, and William F. McCombs, *Making Woodrow Wil-*

*son President* (New York: Fairview, 1921) is a bitter memoir by a man convinced that Wilson had betrayed him.

Edward G. Lowry, *Washington Close-Ups* (Boston: Houghton Mifflin, 1921) and Arthur W. Dunn, *From Harrison to Harding: A Personal Narrative Covering a Third of a Century, 1888–1921* (New York: G. P. Putnam's Sons, 1922) have interesting comments on Bryan, whom both apparently knew well.

Paul S. Reinsch wrote of his experience as minister in *An American Diplomat in China* (Garden City, N.Y.: Doubleday, Page, 1922), but as with most wartime ministers' reminiscences, the volume is weakest in describing the prewar diplomatic scene. Ira Nelson Morris, *From an American Legation* (New York: Knopf, 1923) is another memoir of a minister who arrived too late to assist the overworked secretaries in that difficult period.

The mid-1920s witnessed publication of the memoirs and letters of more important individuals. First in time was Burton J. Hendrick's *The Life and Letters of Walter H. Page*, 3 vols. (Garden City, N.Y.: Doubleday, Page, 1922–25), which uses Page's letters, considerably edited, sometimes to the point of inaccuracy, for a biographical account of the wartime ambassador to the Court of St. James's. Hendrick's admiration for his subject led him to exaggerate Page's importance.

Ray Stannard Baker and William E. Dodd collaborated in editing *The Public Papers of Woodrow Wilson*, 6 vols. (New York: Harper and Bros., 1925–27). The president's private papers plus interviews and correspondence with individuals in the administration became sources for Baker's *Woodrow Wilson: Life and Letters*, 8 vols. (Garden City, N.Y.: Doubleday, Page, 1927–39), until recently the definitive study of Wilson's life. The fourth volume of the series furnished much information for this study. Baker's views of his subject are strongly favorable, and he exerts himself to be fair to Bryan without in any way implying lack of judgment on Wilson's part. Arthur S. Link is editing *The Papers of Woodrow Wilson* (Princeton, N.J.: Princeton University Press, 1966–), which will include nearly everything Wilson wrote. This series will be a most valuable collection. The already published volumes provide insight into Wilson's early opinions on foreign policy, and also refute recent psychological studies.

*The Memoirs of William Jennings Bryan* (Philadelphia: John C. Winston, 1925) were compiled from the recollections of William and Mary Baird Bryan. For the 1913–14 period Mrs. Bryan's journal, an important part of the volume, is useful and honest. She was bitterly disappointed when her husband resigned in 1915, as she enjoyed Washington society. Her occasional hostility to Wilson is ill-concealed.

Volume 2 of Sir Edward Grey, *Twenty-Five Years, 1892–1916*, 2 vols. (New York: Frederick A. Stokes, 1925) covers 1913–14, and while important for other subjects it provided little material for this study.

David F. Houston, *Eight Years with Wilson's Cabinet, 1913–20*, 2 vols. (Garden City, N.Y.: Doubleday, Page, 1926) is reliable. The first volume contains information about Bryan's part in cabinet meetings.

Probably the most important published collection of letters of the period is Charles Seymour, ed., *The Intimate Papers of Colonel House*, 4 vols. (Boston: Houghton Mifflin, 1926–28), which publishes portions of the diary, and House's correspondence, in narrative form. The first volume was used for this book. There are inaccuracies even in Seymour's thorough work, mostly resulting from the editor's inability to use the actual letters sent by House. The colonel frequently dispatched letters with different wordings from the draft copies Seymour used.

Henry Lane Wilson, *Diplomatic Episodes in Mexico, Belgium and Chile* (Garden City, N.Y.: Doubleday, Page, 1927) is biased against Wilson. George T. Marye, *Nearing the End in Imperial Russia* (Philadelphia: Dorrance, 1929) is of little value.

Charles W. Thompson, *Presidents I've Known and Two Near Presidents* (Indianapolis: Bobbs-Merrill, 1929), Archibald Wellington Butt, *Taft and Roosevelt: the Intimate Letters of Archie Butt,* 2 vols. (Garden City, N.Y.: Doubleday, Doran, 1930), and Irwin Hood (Ike) Hoover, *Forty-Two Years in the White House* (Boston: Houghton Mifflin, 1934) contain interesting glimpses of political personalities. William G. McAdoo, *Crowded Years* (Boston: Houghton Mifflin, 1931), despite (or because of) the close connection of its author with the administration, is interesting but needs to be checked against other accounts.

Constantin Dumba, *Memoirs of a Diplomat*, translated from the German by Ian D. Morrow (Boston: Little, Brown, 1932), is hostile to Wilson and more friendly toward Bryan.

Warrington Dawson, ed., *The War Memoirs of William Graves Sharp, American Ambassador to France, 1914–19* (London: Constable, 1931) and Allan Nevins, ed., *The Letters and Journal of Brand Whitlock*, 2 vols. (New York: Appleton-Century, 1936) contain little on the prewar period, although both describe the chaotic situation in the Paris embassy and Brussels legation in the late summer and early autumn of 1914.

Colonel T. Bentley Mott, *Twenty Years as a Military Attaché* (New York: Oxford University Press, 1937), by Herrick's friend and biographer, is episodic but has telling comments on Huntington-Wilson, as does Hugh Wilson, *Education of a Diplomat* (New York: Longmans, Green, 1938). The latter reveals why wealthy young men of the pre–World War period often chose a diplomatic career. Pleasant Stovall, *Switzerland and the World War* (Savannah, Ga.: Mason, 1939), indicative of Stovall's ignorance of European affairs, includes surprisingly incisive comments on the diplomatic service.

Emily Bax, a British-born secretary in the London embassy in 1900–14, provides enlightening comment on American ambassadors and diplomatic secretaries in London in *Miss Bax of the Embassy* (Boston: Houghton Mifflin, 1939).

Josephus Daniels, *The Wilson Era: Years of Peace, 1910–17* (Chapel Hill: University of North Carolina Press, 1944) is good, and E. David Cronon, ed., *The Cabinet Diaries of Josephus Daniels, 1913–1921* (Lincoln: University of Nebraska Press, 1963) is an excellent supplement.

Written during the Second World War, Francis Mairs Huntington-Wilson, *Memoirs of an Ex-Diplomat* (Boston: B. Humphries, 1945) reflects such anti-Japanese and anti-German bias that it must be used with caution. The memoirs illuminate Huntington-Wilson's experience in the Department of State, including the personality of Knox's first assistant secretary, a man who admitted that lack of tact ruined his career.

Thomas E. Sugrue and Edmund W. Starling, *Starling of the White House* (New York: Simon and Schuster, 1946), a memoir of the secret service's presidential bodyguard for many years, comments on Wilson and Bryan with approval.

Joseph C. Grew, first secretary of embassy in Berlin before and during the World War, with the assistance of Walter Johnson, published diaries and portions of letters in *Turbulent Era: A Diplomatic Record of Forty Years, 1904–1945*, 2 vols. (Boston: Houghton Mifflin, 1952), the first volume of which furnished important material. A similar memoir is William Phillips, *Ventures in Diplomacy* (Boston: Beacon, 1953). Phillips did not keep a diary until after the war's outbreak, but his informal commentary on diplomacy and the department in the first part of the work is essential to this study.

Elting E. Morison et al., eds., *The Letters of Theodore Roosevelt*, vol. 7, *The Days of Armageddon, 1909–1919*, 8 vols. (Cambridge: Harvard University Press, 1954) illuminates Republican and Progressive opinion of the Taft and Wilson administrations.

Post Wheeler and Hallie Erminie Rives, *Dome of Many-Coloured Glass* (Garden City, N.Y.: Doubleday, 1955) indicates that both Wheeler and his wife had poor memories and extreme imaginations. A small portion of Wheeler's story about the department's "plot" against his career in 1913–14 is substantiated by the record, but the MacMurray Papers reveal how difficult Wheeler and wife must have been.

Perrin G. Galpin, ed., *Hugh Gibson* (New York: Belgian-American Educational Foundation, 1956) contains reminiscences and portions of letters. There are about ten pages of Gibson's witty commentary on the department and the diplomatic scene before the war. The foreword was by Gibson's friend, former President Hoover, who worked with Gibson in Belgium in 1914–17.

Herbert Hoover, *An America Epic—Introduction, The Relief of Belgium, 1914–1930* (Chicago: Regnery, 1959) is critical of Brand Whitlock. *Felix*

## Essay on Sources

*Frankfurter Reminisces, Recorded in Talks with Dr. Harlan B. Phillips* (New York: Reynal, 1960) is critical of President Wilson and Ambassador Morgenthau. Frankfurter in 1917 accompanied Morgenthau on a mission to persuade Turkey to leave the war. Vincent Starrett, a reporter for the *Chicago Daily News* whose "beat" was the State, War, and Navy Departments in 1914, heaps vitriolic criticism on Bryan, whom he calls "the Juicer" in *Born in a Bookshop: Chapters from the Chicago Renascence* (Norman: University of Oklahoma Press, 1965).

Lawrence E. Gelfand assisted Lewis D. Einstein in editing the latter's memoirs and writings, *A Diplomat Looks Back* (New Haven, Conn.: Yale University Press, 1968), which includes a bibliography of Einstein's published writings. With a foreword by George F. Kennan, this is a useful collection by a longtime career diplomat. Dean G. Acheson, *Present at the Creation: My Years in the State Department* (New York: Norton, 1969) has incisive comments on the secretaryship and on the later careers of personages involved in diplomacy in 1913–14.

### Newspapers and Contemporary Periodicals

The *New York Times* is the most important American newspaper of the twentieth century for accurate reporting of diplomatic and political events. I read daily issues for 1913–14.

Current periodicals include: the *Commoner*, reflecting Bryan's opinion; *Outlook*, reflecting Theodore Roosevelt's; *North American Review*, George Harvey's; *Literary Digest; Harper's Weekly; New Republic; Nation; American Review of Reviews; Century Magazine;* and *Independent*.

For articles on the administration of foreign policy see: Henry White, "American Representatives Abroad," *Outlook*, 101 (April 26, 1913), 889–91; Sydney Brooks, "Mr. Bryan and American Foreign Policy," *Living Age*, 277 (April 26, 1913), 246–48; "Relations of Bryan and President Wilson," *Current Opinion*, 55 (July 1913), 21–23; "The Bryan Scandal," *Nation*, 97 (Sept. 18, 1913), 256–57; "Anglo-American" (pseud.), "American Ambassadors Abroad," *North American Review*, 198 (September 1913), 308–19; William Jennings Bryan, "Our Foreign Policy," *Independent*, 76 (October 9, 1913), 73–75; "The Merit System Attacked," *Independent*, 76 (October 16, 1913), 106–7; James Davenport Whelpley, "Our Disorganized Diplomatic Service," *Century Magazine*, n.s., 64 (November 1913), 123–27; George Harvey, "The Case of Brother Pindell," *North American Review*, 198 (December 1913), 752–59; David Jayne Hill, "Why Do We Have a Diplomatic Service?" *Harper's*, 128 (January 1914), 188–97; George Harvey, "The Diplomats of Democracy," *North American Review*, 199 (February 1914), 161–74; J. Kendrick Kinney, "A Scholar's View of Mr.

Bryan," *North American Review*, 199 (February 1914), 219–27; "An American Diplomat" (pseud.), "The Diplomatic Service—Its Organization and Demoralization," *Outlook*, 106 (March 7, 1914), 533–38; George Harvey, "Mr. Bryan Rides Behind," *North American Review*, 199 (March 1914), 321–36; "The Last Refuge of the Spoilsman," *Atlantic Monthly*, 113 (April 1914), 433–45; David Jayne Hill, "Shall We Standardize Our Diplomatic Service?", *Harper's*, 128 (April 1914), 690–98, and "Can Our Diplomatic Service Be Made More Efficient?", ibid., 130 (January 1915), 190–98.

## SECONDARY MATERIALS

### Biographies and Studies

Notable biographies of secretaries of state in the prewar period, illuminating not only the characters of their subjects but of their departments, include Tyler Dennett, *John Hay: From Poetry to Politics* (New York: Dodd, Mead, 1934); Kenton J. Clymer, *John Hay: The Gentleman as Diplomat* (Ann Arbor: University of Michigan Press, 1975), and Philip C. Jessup, *Elihu Root, 1905–1937*, 2 vols. (New York: Dodd, Mead, 1938). Brief studies of the secretaryships of the early twentieth century, by different authors, are in volumes 9 and 10 of Samuel Flagg Bemis and Robert H. Ferrell, eds., *The American Secretaries of State and Their Diplomacy*, 18 vols. (New York: Cooper Square, 1927–70), and Norman A. Graebner, ed., *An Uncertain Tradition: American Secretaries of State in the Twentieth Century* (New York: McGraw-Hill, 1961).

Bryan suffered at the hands of biographers until after World War II, early studies being prejudiced for or against the Commoner. Examples of the former persuasion are M. R. Werner, *Bryan* (New York: Harcourt, Brace, 1929), and Wayne C. Williams, *William Jennings Bryan* (New York: G. P. Putnam's Sons, 1936), and of the latter, Paxton C. Hibben and C. Hartley Grattan, *The Peerless Leader* (New York: Farrar and Rinehart, 1929), although even Hibben seemingly admires Bryan's sincerity. Merle E. Curti, *Bryan and World Peace*, 16, *Smith College Studies in History* (Northampton, Mass., 1931) is the best account of this aspect of Bryan's career, but Curti overrates Bryan's efforts for peace. Ernest R. May, "Bryan and the World War, 1914–1915," (Ph.D. diss., University of California, Los Angeles, 1951), makes good use of the Bryan and Wilson papers and material in the National Archives. Paul W. Glad, *The Trumpet Soundeth: William Jennings Bryan and His Democracy, 1896–1912* (Lincoln: University of Nebraska Press, 1960) is an interesting account of Bryan's early political career by a scholar sympathetic to Bryan's appeal to the Midwestern farmer. Lawrence

## Essay on Sources

W. Levine, *Defender of the Faith: William Jennings Bryan: The Last Decade, 1915–1925* (New York: Oxford University Press, 1965) is a careful study. Charles D. Tarlton, "Styles of American International Thought: Mahan, Bryan, and Lippmann," *World Politics*, 17 (July 1965), 584–614, analyzes Bryan's idea of morality in international politics. The definitive work on Bryan is the three-volume study by Paolo E. Coletta. The first volume, *William Jennings Bryan: Political Evangelist, 1860–1908* (Lincoln: University of Nebraska Press, 1964) and the second, *William Jennings Bryan: Progressive Politician and Moral Statesman* (University of Nebraska Press, 1969), were of great value to this study. The third, *William Jennings Bryan: Political Puritan* (University of Nebraska Press, 1969) summarizes Coletta's conclusions regarding Bryan's statesmanship, as well as his political achievements, and includes a valuable bibliography. Coletta has exhausted the Bryan sources. He has written several articles on his subject. Most useful were: "Bryan Briefs Lansing," *Pacific Historical Review*, 27 (1958), 383–96; "Bryan, Anti-Imperialism, and Missionary Diplomacy," *Nebraska History*, 41 (1960), 1–27; and "William Jennings Bryan and Deserving Democrats," *Mid-America*, 48 (April 1966), 75–98. The last-mentioned contains material not in the larger work. Since Coletta's third volume appeared, two full-length biographies have been published: Charles Morrow Wilson, *The Commoner: William Jennings Bryan* (Garden City, N.Y.: Doubleday, 1970) is a journalistic account, useful for personal data (the book is dedicated to William Jennings Bryan, Jr.) but inaccurate in detail; and Louis W. Koenig, *Bryan: A Political Biography of William Jennings Bryan* (New York: G. P. Putnam's Sons, 1971) is scholarly and readable.

Woodrow Wilson's biographers have experienced difficulties similar to those of Bryan; it is difficult to be objective about such an individual or to explain his complexities. James Kerney, *The Political Education of Woodrow Wilson* (New York: Century, 1926) is judicious and has the advantage of having been written by a man acquainted with Wilson's political circle. Harley Notter, *The Origins of the Foreign Policy of Woodrow Wilson* (Baltimore: Johns Hopkins University Press, 1937) is scholarly but exaggerates Wilson's knowledge of foreign affairs before he came to office. H.C.F. Bell, *Woodrow Wilson and The People* (Garden City, N.Y.: Doubleday, Doran, 1945) is readable. Tien-yi Li, *Woodrow Wilson's China Policy, 1913–1917* (New York: Twayne, 1952) is a good study, as are Roy Watson Curry, "Woodrow Wilson and Philippine Policy," *Mississippi Valley Historical Review*, 41 (December 1954), 435–52, and the same author's *Woodrow Wilson and Far Eastern Policy, 1913–1921* (New York: Bookman Associates, 1957).

The principal historian of Wilson, Arthur S. Link, began his multivolume biography with *Wilson: The Road to the White House* (Princeton, N.J.: Princeton University Press, 1947). The second volume, *Wilson: The New*

*Freedom* (Princeton University Press, 1956), and the third, *Wilson: The Struggle for Neutrality, 1914–1915* (Princeton University Press, 1960) are of major importance. Link's studies of Wilson's personality are carefully objective and sometimes so full of detail as to constitute almost a primary source. Especially valuable for my volume is his *Woodrow Wilson and the Progressive Era: 1910–1917* (New York: Harper, 1954; rev., 1963), the first published volume in Richard B. Morris and Henry S. Commager, eds., *The New American Nation* series. More recently Link has collected his articles on Wilson in *The Higher Realism of Woodrow Wilson and Other Essays* (Nashville, Tenn.: Vanderbilt University Press, 1971).

Arthur Walworth, *Woodrow Wilson*, 2 vols. (Boston: Houghton Mifflin, 1957; 2nd ed., rev., 1965) is a thorough study, beautifully written. Shorter studies of Wilson include John M. Blum, *Woodrow Wilson and the Politics of Morality* (Boston: Little, Brown, 1956); John A. Garraty, *Woodrow Wilson: A Great Life in Brief* (New York: Knopf, 1956); Alexander L. and Juliette L. George, *Woodrow Wilson and Colonel House: A Personality Study* (New York: John Day, 1956), intriguing; Arthur S. Link, *Wilson the Diplomatist* (Baltimore: Johns Hopkins University Press, 1957); Edward H. Buehrig, ed., *Wilson's Foreign Policy in Perspective* (Bloomington: Indiana University Press, 1957); Lawrence W. Martin, "Necessity and Principle: Woodrow Wilson's Views," *Review of Politics*, 22 (January 1960), 96–114; Sigmund Freud and William C. Bullitt, *Thomas Woodrow Wilson: A Psychological Study* (Boston: Houghton Mifflin, 1967), hostile; N. Gordon Levin, Jr., *Woodrow Wilson and World Politics: America's Response to War and Revolution* (New York: Oxford University Press, 1968), which advances an interesting thesis of Wilson's motives; and Edwin R. Weinstein, "Woodrow Wilson's Neurological Illness," *Journal of American History*, 58 (September 1970), 324–51, an article of high value.

There is no adequate biography of Colonel Edward M. House. Lester H. Woolsey, "The Personal Diplomacy of Colonel House," *American Journal of International Law*, 21 (1927), 706–15, is a useful study. George Sylvester Viereck, *The Strangest Friendship in History* (New York: Liveright, 1932), written after interviews with House, fails to prove its title. Arthur D. Howden Smith, *Mr. House of Texas* (New York: Funk and Wagnalls, 1940), is admiring. Robert S. Rifkind, "The Colonel's Dream of Power," *American Heritage*, 10 (February, 1959), 62–64, 111, analyzes *Philip Dru: Administrator*.

Edwin M. Borchard never published his biography of Moore but wrote a fulsome tribute for the *American Journal of International Law*, 42 (January 1948). Richard Megargee, "The Diplomacy of John Bassett Moore: Realism in American Foreign Policy" (Ph.D. diss., Northwestern University, 1963) explores its title's implications. Megargee is hostile to Wilson and Bryan and friendly to Moore.

## Essay on Sources

There is no full study of Robert Lansing, but Daniel M. Smith, *Robert Lansing and American Neutrality* (Berkeley: University of California Press, 1958) is helpful for its special subject. The only account of Dudley Field Malone apparently is John Reddy, "The Most Unforgettable Character I've Met," *Reader's Digest,* 69 (August 1956), 85–88.

"Veillard" (pseud.), "The Anchor of the State Department," *Nation,* 101 (August 5, 1915), 170–71, gives some account of Alvey A. Adee. His only biographer is George Sheppard Hunsberger, "The Diplomatic Career of Alvey Augustus Adee with Special Reference to the Boxer Rebellion," (M.A. thesis, American University, 1953). The most reliable account, a witty article, is John A. DeNovo, "The Enigmatic Alvey A. Adee and American Foreign Relations," *Prologue,* 7 (Summer 1975), 69–80. Louis G. Geiger, *Joseph W. Folk of Missouri* (Columbia: University of Missouri Press, 1953), indicates Folk's lack of interest in foreign policy. Wilbur J. Carr's assistant, Herbert Hengstler, was interviewed in commemoration of Carr's fortieth year in the department and the result was published in the *American Foreign Service Journal,* 9 (1932), 212–13. Katherine Crane, *Mr. Carr of State: Forty-Seven Years in the Department of State* (New York: St. Martin's Press, 1960) is admiring. The author organized Carr's papers, and missed little information for her book, but she tends to adopt Carr's opinions.

For American diplomats of the time see: Ross Gregory, *Walter Hines Page: Ambassador to the Court of St. James's* (Lexington: University of Kentucky Press, 1970); John M. Cooper, Jr., *Walter Hines Page: The Southerner as American, 1855–1918* (Chapel Hill: University of North Carolina Press, 1977); Theodore L. Gross, *Thomas Nelson Page* (New York: Twayne, 1967); Jack Tager, *The Intellectual as Reformer: Brand Whitlock and the Progressive Movement* (Cleveland: Press of Case Western Reserve University, 1968); Robert M. Crunden, *Hero in Spite of Himself: Brand Whitlock in Art, Politics and War* (New York: Knopf, 1969), a superior study; John Wells Davidson, "Brand Whitlock and the Diplomacy of Belgian Relief," *Prologue,* 2 (Winter 1970); Tertius van Dyke, *Henry van Dyke* (New York: Harper, 1935); Alan Kent, "Down from the Ivory Tower: Paul S. Reinsch, Minister to China," *Wisconsin Magazine of History,* 35 (Winter 1951), 114–18, unfriendly; Noel Pugach, "Making the Open Door Work: Paul S. Reinsch in China, 1913–1919," *Pacific Historical Review,* 38 (May 1969), 157–75, excellent; Waldo H. Heinrichs, *American Ambassador: Joseph C. Grew and the Development of the United States Diplomatic Tradition* (Boston: Little, Brown, 1966), a fine account of a twentieth-century diplomat, invaluable for a study of the diplomatic service.

Other biographies include: Willis Fletcher Johnson, *George Harvey, "A Passionate Patriot"* (Boston: Houghton Mifflin, 1929); Allan Nevins, *Henry White, Thirty Years of American Diplomacy* (New York: Harper, 1930);

## Essay on Sources

George M. Stephenson, *John Lind of Minnesota* (Minneapolis: University of Minnesota Press, 1935); John M. Blum, *Joe Tumulty and the Wilson Era* (Boston: Houghton Mifflin, 1951); Paul A. Varg, *Open Door Diplomat: The Life of W. W. Rockhill* (Urbana: University of Illinois Press, 1952).

### Background

Accounts of the history of the United States in the prewar era drawn from contemporary sources are: Mark Sullivan, *Our Times: The United States, 1900–1925*, 6 vols. (New York: Charles Scribner's Sons, 1926–35), still a remarkably helpful work, and Frederick L. Paxson, *The Pre-War Years, 1913–1917* (Boston: Houghton Mifflin, 1936).

Useful background studies of diplomacy are: George F. Kennan, *American Diplomacy: 1900–1950* (Chicago: University of Chicago Press, 1951); Julius W. Pratt, *Challenge and Rejection: The United States and World Leadership, 1900–1921* (New York: Macmillan, 1967), with an exemplary bibliography; Bradford Perkins, *The Great Rapprochement* (New York: Atheneum, 1968). In a different vein is Walter V. and Marie V. Scholes, *The Foreign Policies of the Taft Administration* (Columbia: University of Missouri Press, 1970) which has able sketches of the administrators of foreign policy during that era.

Walter Millis, *Road to War: America, 1914–1917* (Boston: Houghton Mifflin, 1935) has an initial chapter exploring prewar American sentiment. Ernest R. May, *The World War and American Isolation, 1914–1917* (Cambridge: Harvard University Press, 1959) portrays Bryan, Lansing, Wilson, and House and has the advantage of a multiarchival approach. Daniel M. Smith, *The Great Departure: The United States and World War I, 1914–1920* (New York: Wiley, 1965) is a synthesis.

An exemplary study of European events during the prewar period is Oron J. Hale's fine volume, *The Great Illusion, 1900–1914* (New York: Harper and Row, 1971), in the series edited by William L. Langer, *The Rise of Modern Europe*.

Alan Valentine, *1913: America between Two Worlds* (New York: Macmillan, 1962) is a nostalgic portrayal of life in the United States before the war. Virginia Cowles, *1913: The Defiant Swan Song* (London: Weidenfeld and Nicolson, 1967) views society, politics, and culture in principal European and American cities.

### Special Studies

Among studies of the State Department, one of the earliest is Gaillard Hunt, *The Department of State in the United States: Its History and Functions* (New Haven: Yale University Press, 1914) which recounts the history of the department, its past duties, its work in 1913. Hunt's book cites laws and other regulations establishing divisions and the ranking of officials. Lewis D. Einstein called for further change in a short study, "Reorganization of the State Department," in *Republican Campaign Textbook for 1920* (Washington, D.C., 1920), pp. 231–32, as did Frederic J. Stimson, "An Intimate Discussion on Our State Department," *Scribner's Magazine*, 85 (February 1929), 163–68. Bertram D. Hulen, *Inside the Department of State* (New York: McGraw-Hill, 1939) did not ask for reform, but his account provides sidelights on twentieth-century department personnel not available in other places. Graham H. Stuart, *The Department of State: A History of Its Organization, Procedure, and Personnel* (New York: Macmillan, 1949) is all its title states. Organized according to the secretaries, the chapters on Root, Knox, Bryan, and Lansing indicate change in the department. Alexander DeConde, *The American Secretary of State: An Interpretation* (New York: Praeger, 1962) is a valuable analysis. See also Jerry Israel, "A Diplomatic Machine: Scientific Management in the Department of State, 1906–1924," in Israel, ed., *Building the Organizational Society* (New York: Free Press, 1972).

A study providing a comparative view is Zara S. Steiner, *The Foreign Office and Foreign Policy, 1898–1914* (Cambridge: Cambridge University Press, 1969), proving that the British had problems no less demoralizing than those of the Americans.

On the diplomatic and consular services and their problems, almost a primary source is National Civil Service Reform League, *Report on the Foreign Service* (New York: National Civil Service Reform League, 1919), an excellent guide to salaries, positions, and the inadequacy of the prewar diplomatic machinery. James B. Stewart, "Foreign Service Training School," *American Foreign Service Journal*, 10 (June 1933), 224–27, notes early twentieth-century progress toward professionalism. G. Howland Shaw, "The American Foreign Service," *Foreign Affairs*, 14 (1936), 323–33, called for more specialization. J. Rives Childs, *American Foreign Service* (New York: Henry Holt, 1948) is a concise account by a career diplomat. Graham H. Stuart, *American Diplomatic and Consular Practice* (New York: Appleton-Century-Crofts, 1952) surveys organization and diplomatic machinery. Seymour J. Rubin, "American Diplomacy: The Case for 'Amateurism,'" *Yale Review*, 45 (March 1956), 321–35, furnishes excellent insights. William Barnes and John Heath Morgan, *The Foreign Service of the United States: Origins, Development, and Functions* (Washington, D.C.: Government Printing Office, 1961) outlines the history. Warren E. Ilchman, *Professional Diplomacy in the United States, 1779–1939: A Study in Administrative History* (Chicago: University of Chicago Press, 1961), especially chapter 3, is the first book-length study of the professionalization of the service. C. Maechling, "Our Foreign Affairs Establishment: The Need for Reform," *Virginia Quarterly Review*, 45 (Spring 1969), 193–210, indicates that problems are never-ending. Seward W. Livermore, "Deserving Democrats: The Foreign Service under Woodrow Wilson," *South Atlantic Quarterly*, 69 (Winter 1970), 144–60, is excellent. An important article is Waldo H. Heinrichs, Jr., "Bureaucracy and Professionalism in the Development of American Career Diplomacy," in John Braeman et al., eds., *Twentieth-Century American Foreign Policy* (Columbus: Ohio State University Press, 1971). Robert D. Schulzinger, *The Making of the Diplomatic Mind: The Training, Outlook, and Style of United States Foreign Service Officers, 1908–1931* (Middletown, Conn.: Wesleyan University Press, 1975) is a much-needed study, as is Richard H. Werking, *The Master Architects: Building the United States Foreign Service, 1890–1913* (Lexington: University Press of Kentucky, 1977).

See also Henry M. Wriston, *Executive Agents in American Foreign Relations* (Baltimore: Johns Hopkins University Press, 1929); Thomas A. Bailey, "California, Japan, and the Alien Land Legislation of 1913," *Pacific Historical Review*, 1 (1932), 36–59; Ernest R. May, "American Policy and Japan's Entrance into World War I," *Mississippi Valley Historical Review*, 40 (1953), 279–90; Victor S. Mamatey, *The United States and East Central Europe, 1914–1918: A Study in Wilsonian Diplomacy and Propaganda* (Princeton: Princeton University Press, 1957), pp. 72–87; Robert E. Quirk, *An Affair of Honor: Woodrow Wilson and the Occupation of Veracruz* (Lexington: University of Kentucky Press, 1962); William S. Coker, "Panama Canal Tolls Controversy: A Different Perspective," *Journal of American History*, 55 (December 1968), 555–64; and Kenneth J. Grieb, *The United States and Huerta* (Lincoln: University of Nebraska Press, 1969).

# Index

## Index

# Index

White, Charles D., 32
White, Henry, 30, 95, 104
Whitlock, Brand, 95, 112–14, 131–32, 136, 137
Willard, Belle, 102
Willard, Joseph, 100–102, 131
William II, Emperor of Germany, 89, 91–92
Williams, Edward T., 73
Williams, George Fred, 31–32, 110, 130
Williams, John Sharp, 102
Wilson, Charles S., 45, 106, 118, 121, 133, 136
Wilson, Henry Lane, 48
Wilson, Hugh, 137
Wilson, Woodrow: and Bryan, 24–27, 30, 34, 38–41; and diplomatic appointments, 30, 32, 41–48, 52, 53, 56, 63–71 passim, 78–83 passim, 86–115 passim, 118, 121; and House, 49–55; and Moore, 56–62 passim; and Page, 78–83 passim, 86–87; and Wheeler-Benson incident, 124; peace efforts, 126, 134; reform of diplomatic service, 137; also, 1, 2, 31, 48–49, 62, 77, 85, 127, 128, 130
Wilson, Mrs. Woodrow, 24–25, 44, 66, 128
Winslow, Lanier, 89
Wise, Rabbi Stephen S., 106
Woolsey, Lester, 70
Wyvell, Manton M., 71

Young, Evan E., 19, 74

Zita, Princess, 132

183